DATE DUE

n 1 8 98			
FE 0 00			
J 9 0			

DEMCO 38-296

Pitt Latin American Series

PRIVATIZATION

and

POLITICAL CHANGE

in Mexico

Judith A. Teichman

University of Pittsburgh Press
Pittsburgh and London

Published by the University of Pittsburgh Press, Pittsburgh, Pa., 15260
Copyright © 1995, University of Pittsburgh Press
All rights reserved
Manufactured in the United States of America
Printed on acid-free paper

Designed by Jane Tenenbaum

Library of Congress Cataloging-in-Publication Data

Teichman, Judith A., 1947–
    Privatization and political change in Mexico / Judith A. Teichman.
        p.   cm.—(Pitt Latin American series)
    Includes bibliographical references and index.
    ISBN 0-8229-3928-2 (alk. paper).—ISBN 0-8229-5586-5 (pbk. :
alk. paper)
    1. Privatization—Mexico.   2. Government business enterprises—
Mexico.   3. Mexico—Economic policy   1970–   I. Title.   II. Series.
HD4014.T44   1996
338.972—dc20   95-25839
                                                                 CIP

A CIP catalogue record for this book is available from the British Library.
Eurospan, London

Contents

List of Tables

Acronyms

ALTEX	Programa de Empresas Altamente Exportadora / Program for Important Exporting Companies
AMB	Asociación Mexicano de Banqueros / Mexican Bankers' Association
ANIT	Asociación Nacional de la Industria de Transformación / National Association of Transformation Industry
CANACINTRA	Cámara Nacional de la Industria de Transformación / National Chamber of Transformation Industry
CCE	Consejo Coordinador Empresarial / Business Coordinating Council
CEESP	El Centro de Estudios Económicos del Sector Privado / The Private Sector Center for Economic Studies
CEMAI	Consejo Empresarial Mexicano para Asuntos Internacionales / Mexican Business Council for International Affairs
CFE	Comisión Federal de Electricidad / Federal Electricity Commission
CFM	Comisión de Fomento Minero / Commission for Mining Development
CFLC	Cía de Luz y Fuerza del Centro / Light and Power Company of the Center

CMHN	Consejo Mexicano de Hombres de Negocios / Mexican Council of Businessmen
CNC	Confederación Nacional de Campesinos / National Confederation of Peasants
CNOP	Confederación Nacional de Organizaciones Populares / National Confederation of Popular Organizations
COECE	La Coordinadora de Organizaciones Empresariales de Comercio Exterior / Coordinating Committee for Commercial Export Businessmen's Organizations
CONASUPO	Companía Nacional de Subsistencias Populares / National Basic Foods Company
CONCAMIN	Confederación de Cámaras Industriales / Confederation of Industrial Chambers
CONCANACO	Confederación de Cámaras Nacionales de Comercio / Confederation of National Chambers of Commerce
CONCARRIL	Constructora Nacional de Ferrocarril / National Railway Construction Company
COPARMEX	Confederación Patronal de la República Mexicana / Employers Confederation of the Mexican Republic
CROC	Confederación Revolutionaria de Obreros y Campesinos / Revolutionary Confederation of Workers and Peasants
CROM	Confederación Regional Obrera Mexicana / Regional Confederation of Mexican Labor
CT	Congreso de Trabajo / Congress of Labor
CTM	Confederación de Trabajadores de México / Confederation of Mexican Workers
FAT	Frente Auténtico del Trabajo / Authentic Labor Front

FDN	Frente Democrática Nacional / National Democratic Front
FERRONALES	Compañía de los Ferrocarriles de México / Railway Company of Mexico
FESEBES	Federación de Sindicatos de Empresas de Bienes y Servicios / Federation of Unions of Goods and Services Enterprises
FSTSE	Federación de Sindicatos de Trabajadores al Servicio del Estado / Federation of Unions of State Workers
IMSS	Instituto Mexicana de Seguridad Social / Mexican Institute of Social Security
ISSSTE	Instituto de Seguridad y Servicios Sociales de los Trabajadores del Estado / Institute of Security and Social Services for State Workers
PAN	Partido de Acción Nacional / National Action Party
PARM	Partido Auténtico de la Revolución Mexicana / Authentic Party of the Mexican Revolution
PEMEX	Petróleos Mexicanos / Mexican Petroleum
PMT	Partido Mexicano de los Trabajadores / Mexican Workers Party
PRD	Partido de la Revolución Democrática / Party of the Democratic Revolution
PRI	Partido Revolucionario Institutional / Institutional Revolutionary Party
PRONASOL	Programa Nacional de Solidaridad / National Solidarity Program
PRONAFICE	Progama Nacional de Fomento Industrial y Comercio Exterior / National Program for Industrial Development and Foreign Trade
SECOFI	Secretaría de Comercio y Fomento Industrial / Ministry of Commerce and Industrial Development

SEDESO	Secretaría de Desarrollo Social / Ministry for Social Development
SEMIP	Secretaría de Energía, Minas e Industria Parastatal / Ministry of Energy, Mines and Parastate Industry
SEPAFIN	Secretaría del Patrimonio y Fomento Indusrial / Ministry of Natural Resources and Industrial Development
SME	Sindicato Mexicano de Electristas / Mexican Electrical Workers Union
SNMMSRM	El Sindicato Nacional Minero Metalúrgico y Similares de la República Mexicana / National Mining Metallurgical and Similar Activities Union of the Mexican Republic
SPP	Secretaría de Programación y Presupuesto / Ministry of Budget and Planning
STFRM	Sindicato de Trabajadores Ferrocarrileros de la República Mexicana / Railway Workers Union of the Mexican Republic
STPRM	Sindicato de Trabajadores Petroleros de la República Mexicana / Union of Petroleum Workers of the Mexican Republic
STRM	Sindicato de Telefonistas de la República Mexicana / Telephone Workers Union of the Mexican Republic

Acknowledgments

While privatization—entailing a variety of measures geared toward increasing the reliance on market forces—is a global policy phenomenon, its timing and scope have varied markedly from country to country. For developing countries, privatization has been closely associated with structural adjustment, a package of economic liberalizing measures supported by multilateral lending institutions negotiating agreements with highly indebted developing countries. But even here, the enthusiasm with which privatization has been pursued has varied enormously. The rapidity and depth of Mexico's privatization drive stands out, particularly given the past economic leadership role of the state in that country. This book is the story of how this policy change came about; it is also an examination of the political implications.

For Mexican policymakers, privatization has been a sensitive issue, reflected in the fact that the term *privatization* is not used in public pronouncements. Chapters 2 and 3, dealing with the economic and political role of public enterprises, attempt to illuminate some of the obstacles that have faced Mexico's privatizers. Political obstacles have clearly been among the most important. Due to the political sensitivity of the privatization issue in Mexico, discovering how such decisions were made and implemented has not been easy. I have attempted to piece together events from the press, official documents, and personal interviews. Open-ended interviews of government officials and members of the private sector were carried out during the first five months of 1991. In order to ensure that responses would be as candid as possible, interviewees were guaranteed anonymity. In total, twenty-six interviews were carried out: nineteen were with officials in the public bureaucracy and seven with members of the private sector. Of those in the public bureaucracy, eleven were senior-level officials or their personal advisors, and eight were middle-ranking officials. These officials had or were currently occupying positions in the Ministry of Finance and the Ministries of Budget and Planning (SPP), Industry, Mines, and Public Enterprises (SEMIP), Commerce and Industrial Development (SECOFI), and PEMEX (Petróleos Mexicanos), the state petroleum corporation. The private sector individuals interviewed were owners or senior managers of petrochemical companies. The rationale for this focus was twofold: the economic importance of PEMEX, and the fact that this is a sector where de facto privatization has gone forward despite stiff political resistance. I am indebted to those government officials and businessmen who took the time to speak with me; their perspectives have enriched this study immeasurably.

I owe many other debts, both institutional and individual. The Center for U.S.-Mexican Studies in San Diego, where I began research for this project, was an excellent source of materials on Mexico. The Social Sciences and Humanities Research Council of Canada provided me with initial funding, and support from the Ford Foundation for a collaborative project on hemispheric trade awarded to the Centre for International Studies, University of Toronto, contributed to its completion. I am also grateful to the Centro de Estudios Internacionales of the Colegio de México for affording me access to the college's excellent library facilities. Hugo Ciceri, of the department of economics at the Universidad Nacional Autónoma de México (UNAM), was very helpful in obtaining interviews with members of the private sector. Thanks are due to my research assistant, Remonda Bensabat, and to colleagues Frans Schruyer and Judith Adler Hellman for their helpful comments on an earlier version of the manuscript. I also wish to thank Roderic Camp, who, as one of the reviewers of the manuscript, provided a detailed and helpful commentary. All errors and omissions are, of course, my own.

Most important, a final word of gratitude must go to my family—my husband, George, and daughter Sarah, who have once again provided support and encouragement through the vicissitudes of research and writing.

PRIVATIZATION

and

POLITICAL CHANGE

in Mexico

1

Economic Liberalization and Political Change

Over the past decade, policy reforms in both developed and developing countries have signaled a startling reversal in the relentless postwar expansion of state intervention into economic matters. Trade liberalization, deregulation, and privatization now epitomize the new economic wisdom, replacing the interventionist assumptions of the Keynesian and developmentalist state. While this antistatism has been most enthusiastically adopted by conservative regimes espousing a new neoclassical economic orthodoxy, social democratic regimes in Spain, Portugal, and Greece have also pursued programs to reduce the role of the state and to bring about greater reliance on market forces. Indeed, the pervasiveness of this neoliberal policy thrust reflects a new ideological hegemony that trumpets an unquestioning belief in market forces as its primary article of faith.

Privatization programs have been the most important way in which the state's role has been reduced and redefined. While *privatization* has been used most commonly to refer to the sale of state enterprises to the private sector, the term encompasses a wide range of policy initiatives "all designed to alter the balance between the public and private sectors."[1] Hence in addition to the sale of enterprises, privatization may include the liquidation of public companies, policies opening up economic sectors previously reserved exclusively

3

to the state, and the transfer of public sector activities to the private sector through franchising or contracting out.

While privatization programs have been most complete in a number of the advanced capitalist countries, developing countries have been slower to adopt them. Particularly in Latin America, there has been a considerable gap between rhetoric and implementation. Exceptions are the Chilean case and, more recently, the Argentine and Venezuelan programs.[2] Most dramatic, however, has been the privatization drive in Mexico, a country where the state's leadership role in industrialization and economic growth has been considered one of the most successful in Latin America. In 1991, the Mexican program brought in more money to government coffers (US$9.4 billion) than all other sales of public companies in Latin America combined.[3] From over a thousand state enterprises in 1983, the Mexican state owned around two hundred by 1993. While the participation of the public sector in the economy represented 25.4 percent of gross domestic product (GDP) in 1983, that figure was estimated at 7.5 percent by the beginning of 1993.[4]

This book is a study of the origins, development, implementation, and political impact of Mexico's privatization program—a program initiated by Mexican President Miguel de la Madrid (1983–1988), accelerated by President Carlos Salinas de Gortari (1988–1994), and one that is being pushed even further under current president Ernesto Zedillo Ponce de León. The focus of the work is on the public enterprise sector: because public enterprises in Mexico have played such a central political role, privatization has had important political implications. But while privatization, an integral part of Mexico's broader restructuring process, has domestic origins and effects, the international context played a critical role in patterning the policy reforms that were carried out. In fact, the profound economic changes Mexico has undergone can only be fully understood within the context of the important transformations in the world economy that have occurred since the mid-1970s. These changes not only ushered in new opportunities and constraints but also inspired a new direction in economic thinking—a thinking that came to be reflected in official lending institutions dealing with highly indebted countries such as Mexico. In this way, the international context has narrowly circumscribed the policy options available in Mexico after 1983.

Transformation of the Global Economy and the New Orthodoxy

The nature of recent transformations in the global economy and the alteration in the conventional wisdom in development economics, particularly as it has come to be reflected in the agendas of official banking institutions, have patterned the evolution of the privatization programs in Latin America and in the countries of other less developed regions. Arising in the mid-1970s, those changes coincided with and reinforced the impacts of Mexico's own domestic economic and political crises, pushing its policy makers inexorably toward economic liberalization.

The energy crisis of 1973–1974 initiated a period of economic uncertainty and the transformation of a global system that had been based on U.S. hegemony. The slowdown in world trade initiated by that crisis precipitated the intensification of international trade competition.[5] Hardest hit among Western industrialized nations was the United States: it lost its share of world manufacturing value added to Germany and Japan, which now began to challenge the United States in export markets. The United States, strongly supportive of expanded trade relations prior to 1970, now became increasingly protectionist, and the liberal trading environment of the pre-1970 period began to wane. More and more, trade became subject to some form of protection. The drive for competitiveness, combined with the export-oriented policies of a number of developing countries, propelled the transfer of industrial operations able to utilize cheap labor to a number of those countries. This transfer was facilitated by technological developments that made national boundaries to industry less important than ever before. Due to greater standardization of products and production methods, it became feasible to separate production stages physically. In addition, U.S. legislation encouraged offshore processing, since products assembled from American materials could be reexported to the United States without duty.[6]

Hence, while the development of manufacturing capacity in most developing countries grew slowly, excessive manufacturing capacity developed in a few of them: Taiwan, South Korea, Hong Kong, Singapore, Mexico, and Brazil—the so-called NICs, or newly industrializing countries. Three of these, Taiwan, South Korea, and Hong Kong, together accounted for one-half of developing countries' exports of manufactures to the advanced countries between 1970 and 1980.[7] In this way, the NICs became the arena where competition between the multinational corporations (MNCs) of the advanced capitalist countries was fought out. In the electronics industry, for example, while U.S. companies moved to Mexico and Southeast Asia, many Japanese firms invested in South Korea, Singapore, and Hong Kong.

At the same time, the drive for competitive advantage has meant that MNCs have been one of the most important driving forces behind the creation of regional trading blocks.[8] Indeed, the specter of the European Economic Community acquiring the competitive edge in world trade and prosperity became one of the most important motivations for the pursuit of the North American Free Trade Agreement (NAFTA) by U.S. political and economic elites. At the same time, due to the circumstances discussed below, access to investment capital and markets has become critically important to the Latin American NICs in recent years. Mexico, therefore, was a strong NAFTA supporter—a strategy that has been instrumental in reinforcing that country's privatization drive.[9]

Another implication of the 1973 petroleum crisis was the massive expansion of the debt of most developing countries, plagued with a variety of rising costs including high oil bills, as OPEC petrodollars channeled through the commercial banks aggressively sought borrowers.[10] While oil exporters such as Mexico and Venezuela did not face rising fuel costs, they too borrowed heavily to accelerate petroleum exploitation and take advantage of the bonanza. When interest rates rose in 1981, therefore, developing countries faced a sharp rise in their balance of payments deficits and the onset of economic crisis. When their only recourse was the International Monetary Fund (IMF), the resultant reschedulings and new loans overseen by that organization entailed a variety of economic policy conditions. These conditions, which reflected current economic thinking, strongly encouraged, if they did not dictate, policies conducive to economic liberalization.[11]

Indeed, as a consequence of the economic difficulties that began to emerge after 1973, the consensus that had accepted the efficacy of the mixed economy began to break down. The administrations of

Ronald Reagan in the United States and Margaret Thatcher in Great Britain espoused a set of policy prescriptions that sought to reduce state intervention and to create a greater reliance on market forces: tax cuts, privatization, deregulation, and a weakening of trade unions. These policies were based on the firm belief that production decisions were best made by capitalists in an environment free from government interference.[12]

Similar solutions came to be applied to the problems of the developing countries. With the success of the East Asian NICs, which, unlike their Latin American counterparts, had continued to experience economic growth even after the 1982 debt crisis, influential development economists began to advocate economic liberalization as the panacea for the economic ills of the developing countries.[13] The experience of the "gang of four" (Taiwan, Singapore, Hong Kong, and South Korea) in East Asia was used to argue the superiority of trade-oriented (outward) export-promoting policies that assumed a movement toward a greater degree of laissez-faire.[14] The trade-restricting (closed) import-substitution industrialization policies of Latin America, on the other hand, were seen as responsible for the decline in economic activity in the region and, it was argued, should therefore be replaced by freer economic policies. According to this view, import-substitution industrialization policies had been responsible for the expansion of state enterprises in Latin America during the postwar period. Insulated from market forces and subject to political manipulation, state enterprises are seen as highly inefficient and as representing an unbearable fiscal burden.[15]

Policy prescriptions of both the World Bank and the IMF have reflected the new thinking on economic liberalization in general and privatization in particular. From the mid-1980s, when it became apparent that the Third World debt crisis was a more intractable problem than originally anticipated, structural adjustment, which sought to increase reliance on market mechanisms through reducing the role of the state, was the policy solution Third World debtors were required to follow.[16] Privatization and public sector reform have been among the most important components of this policy package; when combined with or following other measures of economic liberalization, such reforms are believed to bring about greater economic efficiency by shifting the burden of allocation more squarely toward market forces.

The World Bank has recommended a variety of reforms for public enterprises, including tighter financial controls, the adoption of market pricing, and the more drastic solutions of divestiture and liquidation.[17] Addressing its concerns about state enterprise largely through its structural adjustment loans, the World Bank has been particularly critical of the failure of such firms to meet social needs and has recommended that a more efficient method of meeting such needs would be the application of direct subsidies obtained from the profits of reformed market-driven public companies.[18] The IMF's position on public enterprises, on the other hand, springs from its view of the macroeconomic implications of public enterprises due to their large deficits; that is, the impact of public enterprises on monetary instability, inflation, external indebtedness, and balance of payments pressures. The IMF has, therefore, been supportive of public enterprise reform and privatization as a means to reduce public deficits.[19] Moreover, even though privatization may not be specifically called for in agreements with the IMF, these agreements invariably require a drastic reduction in the public deficit—a goal facilitated by privatization, in view of the extreme financial difficulty that public enterprises find themselves in. Finally, a policy environment conducive to privatization has been heavily influenced by strong U.S. support for privatization programs, manifested not only in influence over World Bank and IMF policies but also through the U.S. Agency for International Development (USAID).

Furthermore, while international financial agencies were initially satisfied with efforts to privatize only enterprises on the fringe of the public sector, leaving core companies in state hands, the Brady Plan, announced by U.S. Treasury Secretary Nicolas Brady in March 1989, went considerably further, pledging to grant debt relief to countries that implemented market-oriented reform to promote growth. Striking a deal involved privatization of core sectors. Indeed, one observer has linked the invigorated privatization drives in Mexico, Argentina, and Venezuela after 1989 with the expectations of the Brady Plan.[20]

The leverage imposed by IMF–World Bank conditionality, however, may have been less important than other more subtle means of policy influence. Miles Kahler, for example, argues that generous financing from the IMF and the World Bank was more important than the strictness of conditions in inducing policy change.[21] Furthermore, international financial institutions, convinced that government commitment to policy reform is indispensible to its success, now prefer evidence of prior commitment to policy change before they agree to financing—a factor that could heavily influence the direction of economic policy.[22] Even more important, perhaps, is the existence of a common "international policy culture," which has been described as both a process of emulation and a process of social learning.[23] *Social learning* refers to the spread of new information on which governments can base policy choices. In the case of privatization, it refers to the evolution and spread of "consensual knowledge" among specialists (economists) regarding the way in which public enterprises influence economic growth.[24] Gradually this new knowledge went beyond the professional community and began to influence the thinking of political leaders. As economic crisis discredited the old ideas of both Keynesianism and developmentalism, the "new" ideas of orthodoxy—one of the most important being privatization—took hold.

In the case of developing countries, the most important forum for the social learning of policy elites has been the process of debt negotiation. In this setting, the influence of international financial institutions has occurred not only through bargaining but also through persuasion and debate.[25] Because many of the policy elites of developing countries have been trained in U.S. or European educational institutions, they may already be receptive to the new policy culture. As a result, the technocrats in ministries with macroeconomic responsibilities, such as finance, have become the strongest supporters of structural adjustment and therefore of privatization.[26]

Whether through the direct leverage of conditionality or by means of the more subtle processes outlined above, international lending institutions have played an important role in the initiation and expansion of the privatization programs of developing countries.[27] Indeed, in the words of one scholar writing on the question of policy choice in developing countries, "extensive conditionality and coordination among major financing agencies produced external pressure on internal economic policies unprecedented in scope and detail."[28] But while international factors are important in explaining why developing countries abandoned the statism of the 1970s and moved decisively toward structural adjustment in the mid-1980s, they cannot account for the differences in the timing, scope, and depth of structural adjustment, in general, nor of privatization, in particular. In Latin America, for example, privatization in some countries (Chile and Mexico) was early and rapid; in others (Argentina and Venezuela), it occurred later (after 1989) but has been extensive; while in others (Brazil), despite much rhetoric, it has gone forward haltingly.[29] The interaction of the international context and pressures with domestic economic and political circumstances has patterned the particular direction and depth of adjustment policies.

In the case of Mexico, the interaction between a domestic economic crisis, existent political arrangements, and external circumstances and pressures accounts for the depth and rapidity of that country's privatization program. Measures of economic liberalization rapidly gained ground in Mexico after 1983, following the 1981 decline in petroleum prices and the sudden increase in interest rates in that same year—events that plunged Mexico into its worst recession since the Great Depression. Forced to sign a tough agreement with the IMF in 1982, a further slide in petroleum prices in 1985–1986 resulted in protracted negotiations with both the IMF and the World Bank and an acceleration of economic liberalization. By that time, support for economic liberalization was well established in Mexican official circles. At that time, considerable discussion focused not only on the economic benefits of economic liberalization but also on its supposed political advantages.

Economic Liberalization and Political Transition

Economic liberalization's most well-known advocate has linked the free flow of capital and goods to the expansion of democratic freedom.[30] Privatization is believed to contribute to democratization in a variety of ways. With the reduction of the state's role, public policy more attuned to general public interest will emerge once privatization occurs, since the private sector, unlike public bodies, is less premeated by corruption and rent-seeking behavior and not subject to political manipulation.[31] It has also been argued that with the diminishment of state firms—one of the political elite's principal patronage instruments—the bureaucracies and public enterprise trade unions of developing countries will become increasingly depoliticized, their power will decline, and the power of other, more representative, institutions will be enhanced.[32] This empty political space could, for example, be filled by new social movements, allowing previously politically excluded groups a role in the political process. Economic and political decentralization is another advantage of privatization: decentralization in economic power (as a consequence of the dismantling of monopolistic state companies) will mean a decentralization of political power, as a wide variety of economic actors provide a check on authoritarian political power.[33]

Supporters of privatization have maintained that the dismantling of the public enterprise sector will result in an increase in state capacity—that is, in the state's ability to formulate and implement coherent economic policies conducive to economic growth. Privatization, in this view, is seen as facilitating greater productive efficiency and, in strengthening the economy, as strengthening the state fiscally. The state will now be able to concentrate on carrying out fewer activities effectively, instead of dispersing its capacity over a vast number of areas. Indeed, this has been the rationale given by both Presidents de la Madrid and Salinas in explaining the Mexican privatization drive.

There is, however, good reason to be skeptical about the presumption of a link between economic liberalization, especially privatization, and a march toward democracy. Dismantling the public enterprise sector can severely undermine critically essential sources of regime legitimacy, resulting in an increase in political instability. Here, an understanding of the peculiar role of public firms in developing countries is helpful. Public firms have been important instruments of the economic leadership role assumed in the past by these states—a role that has often been a significant source of public support. In addition, public firms in developing countries are said to have filled the gaps where private sector investment was weak or nonexistent and have had an especially important role in the provision of cheap inputs to the private sector.[34]

Other functions of the public enterprise sector of developing countries have been more explicitly social and political. While failing to show a profit, a public firm may provide such social and political services as distributing low-cost basic products or providing employment. Such activities bolster the state's claim to both development and social roles and in so doing contribute to regime support. Similarly, public firms may play an important legitimating role in their management of strategic resources previously monopolized by foreign capital. Indeed, any one firm may have a variety of functions—economic, social, and political. The elimination of such firms means a loss of the social and political functions provided by them and makes necessary the construction of alternative sources of regime legitimacy. This becomes especially important if the divestiture of public firms, along with other economic liberalization measures, is portrayed by domestic opposition forces as antinational. The adeptness of the political elite at containing political unrest and creating new sources of regime legitimacy at this stage becomes critical. Greater political liberalization may be a way to shore up regime legitimacy, but it may well threaten the political survival of the current political elite by allowing opposition groups more leeway. Furthermore, the ensuing political agitation will likely have a deleterious impact on the business investment climate. Such a scenario can set the stage for the forces of authoritarian repression.

Another reason to question the democratizing power of economic liberalization measures such as privatization is the recognition that in the absence of developed capital markets, as is the case in most developing countries, public enterprises will be passed onto an already wealthy elite, worsening the problem of income distribution.[35] The enormous disparity between the economically powerful and the dispossessed in most parts of the developing world has undoubtedly reinforced the inequality in political power. Increased economic concentration is not likely to alleviate the authoritarian features of most regimes.

Such concerns appear to be particularly germane to the experience of Latin America, a region in which public enterprises have played a predominant role. Here, the share of public enterprises in gross fixed capital formation increased from an average of 13.7 percent in the 1960s to an average of 20.5 percent by the mid-1970s.[36] By the early 1980s, public firms represented about 30 percent of total public sector budgets in Argentina, Chile, and Colombia and over 50 percent in Brazil, Mexico, Peru, and Venezuela.[37]

Public enterprise expansion has occurred during a variety of regime types in Latin America, from military regimes to those with populist and democratic features. The public enterprise sector in Latin America experienced steady growth from the 1940s to the early 1970s and came to encompass a broad spectrum of activities, from the traditional areas of transportation, communication, public utilities, and natural resources to direct production, particularly in iron, steel, chemicals, and cement as well as in food processing and sugar production. In a number of countries in the region, public enterprises also became involved in agricultural marketing.

While the origins of the modern Latin American interventionist state are to be found in the establishment of state development banks in the early part of the twentieth century, rapid public enterprise expansion has been commonly associated with nationalist political projects of the immediate postwar period. Policy during this time, usually referred to as the easy import-substitution phase, was geared toward the stimulation of industrial growth in light consumer goods and to the protection of employment through state expenditure and investment. Such regimes, usually described as populist, instituted a variety of measures to stimulate domestic industry: tariff and quota protection, the provision of cheap inputs through state firms, and the supply of credit and other incentives through state development banks. Some of these regimes (such as the administration of Lázaro Cárdenas of Mexico, 1934–1940, or that of the Unidad Popular of Chile, 1970–1973) viewed state enterprises as the means by which the state could gain control of the commanding heights of the economy, wresting control from foreign capital and domestic propertied classes. State enterprises in such cases became important national symbols. Some observers saw state enterprises as a manifestation of relative state autonomy, reflecting the ability of such states to act contrary to the short-term wishes of both their own capitalist classes and international capital, although within the limits established by the requirements of capitalist reproduction. Others went so far as to suggest the presence of absolute autonomy in state action.[38]

However, expansion of public enterprises has also occurred under regimes whose objective was to reverse the populist/inclusionary character of earlier administrations—regimes described as bureaucratic authoritarian.[39] Since the objective was now to exclude the masses both politically and economically, state structures and their ties with society become more controlling. Observers of state expansion under the auspices of bureaucratic authoritarian regimes stress not only its popular exclusionary character but also its autonomy in the face of international capital—an autonomy that, although it allows the state to renegotiate the terms of dependence, is transitory, given the rapid rise in foreign debt.[40]

While populist and statist bureaucratic authoritarian regimes differ fundamentally in a number of respects, most importantly over the question of the political and economic exclusion of the popular classes, the centrality of the state is a common feature: the state's economic leadership role and public enterprise remain pivotal. Because of the extensiveness of state activities, because the state's decisions impinge on the interests of so many groups, the state becomes the focus of political struggle. This is especially so during the populist-inclusionary phase but remains the case even during bureaucratic authoritarian stages, as far as the more privileged groups are concerned. State institutions and agencies come to reflect the interests of competing groups and class factions.[41] At the same time, however, the concept of bureaucratic authoritarianism introduced the idea of the emergence of a technocratic policy elite, and while this group had important allies outside the state, it was seen as a crucially important source of policy initiation and change.

The extrastate coalitional bases of populist and bureaucratic authoritarian regimes, however, remains important in explaining the distinct policy thrusts of such regimes. In the case of the populist regimes, the state is believed to have been in the hands of an alliance of elements of the petite bourgeoisie and the popular classes. In these circumstances, public enterprises are said to have played a redistributive role by stimulating labor-intensive small and medium businesses, making possible employment opportunities and increased wages to workers, and through the provision of subsidies to consumers. In the case of bureaucratic authoritarianism, on the other hand, since the dominant alliance consists of the local bourgeoisie, MNCs, and state bureaucrats (among the most important, the directors of state enterprises), whose objective it is to remove the obstacles to economic growth, state policy abandons its redistributive character and moves decisively toward measures to guarantee capital accumulation. In Brazil, joint ventures between the state, multinational corporations, and local capital provided the basis for the renewal of economic growth. Hence, the years 1968 to 1973 were ones of rapid public enterprise expansion in Brazil.[42]

Just as the expansion of state enterprises cannot be neatly linked to regime type (whether authoritarian or populist), so privatization has gained ground, in the Latin American context, in harshly authoritarian (Chile), benignly authoritarian (Mexico), and democratic (Argentina and Venezuela) regimes. Hence the argument, made by those examining the Chilean case, that the depth of Latin America's first extensive privatization program has to be understood in terms of the isolation of the Chilean military government from political concerns[43] cannot be generalized. Since, outside of the Chilean case, the literature on the Latin American privatization policy process is sparce, this book draws largely on the work dealing with stabilization and structural adjustment policies (of which privatization has become an important part) for insights into the process and circumstances of neoliberal policy reform. This literature links the successful implementation of orthodox structural adjustment to an exclusionary decision-making process, regardless of formal regime type—that is, whether procedurally democratic or not. Stephan Haggard, in an examination of structural adjustment in seven developing countries, suggests that successful structural adjustment policies are likely to be associated with "a cohesive group of sympathetic technocrats forming the domestic half of a transnational alliance with the [International Monetary] Fund"[44] capable of resisting societal political pressures.

Similarly, Merilee Grindle and John Thomas acknowledge that the policy reforms of the 1980s sprang from the enhanced role of lending institutions and local technocrats responsible for the implementation

15

of structural adjustment programs.[45] Successful structural adjustment, it has been argued, requires state managers to reduce the size of their support coalition, because the smaller the coalition, the more compatible the interests of its components and the lower the level of resources required to maintain it—especially important in times of fiscal austerity. This is so because fiscal austerity (one of the most important aspects of structural adjustment) limits the rewards state elites can make available to supporters and therefore reduces the maneuverability of those policy elites. Under such circumstances, it is tempting to shed labor as a coalitional partner, despite the long-term political risks.[46] These observations, which suggest an authoritarian style of decision making, appear to be relevant even to those Latin American regimes that have been described as democratic.

While a simple association between orthodox structural adjustment and authoritarianism has been shown to be problematic,[47] one recent study distinguishes between authoritarian regimes and established democracies, which are more likely to successfully pursue orthodox stabilization or structural adjustment programs, and transitional or new democracies, which are much more subject to pressures for expansionary policies, such as growth in public expenditure and the expansion of credit.[48] Another study lends support to this argument, pointing out that regime change (from military to civilian) is associated with labor gains in wages, while "old" democratic regimes do not guarantee any better distribution of the costs of austerity than do authoritarian regimes.[49] This is the case because new or transitional democracies have increased levels of political mobilization and conflict, as leaders are now confronted with previously repressed demands. Leaders are likely to give in to those demands because of the fear of increased political unrest, which could set the stage for a return to authoritarian rule. Such regimes, dependent on labor and popular support, are likely to generate heterodox programs, while those dependent on the support of business and finance will tend to support orthodox programs. Trade unions have been described as the most important threat to successful stabilization and structural adjustment.[50] Particularly patronage-laden regimes, it is argued, are unlikely to implement structural changes, as such systems are believed to steadfastly resist the shifting of allocative responsibilities to impersonal market forces.[51]

A clue to the ability of established procedurally democratic regimes to implement orthodox structural adjustment is perhaps to be found in their marked authoritarian executive decision-making styles. Due to the unpopularity of stabilization and structural adjustment measures, their implementation in such countries as Bolivia, Ecuador, and Peru has involved highly exclusionary political styles, in which decision making is heavily centralized in the executive. In all of these countries, neoliberal policies were carried out through executive decrees, producing what has been described as a "hybrid form of government" in which a "formal democratic facade marks a real authoritarian bent."[52]

Moreover, even within the subtype of "new democracies," believed more open to popular pressure, authoritarian decision-making styles are in evidence. Within their category of countries in democratic transition, Stephan Haggard and Robert Kaufman identify three subtypes and conclude that those countries with a highly concentrated executive decision-making authority and less popular mobilization have been the most successful at structural adjustment.[53] Other studies have pointed to highly concentrated forms of executive decision making even in the cases of heterodox adjustment programs. Both President José Sarney, of Brazil, and President Raúl Alfonsín, of Argentina, retained considerable discretionary authority (a legacy of the previous period of military rule), with the result that both labor and business were largely excluded from executive decision making.[54] In Argentina, the heterodox policy package known as the Austral Plan was prepared in secret, involving the participation of neither business nor labor, and was implemented without legislative approval and over the vigorous opposition of labor.[55]

On the basis of the literature discussed above, it is reasonable to conclude that the political opposition to privatization, likely responsible for slowing down the process in many countries,[56] suggests the need for a state with the capacity to overcome popular opposition and intrastate bureaucratic resistance if privatization is to go forward. The obstacles to privatization are enormous, since the process inevitably calls for the dismantling of what in many cases has been not only instruments of patronage but also symbols of national pride and economic prowess.[57] At the same time, massive debt and fiscal crisis have severely weakened those state enterprises remaining in state hands, thereby rendering them less able to carry out the various political, social, and economic functions for which they were created. Moreover, the fact that privatization is widely seen as an IMF/World Bank–induced policy prescription cannot help but taint governments that pursue such policies with vigor.

While most of Latin America has traded highly repressive military regimes for civilian regimes with formal democratic procedures, authoritarianist decision-making styles stubbornly persist. Driven by the force of circumstances toward economic liberalization, neoliberal political elites must increasingly insulate themselves from opposition pressures in order to successfully implement their policies. State managers invariably face growing political alienation from civil society as they attempt to redefine the role of the state. Lacking the co-optative mechanisms of previous regimes, given the severity of fiscal restrictions, they must seek alternative mechanisms to obtain support and legitimacy. State managers may take measures to establish new links with civil society, or they may seek to politically weaken civil society by ensuring its segmentation. Nevertheless, the temptation to use various forms of repression remains great. Forced to abandon many of the symbols of nationalist rhetoric, such as state enterprises, along with their historic vocation as managers of the developmentalist state, neoliberal political elites will have to develop a new political discourse—one that merges the policy requirements of neoliberalism with some of the old ideals of a populist nationalism. Neoliberal political elites who fail to make these sorts of adjustments may not survive politically, even with considerable repression. At the same time, the political elite's success in establishing a new coalitional base and new sources of regime legitimacy may influence its willingness to tolerate political liberalization.[58]

The pursuit of structural adjustment, therefore, involves changes more profound than a modification of existent political arrangements. The groups backing bureaucratic policy leaders must change in fundamental ways. It will likely become necessary to discard previous support groups, particularly labor, as the new economic program makes it impossible to satisfy its interests even minimally. At the same time, the emergence of global capitalism, combined with the policy implications of a high degree of indebtedness manifested in pressures, whether through leverage or influence, to implement the policy prescriptions of the IMF and the World Bank makes the cultivation of private sector interests, particularly MNCs offering export capacity, increasingly important for the state.[59]

The extent of Mexico's economic liberalization program, combined with the past centrality of its state both politically and economically, makes an examination of the links between privatization, changes in the coalitional basis of the state, and changes in the institutional arrangements of political control especially pertinent. Ruled for over fifty years by the Institutional Revolutionary Party (PRI), Mexico has avoided the swings between political chaos and highly repressive military rule that have characterized many Latin American countries. Between 1940 and 1970, a highly interventionist state, spawning a mammoth state enterprise sector, led an industrialization project that achieved average growth rates of 6 percent per year along with severe inequalities.[60] And as noted, Mexico's privatization process, under way since 1985, has been an extensive one. Certainly, stiff political resistance was present in the Mexican case, but Mexico's unique political arrangements enabled the state to readily overcome that resistance. At the same time, however, privatization has been integral to the transformation of those very arrangements. In the process, privatization has involved a fundamental alteration in the power structure within the state.

Mexican Authoritarianism in Transition

Most of the literature characterizes Mexico's postrevolutionary regime as authoritarian in nature. One well-known analysis points to the characteristics of limited pluralism, low political participation, and patron clientelism as being its major traits.[61] In such a context, the role of organized groups, particularly popular groups, has tended to be reactive, since limited political mobilization and patron clientelism reduce political demands. The limited pluralism of organized groups, usually characterized as a product of the interaction of corporatist structures with patron clientelism, has been instrumental in maintaining the relative stability of the system: it has been essential in limiting the independent political action of potentially oppositional groups. While care must be taken not to characterize the Mexican political system as monolithic, the two hierarchical principles of corporatism and patron clientelism have been instrumental in containing dissent from some of the best-organized groups within the popular classes in strategic economic sectors.[62]

Most discussions of the co-optative–control capabilities of Mexico's political system have focused on the operation of the dominant Institutional Revolutionary Party (PRI). Under its corporatist structure, popular organizations purporting to represent workers and peasants have been incorporated into the party apparatus in such a way as to minimize, if not eliminate, the potential for popular dissent. Patron clientelism, a "tie between two parties of unequal wealth and influence" that "depends upon the exchange of goods and services,"[63] has operated to reinforce the subordination of these organizations. Premised on the economic vulnerability of a weaker client, patron clientelism involves the exchange of material rewards (from the more powerful patron to the weaker client) for political support from the client. Hence, cooperative worker and peasant leaders have been rewarded with opportunities to run for electoral office and plum positions within the party and at the top levels of the union bureaucracies.

Corporatism has its roots in Mexico's postrevolutionary history. Formal incorporation of popular organizations within the official party occurred during the presidency of Lázaro Cárdenas (1934–1940). In 1938, the regional groupings within the party were dropped and replaced by sectoral representation from labor, peasants, the popular sector, and the military, which later disappeared from the coalition. Cárdenas sponsored the Confederación de Trabajadores de México (Confederation of Mexican Workers, or CTM) and the Confederación National de Campesinos (National Confederation of Peasants, or CNC) and incorporated them into the official party as sectoral representatives. The popular sector, known as the Confederación Nacional de Organizaciones Populares (National Confederation of Popular Organizations, or CNOP), comprised organizations representing a number of important middle-class interests, along with elements of the urban poor, and was also incorporated into the party.

In the years following the Cárdenas presidency, the party became a mechanism of popular control. Particularly during the Second World War, control over labor unions was tightened, as radical leaders were replaced by more acquiescent ones bound to the system by means of material rewards. Control of the party, through the choice of candidates and their sectoral distribution, came to be exercised from the top downward—by the president, governors, and sectoral leaders. Hence, the minimization of dissent and potential dissent from labor groups was premised on control through nationwide organizations incorporated into the party apparatus. Labor resistance to this strategy presented some difficulties for the regime: some of the country's most important trade unions chose to stay out of the CTM. In 1966, therefore, the government of President Díaz Ordaz promoted the establishment of a new umbrella labor organization, the Congreso del Trabajo (Labor Congress, or CT), to allow centralized state control of all the country's most important trade unions.

In addition to the hierarchical arrangements described above, other mechanisms have contributed to the legitimacy and relative stability of the regime: healthy economic growth rates of over 6 percent per year between 1940 and the late 1960s, improved living standards for selected working-class groups, and a powerful nationalist revolutionary mythology that has regarded the PRI as the purveyor of the ideals of the Mexican Revolution. Violent repression has certainly not been absent from the PRI's arsenal of political weaponry, but it has usually been a last resort.[64]

On the other hand, the relationship between the private sector and the state has been qualitatively different from that between the state and popular groups. While the degree of independence of the private sector from the state is a subject of considerable debate,[65] the consensus is that the state in no way controls the private sector to the extent it controls labor, peasants, and other popular groups. Indeed, some of the most well-known work on the subject has argued that the state and the private sector are able to act independently of each other: while the state cannot control the private sector, neither can the private sector control state action.[66] Absent has been the top-down corporatist and clientelist control that have characterized the state's relationship with other social groups. Although there has been considerable debate over the extent of business influence over public policy, it is generally agreed

21

that business has not only had a major influence on public policy but has also been its major beneficiary.

Despite its authoritarian features, however, the Mexican case has usually been regarded as considerably more inclusionary than the now terminated military-bureaucratic authoritarian regimes of the Southern Cone. A substantial body of work on Mexico has stressed the fact that the Mexican political elite has displayed a considerable degree of heterogeneity.[67] A variety of views were accommodated within the state, and a process of bargaining between competing interests and ideological tendencies is believed to have taken place—even after 1970, when the recruitment basis of Mexico's political elite moved from the party to the state bureaucracy.

A study published by Susan Kaufman Purcell and John F. Purcell over a decade ago points to "a constantly renewed political bargain among several ruling groups and interests, representing a broad range of ideological tendencies and social bases."[68] It is argued that a diversity of elite groups share power in Mexico, each with quite differenct interests and constituencies—some with constituencies within the state, others with power bases outside the state. Indeed, while the initiative in policy may have rested in the hands of the political elite,[69] the need to consult elite groups outside the state bureaucracy has long been recognized. The "revolutionary family" comprised of former presidents, regional strongmen, certain state governors, the heads of the CTM, the CNC, and the CNOP, and the country's wealthiest businessmen (and anyone else the president of the day deemed it necessary to consult) joined the country's most important cabinet ministers and directors of the key public companies in influencing policy.[70] Hence, although the policy process was certainly heavily centralized in the hands of the president and his closest advisors, those able to influence policy were a heterogeneous lot.

Moreover, although big business may have had priviledged access to the state, small and medium business has been able to make its policy preferences felt. In fact, in a number of notable cases (the last years of the administrations of Luis Echeverría and José López Portillo, for example) relations between the country's political elite and the most powerful business interests were extremely tense, while some decisions, such as the 1980 decision not to enter the GATT, reflected many of the concerns of small and medium business.[71] Furthermore, the method of political incorporation allowed privileged labor leaders to accumulate substantial wealth and to join the business class. The system also afforded the most powerful among them a certain amount of political influence.

The tension between the political and economic elites has, at times, been particularly tense, a fact probably contributing to the system's incorporative capacity as far as the popular classes and small and medium business were concerned. Indeed, the resilience and durability of Mexican authoritarianism has stemmed from its incorporative features, as later chapters demonstrate. State and regime, then, in Mexico were mutually reinforcing: flexible authoritarian institutional arrangements allowed a heterogeneous coalition to maintain political control with a minimum use of overt violent repression.

The literature on Mexico points to changes in Mexico's traditional co-optative-clientelist regime arrangements, beginning with the economic crisis of the late 1960s and the ensuing political crisis that culminated in the 1968 massacre at Tlatelolco of some two hundred student demonstrators. From this time onward, alienation from and opposition to the predominant PRI party has gained ground. The economic crisis of the 1980s and the following economic restructuring program have accelerated the deterioration of many of the features of Mexico's traditional political system.[72]

This book focuses on the impact of privatization on the process of political transition. Its starting point is a discussion of the economic and political role of state enterprises—a role, given the strategic importance of the economic sectors concerned and the militancy of their workers, that became integral to the traditional system of co-optation and control. Under this system, the powerful trade unions of the public enterprise sector formed the core of the state's corporatist-clientelist control of the working class. Indeed, given the strategic nature of these economic sectors, the control of these unions was essential to the success of the government's economic model.

Furthermore, the extensiveness of public enterprise activities had important implications for the distribution of power within the state: it assumed a decentralization of bureaucratic power favoring public firms that facilitated the co-optative capabilities of the state. Privatization has brought about basic alterations in these arrangements: it has involved a fundamental adjustment in the power structure within the state and in state-societal relations. While the impact of the dismantling of the state has important implications for the process of political transition, it must be born in mind that Mexico's privatization drive was formulated as part of a broader restructuring program focused on trade liberalization and a tough adjustment involving a drastic reduction in government investment and expenditure. The nature and direction of Mexico's privatization must be understood within this context. Nor can the political implications of privatization be neatly disentangled from the political impact of other economic policies in the economic restructuring and adjustment package.

The debate about the direction of political change within Mexico is becoming increasingly heated. There are those who argue that the opening of the Mexican economy is destined to produce broadened political participation and an inevitable process of democratization. Such factors as the decentralization of economic and political power brought about by privatization, the reduction of corruption, and the pressure exerted by Mexico's NAFTA partners for more political freedoms are among the forces pushing Mexico toward greater democracy.[73] Others are hopeful for some degree of political liberalization, pointing to such encouraging trends as past political reforms and President Salinas's apparent commitment to further such political reform.[74] Still others anticipate a trend toward more authoritarianism in light of IMF-imposed austerity measures.[75] I take the position that there is no clear trend toward democratization. However, important changes have occurred in the nature and operation of Mexican authoritarianism and in the composition of the societal coalition guiding state policy: statist bureaucrats, the most powerful sectors of organized labor, and small and medium business have been shed as coalitional partners.[76] The most important groups are now state bureaucrats closely identified with the finance functions within the state bureaucracy and their big-business allies.

In the policy-making realm, certain authoritarian features have intensified: policy making is no longer influenced by a heterogeneous elite with a wide variety of constituencies; pluralism remains limited, and clientelism remains a central feature of the system. The massive reduction of the state apparatus has meant an alteration in the functioning and target groups of clientelism. Authoritarian control through the centralized clientelist control of the country's most powerful labor leaders has been partially replaced by a decentralized cultivation of certain organized groups (those linked with the current economic model) along with the parallel co-optation (usually unmediated by the party) of marginalized groups.

While privatization has meant that the state may have divested itself of the inordinate influence of certain labor and bureaucratic sectors, the influence of international economic and domestic business pressures is now greater than ever. The ruling group now consists of a homogeneous circle of finance sector political bureaucrats who must be open like never before to the policy preferences of the country's biggest business interests. And while Mexico's political elite has been able to override popular pressures, it operates within a policy environment of severely limited options. The government now has the country's powerful business interests and international capital onside, but with the move to privatization, it is now more dependent on them than ever to ensure the success of its new economic model and, with that, its own political survival.

2

The Evolution of Public Enterprise in Mexico

Until the recent economic liberalization drive, Mexico's postrevolutionary economic experience, particularly its industrialization strategy, had been characterized by a strong and expanding state leadership role. State enterprises have been indispensable instruments of this role. They have also had important social and political responsibilities—functions that often emerged as a consequence of attempts to make the chosen economic model palatable to mobilized sectors of the popular classes. Through various means, state firms have expanded the state's co-optative capacities and contributed to regime legitimacy. A severe fiscal crisis, however, became the major contradiction of this extensive public enterprise activity, a contradiction that would set the stage for the state's eventual dismantling.

In Mexico, public enterprises, known as parastatals, have included a wide variety of types of firms. *Decentralized agencies* are state enterprises entirely owned by the state, created by an act of congress or by the federal executive, while *enterprises of majority state participation* include a variety of financial institutions and other companies in which the federal government or its agencies own 50 percent of the shares. *Enterprises of minority state participation* are those in which the state owns between 25 and 50 percent of the shares. By 1982, this varied public enterprise sector was comprised of over a thousand firms spanning industrial, commercial, and banking activities.

Public Enterprise from the Revolution to 1940

Born of the revolutionary struggle of 1911–1917, the new constitution of 1917 provided norms that would become the basis for the subsequent proliferation of state firms. Its article 27 gave the nation direct ownership of all minerals and deposits beneath the soil, ownership of all water, lakes, and principal rivers, and the right to dispose of private property in the public interest.[1] Article 73 established the state's jurisdiction over credit institutions and the issuance of money, while article 123 empowered the state to solve disputes between capital and labor. Article 28 reserved the issuance of money to a single bank controlled by the federal government.[2] With these responsibilities established in law, the period 1920–1934 was one of transition and reconstruction, during which the basis for later growth was established. Public expenditure moved from its earlier emphasis on mining to the reconstruction of infrastructure, particularly irrigation works, roads, and electrical energy. Public enterprises emerged slowly during this period (see tables 2.1, 2.2). Institutional reconstruction occurred first in the banking industry in the 1920s, with the establishment of the first postrevolutionary public enterprises: the Bank of Mexico (Banco de México) and the National Bank of Agricultural Credit (Banco Nacional de Crédito Agrícola).

Although important institutional innovations occurred during the 1920s, the economic structure of the country remained unchanged: land ownership continued to be highly concentrated, and the country's most important economic activities (mining, railways, petroleum, and electricity) were in the hands of foreigners. By 1910, U.S. investment controlled 80 percent of mining, and between 1891 and 1910, mining exports represented between 73 and 65 percent of total Mexican exports, most of this going to the United States.[3] Closely tied to mining was the construction of railways that carried mineral exports to Mexican ports and northward to U.S. markets. Between 1890 and 1905, four or five foreign companies controlled the railway system. Indeed, the near monopoly prompted the government to purchase a

27

TABLE 2.1

Establishment of Major Public Enterprises

1908	Ferrocarriles Nacionales (51%)
1925	Banco de México
1926	Banco Nacional de Crédito Agrícola
1934	Nacional Financiera (NAFINSA) (development bank)
1934	Comisión de Fomento Minero (mining)
1937	Compañía de los Ferrocarriles de México (FERRONALES) (railways)
1937	Comisión Federal de Electricidad (CFE). Industry nationalized in 1960
1938	Petróleos Mexicanos (PEMEX) (petroleum)
1942	Altos Hornos (AHMSA) (steel)
1943	Guanos y Fertilisantes (GUANOMEX) (fertilizer). Industry nationalized 1965–1967; established as FERTIMEX in 1977.
1952	La Constructora Nacional de Ferrocarril (CONCARRIL) (railway cars)
1951	Diesel Nacional (DINA) (buses, motors)
1944	Instituto Mexicano de Seguro (IMSS)
1947	La Cía Minera Santo Roselía (mining)
1947	La Cía del Real del Monte y Pachuga (mining)
1959	AEROMEXICO (airline)
1960	Instituto de Seguridad y Servicios Sociales de los Trabajadores del Estado (ISSSTE)
1961	Compañía Nacional de Subsistencias Populares (CONASUPO). Expanded 1970–1976. Precursor: Comité Regulator del Trigo (1937).
1971	Siderúrgica Lázaro Cárdenas–Las Truchas (SICARTSA) (steel)
1971	Cananea (copper) (51% of shares acquired by (NAFINSA)
1972	TELMEX (51%)
1978	Fundidora Monterrey (steel)
1982	Mexicana de Aviación (airline)
1982	Nationalized Banking Sector (18 banks)
1983	Instituto Mexicano de Televisión
1983	Azucar S.A. (sugar) (grouped state sugar refineries), majority of which were statized 1970–1976.

The group of entries from 1942 (Altos Hornos) through 1951 (Diesel Nacional) are bracketed together under the label **NAFINSA**.

Note: Dates indicate when the company was established as a solely owned state company or awhen the state acquired more than 50 percent of the shares of an existing company.

TABLE 2.2

Creation of Public Enterprises, by Type and Year

	Enterprises with State Participation	Decentralized Agencies	Fiduciary Institutions	Total
1917–1921	2	—	—	2
1921–1930	8	2	—	10
1930–1933	6	—	—	6
1934–1940	29	10	—	39
1940–1945	37	14	—	51
1945–1950	30	20	—	50
1950–1959	65	36	—	101
1960–1970	105	27	—	132
1970–1976	458	176	211	845
1976–1982	829	103	223	1,155

Source: 1917–1982: Tamayo, "Relación gobierno federal," 228; 1976–1982: Secretaría de la Contraloría General de la Federación, Restructuración del sector parastatal, 74.

majority of the shares in two companies in 1908, consolidating Ferrocarriles Nacionales de Mexico, in which it held 51 percent of the shares.[4] Two foreign conglomerates controlled the electricity sector: Mexican Light and Power maintained a monopoly in central Mexico, while the American and Foreing Power Company operated throughout the national territory. Encouraged by land grants and other concessions, foreign capital (British and American) entered Mexico's petroleum industry at the turn of the century, with the result that the industry came to be controlled by British and American interests.[5] By the First World War, petroleum had become an important export, with Mexico supplying nearly 25 percent of the world's supply of crude.[6]

The Great Depression was the catalyst for the deepening of the state's interventionist role. Between 1926 and 1932, the value of Mexican exports was reduced 71 percent, the value of imports declined 69 percent, and GDP dropped 27 percent.[7] The exhaustion of Mexico's international reserves, the collapse of the capacity to import, and the contraction of government revenue forced the authorities to reformulate their ideas of economic management. Beginning in 1932, the government pursued a countercyclical monetary policy, and beginning in 1936, it began to run deficits as an explicit component of its antidepression policies.[8] The administration of Lázaro Cárdenas (1934–1940) not only increased the amount spent on economic infrastructure and social programs but also dramatically expanded the role of the state in the economy, particularly through the establishment of public firms. Indeed, it was during Cárdenas's administration that Mexico's most important public enterprises were established.

The expansion of the state enterprise sector during the period was driven by a combination of factors: the requisites of economic growth, the force of nationalist sentiment, especially on the part of workers in foreign enclaves such as petroleum, mining, and electricity (discussed further in the following chapter), and worker discontent over deteriorating economic conditions. The 1936 Expropriation Law (Ley de Expropriación) gave the state the unlimited right to intervene in the economy and set the stage for the state takeover of a number of key industries.[9] Nationalizations carried out during the Cárdenas administration resulted in the formation of new public firms occupying strategic economic sectors in railways, electricity, and petroleum.

The most important expropriation of the period was the state takeover of foreign companies in the petroleum industry. Although the catalyst was a labor dispute with the foreign management of the companies, the expropriation responded also to the growing nationalist opposition to foreign control of the industry.[10] There was a growing belief that domestic consumption demands were not being met by foreign companies, that the decline in petroleum production was a consequence of the companies' failure to carry out an adequate exploration and drilling program, and that consequently any further decline in the industry represented a serious threat to the national economy.[11] Petróleos Mexicanos (PEMEX) was created in 1938 to carry out exploration, production, and refining, with marketing functions added in 1940, making it Latin America's first fully integrated state-owned petroleum company. The period also witnessed an expansion of the state's regulatory role into other strategic sectors, such as mining, where the state, with the strong support of the mine workers, sought to reduce the role of foreign mining companies.[12]

The rate of growth of federal public investment accelerated markedly during the 1934–1940 period.[13] The expanding role of public development banks (Cárdenas established seven of them) provided the funds for public sector investment in roads, irrigation, and energy production.[14] Hence, whereas the public enterprise sector was practically nonexistent at the beginning of the 1930s and involved largely financial institutions, by 1940 the state had become involved in the direct production of a number of important industrial inputs: petroleum, electrical energy, and mining. Public expenditure as a percentage of GDP continued to increase, from 6.6 percent in 1935 to 7.7 percent in 1940, while the investment made by public enterprises as a percentage of total public investment increased substantially, as did its percentage of GDP (tables 2.3 and 2.4).

With expansion of the state's responsibilities, government expenditure expanded beyond the state's financial capabilities. In 1936, the expenditure of the government was greater than its income, and a deficit situation characterized government finances for the remainder of the administration.[15] As a consequence, the domestic debt grew 71 percent between 1934 and 1940.[16] Two public enterprises, FERRONALES (Compañía de los Ferrocarriles de México, the railway company) and PEMEX, accounted for over 90 percent of public enterprise investment during the period.[17] Conflict within the state over the rising level of government expenditures emerged almost from the beginning of the Cárdenas administration between the president and his bureaucratic supporters, on the one hand, who championed the state's highly interventionist role, and Central Bank and Ministry of Finance officials, on the other, who opposed the use of banking credit to finance investment programs.[18] Sylvia Maxfield argues that two competing alliances arose in this period: the Cárdenas alliance, with its bureaucratic faction centered in such ministries as labor, agriculture, and property and industry, among others, and allied to the worker and peasant sectors of the PRI, espoused expansionary policies and state control of strategic economic sectors, while the Bankers' Alliance, located in the Ministry of Finance and the Central Bank and allied with the country's most powerful financial interests, was guided by a laissez-faire ideology and supported tight monetary policy.[19] This intrabureaucratic conflict became a common feature of the Mexican policy process and would be integral to the evolution and ultimate dismantling of most of Mexico's

TABLE 2.3

State Participation in the Economy: Basic Indicators, 1925–1982
(as percentage of GDP)

	Public Expenditure	Public Investment	Public Enterprise Investment
1925	5.6	1.6	0.9
1930	6.0	2.2	0.9
1935	6.6	3.0	0.9
1940	7.7	3.5	1.7
1945	7.7	4.1	1.8
1950	8.2	6.3	3.6
1955	9.9	4.9	2.8
1960	12.6	5.2	3.5
1965	23.9	6.1	4.0
1970	24.6	6.6	4.3
1975	36.4	8.7	6.2
1980	41.6	11.4	7.3
1982	58.6	10.8	8.4

Source: Calculated from Ayala Espino, *Estado y desarrollo*, 52, 59–61, 396.

public enterprises. Meanwhile, the state's heavily interventionist role during the Cárdenas years, combined with the populist nature of many Cardenista reforms (land redistribution, support for workers' economic and social demands, and the integration of workers and peasants into the political process) produced growing business opposition.[20] As a consequence, the years after 1940 saw a reversal of a number of Cardenista policies, particularly land reform, and the pursuit of an economic model offering generous advantages to Mexico's industrialists.[21]

Public Enterprise and State-Led Industrialization (1940–1970)

The period between 1940 and 1970 was one of unabashed pursuit of industrialization by the state and of agricultural neglect. While public policy prior to 1960 favored agriculture for commercial export, post-1960 policy was generally less favorable toward agriculture.

TABLE 2.4

Structure of Public Expenditure and Investment
(in percent)

	Expenditures		Public Enterprise Investment
	Federal Government	Public Enterprise	
1925	—	—	54.8
1930	—	—	39.7
1935	—	—	29.8
1940	63.5	22.6	49.2
1945	43.9	37.9	44.1
1950	35.3	51.4	60.0
1955	55.6	44.3	56.5
1960	59.3	40.6	66.8
1965	48.5	51.7	66.5
1970	47.1	51.0	—
1975	50.0	50.0	73.1
1982	47.7	52.3	65.5

Source: Calculated from Ayala Espino, *Estado y desarrollo*, 299–300, 396, 451.

Note: Figures for 1940–1950 exclude payments on the debt.

Economists usually divide the years 1940 to 1970 into two subperiods, 1940–1957 and 1958–1970. During the second period, known as stabilizing development, the government abandoned its inflationary financing of government expenditure and turned to noninflationary methods, such as increasing the legal reserve requirement, external indebtedness, and direct foreign investment. This strategy reflected the dominance of the Finance Ministry within the state and its predisposition for reliance on the private sector, as reflected in a wide variety of stimulative measures: tax incentives, credit, and industrial protection.

As well as continuing to provide and improve essential infrastructure, the state moved further into the production of strategic inputs for industry, which it made available at below-international-market prices. The production of these inputs was carried out by public enterprises, which became the axle of the government's industrialization program.[22] In order to maintain the confidence of the private sector, President Manuel Avila Camacho initiated the practice of appointing private sector representatives to the boards of directors of some of these firms.[23] Meanwhile, the private sector predominated in the consumer goods branches and carried out an increasing proportion of total investment.[24]

State credit played a critical role in the industrial expansion that occurred during the period. Between 1942 and 1970, fiduciary institutions (trusts), which focused resources on the stimulation of priority development areas, and national banks supplied more capital to industry than did the commercial banks.[25] In 1941, Nacional Financiera (NAFINSA) was reorganized as an industrial development bank, and over the next twelve years it promoted enterprises in almost every sector of the Mexican economy.[26] By the mid-1950s, it was supplying over 36 percent of total financing, most of which went to the public sector.[27] By 1961, NAFINSA was creditor, investor, or guarantor of 533 business enterprises of all kinds.[28] Although NAFINSA's dominant role was that of creditor, it also acquired ownership shares in many enterprises over the years. This occurred when it provided capital to debt-ridden firms, when it accepted stock ownership in payment for loans, and when it rescued failing companies by buying out private owners. NAFINSA also played a key role in the establishment of a number of important enterprises. With these enterprises, NAFINSA continued the state's march into the production of essential industrial and agricultural inputs and equipment—steel, fertilizer, and the manufacture of railway cars and trucks.

The requirements of industrial expansion were not the only motive behind the state's expansion: social and political factors continued to motivate the establishment of state enterprises. The state's expansion into the mining industry, for example, sprung not just from nationalist criticism of the monopoly structure and foreign control of the industry but also from concerns about the economic stagnation and the desire to preserve employment in local and rural communities. Hence, the government rescued a number of mines, usually abandoned by the private sector. The acquisition of mining companies by the Commission for Mining Development (Comisión de Fomento Minera, or CFM) in 1947 signaled a new stage in government mining policy, away from the promotion of co-ops and toward the use of state enterprises.[29] In 1961, legislation regulated article 27 of the constitution, establishing national sovereignty over mineral resources and their exploitation.[30]

The combination of a desire to respond to popular nationalist sentiments and a commitment to keep the price of electrical energy down and extend service prompted the nationalization of the electrical industry in 1960,[31] bringing the two most important private sector electrical enterprises (the Mexican Light and Power Company and the American Foreing Power Company) under the administration of the Federal Electricity Commission (Comisión Federal de Electricidad, or CFE).[32] The responsibilities of the state-owned petroleum company (PEMEX) also expanded during the period. Under President Adolfo Ruiz Cortines, legislation was passed reforming article 27 of the constitution, giving PEMEX the exclusive right to the production of basic petrochemicals and to the transportation and distribution of all products of petroleum and gas.[33]

Public enterprises having strictly social welfare responsibilities also began to emerge during this period. The Mexican Institute of Social Security (Instituto Mexicano de Seguro Social, or IMSS) was established to provide health and social security services to urban salaried workers, and the Institute of Security and Social Services for State Workers (Instituto de Seguridad y Servicios Sociales de los Trabajadores del Estado, or ISSSTE) was set up in 1960 to provide social security to state employees.[34] In 1961, the Companía Exportadora e Importadora Mexicana S.A. (Mexican Import and Export Company, or CEIMSA) was restructured to form the Companía Nacional de Subsistencias Populares (National Basic Foods Company, or CONASUPO), responsible for the provision of basic foodstuffs to marginal populations.

Once again, this expansion of the state was reflected in the dramatic increase in the levels of expenditure and investment. But by the 1960s, the public sector was borrowing to finance its expanding role in the economy. As noted, this situation was linked to the economic strategy of stabilizing development employed by Mexico's policy elite after 1958: the abandonment of inflationary financing of public sector investment now meant a reliance on increased foreign capital inflows. Mexico's foreign debt became the "adjustment mechanism" that would allow the continued expansion of the public sector.[35] Hence, public expenditure as a percentage of GDP increased from 7.7 percent in 1940 to over 24 percent by 1970 (table 2.3). Public investment grew at over 8 percent between 1940 and 1954 and at over 12 percent between 1954 and 1970[36]—that is, faster than the growth rate in GDP. Public enterprise investment increased particularly rapidly. As well, Mexico's debt-service ratio increased from 16.3 percent in 1960 to 23.2 percent in 1970.[37] With such strong state support, industry surged forward during the period: its proportion of GDP increased, while those of mining and agriculture decreased.[38]

The public enterprise sector was the most dynamic element of public sector expansion. By 1970, public enterprise expenditure accounted for slightly more than one-half of federal public outlays (table 2.4), up from 22.6 percent in 1940. Public enterprise investment as a proportion of total public investment increased substantially, as well (table 2.4). Over 80 percent of state industrial production was in petroleum, capital, and intermediate goods—that is, inputs for industry.[39]

Public policy neglect of agriculture and consequent declining agricultural production and exports, along with an industrial structure heavily dependent on expensive imported inputs and technology, contributed to a growing balance of payments deficit. The failure to invest adequately in agriculture and petroleum set the stage for Mexico to become a net importer in both food and petroleum by the early 1970s. At the same time, the import-substitution industrialization that had occurred during the 1960s had promoted the manufacture of consumer durables, the market for which was becoming saturated. As economic growth stagnated, unemployment and underemployment reached an estimated 40 to 50 percent.[40] Two economic strategies, spanning the years 1970 to 1982, attempted to find a way out of these economic difficulties; both entailed extensive expansion of the public enterprise sector.

Public Enterprise Expansion During Stagnation and Boom (1970–1982)

The period 1970–1982 witnessed an even more dramatic expansion of the public enterprise sector. While during the administration of Luis Echeverría (1970–1976) this expansion reflected the state's efforts to end economic stagnation, the growth of the sector under José López Portillo (1976–1982) was linked to the central role of PEMEX during the petroleum boom years, the massive inflow of capital that made possible further expansion of the public enterprise sector in general, and the 1981 economic collapse that precipitated the bank nationalization. The public enterprise sector continued to lead economic growth, providing cheap inputs and services to the private sector and expanding employment opportunities. By the end of the period, the contradictions of this role surfaced in the form of a severe fiscal crisis.

President Luis Echeverría's strategy to overcome the economic stagnation that had set in by the late 1960s was known as shared development. It involved a substantial expansion in state expenditure, calling for increased investment in agriculture, especially small and ejidal agriculture. In other areas, such as petroleum, spending was increased in order to remove the bottlenecks to economic growth. The strategy also emphasized redistributive and social welfare measures and entailed extensive state intervention to save failing industries. Total expenditure and investment increased rapidly during the Echeverría years, increasing from 23.6 percent of GDP in 1970 to 36.6 percent by 1975.[41] Between 1970 and 1975, the state acquired a large number of enterprises spanning a variety of sectors, many rescued by the state to protect employment. The most important ones are listed above. Between 1970 and 1976, the number of state enterprises increased by over 700 (table 2.2), while public enterprise investment as a proportion of GDP increased (table 2.3).

The discovery of vast petroleum reserves and the decision by the new administration of President López Portillo to use petroleum as the new *palanca* (lever) of economic development removed the necessity of instituting painful structural reforms and made possible a period of uncontrolled expansion of public enterprises, particularly of PEMEX. With Mexico's vast petroleum reserves attracting an abundance of foreign financing, the public enterprise sector experienced a period of unrestrained growth. The original aim, that Mexican petroleum exports would finance industrial growth, was lost sight of as the extraction and exportation of petroleum became an end in itself. Between 1975 and 1979 and again between 1982 and 1983, the participation of public enterprises in GDP more than doubled.[42] The economic crisis itself brought about an unprecedented expansion of the state in 1982, when, in the face of capital flight and political crisis, the López Portillo government nationalized eighteen private sector banks. Although ostensively linked to efforts to stem the outflow of capital, political motivations were by no means absent from the bank nationalization.[43] The state immediately acquired shares in 480 companies owned by the banks, by virtue of the fact that the banks held shares in a variety of firms, 40 percent of which were manufacturing concerns.[44] The number of public enterprises continued to increase (table 2.2). Public enterprise investment increased its proportion of GDP (table 2.3), while private investment lagged.[45]

Whereas state manufacturing had increased its participation in the total value of state production up to 1975, after that date primary activities, particularly the production of petroleum and natural gas, came to predominate as the exploitation and exportation of petroleum led economic growth. Petroleum and natural gas increased their proportion of total gross state production from 17.1 percent in 1970 to over 45 percent by 1980.[46] Public enterprise growth, particularly that of PEMEX, led economic growth. Between 1970 and 1980, the annual growth rate of the sales of goods and services of public enterprises was 10.4 percent, while the national economy grew at the rate of 6.6 percent per year.[47] PEMEX paid the lion's share of taxes, and its exports were by far the country's most important source of foreign exchange.[48]

But it was the nature of the role of the public enterprise sector, as much as its extensiveness, that would produce an unbearable fiscal burden. The financial situation of Mexico's major public firms deteriorated throughout the period; by 1982, public firms accounted for nearly one-half of the public sector deficit.[49] Although a variety of factors account for this situation, including laxity of financial control and the clientelist ways in which public firms operated, underpricing of public enterprise goods and services was probably the most important factor.[50] The growth of prices of the public sector were maintained, on average, up to 10 percent below the general level of inflation.[51] The private sector was the major beneficiary of the low prices for public goods and services, although consumers and lower socioeconomic groups also benefited in certain cases. According to one estimate, toward the end of the period, public subsidies to the private sector through low prices (a policy designed to stimulate private investment) represented 6 percent of GDP—a figure close to the consolidated debt of the public sector.[52]

The expansion of the public sector also provided benefits, although less generous ones, to the population in general. One of the most important of these was jobs. By 1983, the public sector employed 20.4 percent of the economically active population.[53] The contribution of the public enterprise sector to employment was on the rise: between 1970 and 1980, public enterprise employment increased at an average annual rate of 7.9 percent, significantly higher than the 3.1 percent average annual increase in the population,[54] while its proportion of the economically active population went from 3.0 percent in 1970 to 5.1 percent by 1983.[55] The most rapid increase in employment occurred between 1977 and 1980 (the height of the petroleum boom), during which the average annual increase in the number of jobs was more than double that of 1970–1976.[56] As a consequence of its efforts to stem unemployment by taking over failing industries, by the early 1980s the state participated in the production of all types of manufactured goods, producing in thirty-five of the forty-nine industrial branches found in the national accounts.[57]

The economic deterioration of public enterprises meant that they relied decreasingly on their own resources and increasingly on transfer payments from the federal government and on loans.[58] By 1981, 17 percent of public enterprises' funds came from transfer payments, while nearly 30 percent came from loans, mostly foreign.[59] The biggest borrowers were PEMEX and the Federal Electricity Commission (CFE), which together accounted for more than half the controlled public enterprise debt (table 2.5), while the bulk of federal government transfer payments went to CONASUPO and the CFE.[60] Because of their weak finances, state enterprises lacked any reserves with which to bear the burden of devaluation and indebtedness that came with the 1982 economic crisis.

Both the rapid explosion of the public enterprise sector and its financial weakness had an important impact on the distribution of power within the state. The growth of public firms created a serious problem of executive control, producing a myriad of administrative regulations. As public enterprise autonomy increased, opposing bureaucratic groups competed for control over powerful public sector firms. And as the financial situation of public firms deteriorated, those bureaucratic groups opposed to their expansion strengthened.

Intrabureaucratic Conflict and the Growth of Public Enterprise Autonomy

Concern over centralized supervision and control of public enterprises emerged as early as 1947. The evolution of public enterprise control between that date and 1982 involved a process that eroded the power of the Ministry of Finance and produced a dispersal of control over public firms. This dispersal of power in fact signaled the growth in public enterprise autonomy. The major stages in this process are outlined below.

The period from the 1920s to the late 1940s, a period witnessing the political predominance of what Sylvia Maxfield has described as the expansionary Cardenista alliance, constitutes the first stage.[61] During this phase, state enterprises were created in an ad hoc manner, with the absence of any sort of systematic control from the federal executive. The federal government's mandate to establish and exercise control over public enterprises was inferred from various articles in the constitution, such as those giving the national government ownership of water and the subsoil and the exclusive responsibility for the issuance of money. Legislation establishing specific enterprises, such as PEMEX and the CFE, stipulated the role of the various ministries of state in the public firm's administration and sought to ensure federal executive control by presidential appointments of the director general and boards of directors.[62] In view of the government's reorganization and strengthening of the financial system, financial entities were important, and they remained under the control of the Ministry of Finance.

The 1947 Law for the Control of Decentralized Agencies and Enterprises with State Participation initiated the second stage, which ended in 1957 with a significant diminishment in the Finance Ministry's power over public firms. This was a period of struggle for con-

TABLE 2.5

External (Short-Term) Debt of the Public Enterprise Sector

	Public Enterprise as % of Pulic Sector Debt	% of Public Enterprise Debt	
		PEMEX	CFE
1973	75.8	13.1	—
1974	75.6	14.2	—
1975	81.3	15.3	—
1976	77.8	14.8	—
1977	78.8	18.5	23.5
1978	78.3	22.0	24.6
1979	70.4	25.5	25.5
1980	81.5	28.3	25.5
1981	81.9	33.0	23.8
1982	73.5	34.5	22.5

Source: de la Madrid Hurtado, *Primer Informe de Gobierno*, 577.

trol of the public enterprises between the Ministry of Finance and the Ministry of National Wealth and Administrative Inspection. The 1947 legislation represented the first attempt to legally supervise and financially control decentralized agencies and enterprises with majority state participation. The Ministry of Finance was confirmed in its exclusive responsibility for all financial institutions and was also given responsibility for all nonfinancial public enterprises. However, opposition to this expansion of the Finance Ministry's power quickly arose from other areas within the public bureaucracy.[63] As a consequence of this bureaucratic opposition, nonfinancial firms gradually came under the control of the Ministry of National Wealth and Administrative Inspection. In fact, the Ministry of National Wealth was given formal supervisory and financial control responsibilities for FERRONALES (the railway company) in 1948 and for the Federal Electricity Commission in 1951.

The 1958 Law of Secretaries of State and Administrative Departments initiated the third stage, known as triangular control, a stage which in fact involved the definitive transfer of responsibility for nonfinancial firms to the Ministry of Natural Resources (formerly the Ministry of National Wealth and Administrative Inspection). While the Finance Ministry remained dominant within the public bureaucracy, especially with regard to financial policy, its power was now being challenged.[64] The Ministry of Natural Resources was given formal responsibility for the control, supervision, and dissolution of all nonfinancial companies, while the newly created Ministry of the Presidency became responsible for the investment projects of nonfinancial public firms. The only responsibility retained by the Ministry of Finance for nonfinancial firms was for their loans and payments. The 1970 Public Enterprise Control Legislation further eroded the power of the Finance Ministry in handing over to the Ministry of Natural Resources control over all fiduciary institutions tied to specific programs.

The administration of Luis Echeverría witnessed a further marked decline in the influence of the Ministry of Finance, as the bureaucratic expansionary forces gained momentum and public enterprises multiplied.[65] A variety of control mechanisms were tried, from industry and ministerial commissions to budget surveillance by the Ministry of Natural Resources. But these attempts failed to stem the growing centrifugal tendencies. By the early 1970s, as economic stagnation set in, there was growing concern expressed about the need for administrative reform. A report from the Ministry of the Presidency outlined the principal problems in the public enterprise sector as duplication and competition, problems it said had not been adequately solved by the existing mechanisms of coordination.[66] But the root of these difficulties did not involve only the issue of divided jurisdiction for public enterprise administration. Equally important were the problems created by the increasing autonomy of public enterprises; divided jurisdiction simply increased the autonomy of public firms.

The 1976–1982 period is the fourth and final stage—one in which further administrative reforms were instituted with the objective of achieving greater policy coordination. Twenty-eight public firms, for example, were incorporated into the budget of the federal government, thereby giving the executive direct budget control and requiring approval of their budgets by the Chamber of Deputies. However, public enterprise autonomy increased, and central administrative confusion deepened.

The power of the Finance Ministry also continued to be seriously challenged. Legislative changes introduced during the period eroded the power of both the Ministry of Finance and the Ministry of Natural Resources and Industrial Development[67] in favor of the newly created Ministry of Budget and Planning (Secretaria de Programación y Presupuesto, or SPP).[68] Created in 1976 to plan and enhance the coordination of economic policy, the SPP acquired the responsibilities of the old Ministry of the Presidency (approval of the investment programs of public firms) and added to those responsibilities the global management of economic and social policy. The SPP became responsible for global economic planning and for the control, supervision, and evaluation of all federal public expenditures, including those of public enterprises. These changes meant an erosion of the powers of both the Ministry of Finance, which had been responsible for federal government expenditures, and the Ministry of Natural Resources and Industrial Development, which had been responsible for the operating budgets of public firms. The Ministry of Finance remained in charge of the collection of revenue—that is, taxes and loans.[69] Furthermore, the SPP acquired the Ministry of Finance's exclusive right to establish fiduciary institutions. And with the Law of Budget Accounting and Public Expenditure (1976), the SPP was given exclusive power to liquidate, fuse, or alter the organization of public enterprises, a responsibility that had rested in the hands of the Ministry of Natural Resources and Industrial Development.

Jurisdiction over public enterprises was further divided with passage of the 1976 Organic Law of Public Administration. This law grouped together public enterprises according to affinity of economic activity and assigned responsibility for them to sectoral coordinators, who were, in fact, the various secretaries of the state. Hence, agricultural enterprises, for example, now came under the jurisdiction of the Ministry of Agriculture, enterprises involved in marketing and distribution under the Ministry of Commerce. The bulk of enterprises, and certainly the most powerful among them, however, remained with the Ministry of Natural Resources and Industrial Development. This dispersal of formal control gave rise in 1979 to a further effort at policy coordination, which excluded the Ministry of Natural Resources and Industrial Development: the establishment of the Intersecretarial Expenditure-Finance Commission. Composed of the secretary of finance and the secretary of budget and planning (SPP) and various officials from these two ministries, the commission was responsible for the coordination of revenue and expenditure and for analyzing the financial situation of public firms.

Despite the formal erosion of many of its powers pertaining to public enterprise, however, the Ministry of Natural Resources and Industrial Development overshadowed the Ministry of Finance and the SPP until the end of the López Portillo administration in 1982. This situation was largely due to the personal power of the secretary of natural resources, José Andrés de Oteyza, who retained enormous influence over the presidency throughout the period.[70]

The difficulty of effective administrative control over public firms was made worse by the enormous infusion of resources that occurred as a consequence of the petroleum boom, especially in the form of foreign credits. PEMEX was certainly the major beneficiary of the petroleum boom years. In fact, for a brief period, its power rivaled that of the Ministry of Natural Resources and Industrial Development, to which it was theoretically subordinate. Even in past administrations, the director general of PEMEX had had direct access to the president. As petroleum increased in importance in the Mexican economy, the PEMEX chief under President López Portillo, Jorge Díaz Serrano, became one of the most powerful figures of the country.[71]

But while PEMEX was by far Mexico's most powerful public firm, many other public companies also became power centers that eluded centralized control. The growth of public enterprise and departmental autonomy has been observed by a variety of analysts.[72] There were a number of reasons for this, in addition to the chaotic division of authority outlined in previous paragraphs. The size of public firms, in combination with their monopoly of technical knowledge and highly specialized activities, made monitoring their activities by officials in the ministries difficult. Requests for information could be and were ignored, misinformation supplied, and technocratic arguments used to hide goals of expansion and aggrandizement. Requests for budget overruns by the directors of public firms could and were often made directly to the president, without the knowledge or approval of the appropriate secretary.

Public enterprise autonomy, along with that of other agencies and departments, has been further fostered by the fact that public sector institutions tend to develop their own distinct clienteles—indeed, one author has described such clientelelist arrangements as "fiefdoms."[73] The facility with which they have been able to build clienteles has been enhanced by the wide discretion they have had in the dispensing of moneys for contracts and purchases. Through such contracts, government agencies make allies of the firms with which they do business. These firms act as pressure groups, providing support for projects that benefit them. One of the most common consequences of such close ties has been the emergence of "bureaucratic capitalists"—bureaucrats engaged in numerous financial and economic enterprises while remaining officials of the government.[74]

But public enterprise autonomy, particularly for PEMEX during the petroleum boom years, was also the consequence of the ambitions of public enterprise leadership. Bureaucratic imperatives and the quest for career advancement were additional factors propelling the building of clienteles—bureaucratic, private sector, and union—clustered around public firms. For the director general of a public company to advance, he must demonstrate success at attracting and maintaining a support base, and to do so requires constant enterprise expansion in order to produce jobs and benefits for bureaucrats, union leaders, and workers and contracts for the private sector. Indeed, the direct representation of labor and business on the boards of directors of public firms (such as the state railway and petroleum companies) institutionalized and stimulated this process. But even when such representation was not formally present, union and business representatives acted informally as advisors in a system that has been described as "decentralization by collaboration."[75] These groups of top public enterprise officials, labor leaders, and owners of private sector companies became important sources of pressure for the expansion of public companies, while public firms became, at the same time, important channels of co-optation.[76] While the power of Díaz Serrano (director general of PEMEX between 1976 and 1981) hinged largely on his personal relationship with the president and the momentary success of his petroleum export strategy, that influence was reinforced by his powerful basis of support among the petroleum workers and private sector petroleum contractors.

The dispersal of bureaucratic power centers and interests might present problems of elite cohesion were it not for (or so it has been argued) the *camarilla,* a network of vertical and horizontal patron-client ties (based on strong interpersonal loyalties) that most, though not all, observers have confined to the state apparatus proper.[77] Such groupings, clustered around a key leader, strive to foster the influence and career advancement of both the key leader and his followers. Because they span a variety of government ministries, agencies, and public enterprises, *camarillas* are believed to have played an important role in maintaining elite cohesion, since they mitigate divisions based on institutional loyalties.[78] And since they are based on personal loyalties, they are also believed to have discouraged serious divisions along policy lines. Divisions tend to be not over issues of policy but rather power struggles between *camarillas* and their key leaders.[79] At least two observers, however, suggest that in recent years the cohesive impact of the *camarillas* has begun to break down.[80]

By 1982, the lack of central coordination and control of the public enterprise sector, and particularly of the most powerful ones, had become a serious problem, which neither *camarillas* nor various institutional reforms had been successful in mitigating. Moreover, the chaotic expansion of the sector had been the subject of an ongoing power struggle between the most powerful economic ministries of the state, a struggle characterized by distinct policy differences— again, an institutional struggle, apparently not blunted by *camarilla* networks.[81] The biggest loser was the Ministry of Finance, which lost almost all control over the nonfinancial public enterprise sector. The Finance Ministry was the most opposed to the rapid expansion of state expenditure and investment and, therefore, to the extensive expansion of the public enterprise sector. It would become the architect for the dismantling of the state's vast network of public companies when the opportunity arose with the 1982 crisis.

Conclusion

Public enterprises played a crucial role in Mexico's postwar economic success, providing financing, infrastructure, and cheap inputs for the private sector, which prospered under state tutelage. Public firms have also had important social and political functions. The high economic growth rates to which public enterprises contributed helped to bolster popular support for the PRI. Placed in charge of economic activities previously dominated by foreigners, public firms became symbols of national pride. State companies set up explicitly for social purposes provided benefits that bolstered the regime's claim to popular welfare concerns. All provided expanding sources of employment, a function that increased in importance as the economy began to stagnate by the late 1960s. The system offered considerable co-optative advantages—to bureaucrats in the form of career advancement, power, and opportunities to acquire wealth, to labor leaders in the form of economic opportunities, to workers in the form of jobs, and to the private sector in the form of cheap inputs and lucrative government contracts. But the contradictions of these arrangements were readily becoming apparent in the form of a growing fiscal crisis and the absence of adequate policy control over public firms. This situation was rendered even more unmanageable by the presence of powerful and demanding trade unions. The story of the state's ongoing struggle to control these unions and their place within the system of political control is the subject of the following chapter.

3

Labor Relations in the Public Enterprises

Insurgency and State Control

The trade unions of Mexico's public enterprises—in the railway, petroleum, electricity, and mining sectors—have been among the most well organized and the most combative in Mexican labor history. These industries began as foreign enclaves and came under state control due to both economic necessity and the force of revolutionary nationalism. While the public enterprise sector came to represent tangible evidence of the state's commitment to the ideals of the Mexican Revolution, the workers of these enterprises became the country's most important and ardent exponents of revolutionary nationalism. Given the nationalist appeal used to justify the state's direct participation in the economy, these trade unions have regarded it as their right to obtain control over management decisions. Indeed, labor demands in these sectors, such as those for worker participation in enterprise administration and control over firm purchasing and pricing policies, stand out for their militancy.

The industries of highest state participation have experienced the most advanced unionization: whereas the rate of unionization in industry in general was 26 percent in 1975, it was 78.6 percent in extractive industries, including petroleum, 97.9 percent in electricity and gas, and 84.9 percent in transportation.[1] Nowhere else in the Mexican economy have such large concentrations of workers been found. The most important state enterprises had between 50,000 and 90,000 workers per enterprise, compared with 15,000 workers spanning twenty-six enterprises in the largest private sector company, ALFA.[2]

The political importance of the labor relations of Mexico's major public enterprises has been a function of their strategic economic importance, particularly after 1940, when the government launched its industrialization drive. Petroleum, electricity, railways, and mining—economic sectors providing industrial inputs and transportation—were all necessary for industrial expansion. It was in these sectors, therefore, that the state had the greatest need for a compliant labor force. As a consequence, the history of the struggles of these unions has been marked by resistance to intense pressure for control by the state, a resistance that has occasionally burst forth into sporadic insurgency. At the same time, there is a history of mutual support among these unions in their struggles for union autonomy.

The state's need to contain labor unrest resulted in the imposition of a particular form of labor relations, which, although present in the majority of worker organizations, has been most marked in public enterprises, due to the historical combativeness of workers and the economic importance of their sectors. Labor-management relations came to be ruled by two hierarchical, reinforcing principles, arrangements that have functioned to minimize opposition and potential opposition from trade unions: patron clientelism, which operated in Mexican official unionism through *charrismo,* union domination by corrupt labor leaders loyal to the state; and corporatism, the incorporation of trade unions into the party apparatus. The importance of these mechanisms in the public enterprise sector and their significance for the Mexican political system as a whole has led one observer to characterize the public enterprise unions as constituting the "heart of [Mexican] corporatism."[3]

The distinct labor-management relationship found in Mexico's public enterprises eventually created an important basis of regime support. Most public companies are not part of the public sector proper, and therefore, like trade unions of the private sector, are not subject to the limitations imposed by Section B of the Labor Code, which prohibits collective agreements and restricts the right of public servants to strike. However, since, as one observer has pointed out, the state is "at the same time arbiter and management"[4] during times of labor disputes, the relationship between public sector unions and the state is a much more direct one than is the case for private sector unions.[5]

The selective distribution of material rewards has been essential in the maintenance of the alliance between the leadership of the labor unions of public firms and the state. While the corporatist incorporation of labor unions into the state apparatus has been important, it was not sufficient to contain mounting labor unrest. Direct manipulation of corrupt labor leadership and the distribution of material rewards became an essential ingredient of the system. These arrangements have shown the greatest stress at those times when economic difficulties have constrained the ability of the system to deliver selective benefits. While these arrangements account for the state's ability to overcome labor opposition to privatization, the process of privatization, paradoxically, set in motion their disintegration.

Early Labor Combativeness
and Attempts at Incorporation

Nationalist opposition to foreign economic domination has been an important source of labor mobilization in the mining, petroleum, and, particularly, railway industries. Demands for improvements in salaries and protests against layoffs were linked to the considerably more favorable situation experienced by foreign employees. In the railway industry, clashes between Mexican and American workers occurred as Mexican workers demanded comparable salaries and working conditions.[6] Indeed, one author has argued that the nationalism of Mexican workers as ideology had its roots in the foreign domination of the railway industry.[7] The 1906 strike in the American-owned Cananea copper company, where Mexican workers earned half as much as their American counterparts, fanned the flames of Mexican nationalism, particularly among the organized working class. Some one hundred Mexican workers were killed when police, the Mexican army, and U.S. rangers were sent in to end the strike,[8] an event that became symbolic of the workers' nationalist resistance to foreign economic domination.

Due to its historical combativeness and level of organization, industrial labor's political importance has been much greater than its numbers might suggest. While in 1921, only 14 percent of the economically active population was in industry, national political contenders continually recruited it in their leadership struggles: labor was recruited by Venustiano Carranza in his struggle against Adolfo de la Huerta (1914), by Alvaro Obregón in his struggle against Carranza (1919), by Plutarco Elías Calles against Obregón (1923) and by Lázaro Cárdenas in his efforts to consolidate his power against Calles.[9] Workers in the railway, mining, electricity, and petroleum industries had important roles in these struggles. The railway workers, for example, played a key role in Obregón's success: a strike at the South Pacific Railway furnished the signal for the beginning of the Obregón uprising.[10] And public enterprise unions were an important basis of Cárdenas's support.

At the same time, these unions offered the stiffest resistance to incorporation by the state. Even in pre-Cárdenas times, there was a clear state strategy to stimulate the establishment of an officially recognized national labor confederation that could be induced to work closely with the state in order to contain labor demands. Instigated by Carranza, the Regional Confederation of Mexican Labor (Confederación Regional Obrera Mexicana, or CROM) was established in 1919. However, given Carranza's repression of labor, the CROM quickly forged an alliance with Obregón, pledging its support in return for, among other things, a labor law and consultation on labor matters. When Obregón won the presidency in 1920, the CROM gained enormous influence in government. The height of its power occurred when its head, Luis M. Morones, was appointed secretary of the Ministry of Industry, Commerce, and Labor[11] in Calles's cabinet in 1924.[12] The government pursued an active policy of cooperation with CROM unions, giving them both money and special privileges. While the CROM's influence lasted (until 1928), it became a staunch ally of the state in the repression of labor.[13]

The major railway union at the time (Confederación de Transportes y Communicaciones) did not join the CROM and remained a strong opponent throughout the period. This created difficulties for the government, as the CROM could not be used to deal with the ongoing labor unrest in this strategically important sector of the economy. And while the Mexican Miners' Union (Union Minera Mexicana) had contributed to the establishment of the CROM, the miners soon rejected the CROM's collaborationist stance and its attempt to dampen the radical positions of labor organizations. It accused the CROM of never having carried out an effective campaign in favor of the miners, petroleum workers, "or in general workers in the basic industries of the country which, as we know, are controlled by Yanqui capital."[14]

Unable to use the CROM to quell labor unrest in sectors such as railways, mining, and petroleum, the government resorted to other means to enable it to more readily intervene directly in labor conflicts and change the orientation of unions. In 1926, jurisdiction over labor conflicts in the railway industry was removed from the Ministry of Industry, Commerce, and Labor, whose effectiveness was blocked by the fact that the ministry was in the hands of a CROM man, and placed in the hands of a newly established Federal Board of Conciliation and Arbitration. One year later, the mining and petroleum industries were also incorporated under the federal jurisdiction of the board.[15]

The devastating impact of the Great Depression hit workers in the export enclaves particularly hard. The first nine months of 1931 witnessed the closing of nine mining companies. The petroleum company, El Aguila, threatened to close its refineries unless it was allowed to carry out layoffs and salary reductions, and FERRONALES, the state-owned railway company, let go 4,000 workers and reduced salaries.[16] Labor conflict escalated. Strikes were carried out by miners and telephone, railway, and petroleum workers, with the majority of strikes during the period being declared illegal.[17]

The government, therefore, sought measures by which it could contain labor unrest. The Federal Labor Code (Ley Federal de Trabajo), enacted in 1931, provided the legal framework for the state to select which labor organizations were to be allowed into the political struggle. The law required that trade unions obtain legal recognition from the state before placing an intent-to-strike declaration before the Federal Board of Conciliation and Arbitration. Since any strike not first put before the board was automatically illegal, a union without legal recognition could not lead a strike. The law also made legal the closed shop, which, although originally enacted to protect labor by inhibiting the use of scabs, became a means by which union leaders could rid themselves of dissident workers, since expulsion from the union meant automatic dismissal from the enterprise.[18]

Public Enterprise Unions and the Corporatist Control of the Working Class

As the effects of the Great Depression lingered, Cárdenas's first two years in power were greeted by an epidemic of work stoppages. Worker agitation was particularly marked in those sectors soon to be either nationalized or subject to greater state control: railroads, petroleum, electricity, and mining.[19] Worker demands revolved around calls for single-industry-wide labor contracts and salaries and working conditions comparable to those of foreign workers. In the face of stiff foreign management resistance, worker demands for the government takeover of foreign-owned firms increased. Labor unrest and pressure for nationalization was instrumental in the 1937 nationalization of the railway industry and the 1938 takeover of foreign firms in the petroleum industry.[20] Pressures for nationalization from miners and electrical workers were strong, as well, but were resisted.

The administration's response to the high degree of worker agitation was a positive one in the early years.[21] The presidency of Lázaro Cárdenas is noted for its support for labor organizing, as well as for the encouragement it gave to the establishment of the corporatist structures that laid the basis for the incorporation of the official workers' movement to the party apparatus. Cárdenas succeeded in bringing about the establishment of the Mexican Workers Confederation (Confederación de Trabajadores de México, or CTM) in 1936 by offering financial aid, a new building for its headquarters, and seats in the senate for CTM leaders.[22] The CTM therefore felt obliged to acquiesce in the government's wishes. Cárdenas's reorganization of the official National Revolutionary Party (Partido Nacional Revolucionario, or PNR), reconstituted as the Party of the Mexican Revolution (Partido de la Revolución Mexicana, or PRM) along sectoral lines, incorporated the CTM as the worker sector. While the establishment of the CTM greatly enhanced the political influence of organized labor,[23] the official party's sectoral organization and representation constituted the legal mechanisms by which the state could reward cooperative trade unions and punish uncooperative ones.[24]

Worker organizations, particularly the more militant ones of the public enterprise unions, continued to resist incorporation to the state. When, almost immediately after its formation, the CTM leadership began to use antidemocratic methods, about twenty unions, including the Mexican Electrical Workers' Union (Sindicato Mexicano de Electricistas, or SME) and the National Mining Metallurgical Union[25] withdrew in 1937.[26] At the same time, a new type of union tied closely to the state, a type that would become the norm in later years, emerged in the newly created Federal Electricity Commission (Comisión Federal de Electricidad, or CFE). From its earliest years, the leaders of this union, the National Union of Electricity Workers (Sindicato Nacional de Electricistas), amassed wealth by using extortion and used repression to maintain control over their rank and file. This organization became an important member of the CTM.

The nationalizations in the petroleum and railway industries marked the high point of labor conflict and initiated a process during which labor unrest was increasingly dampened. Indeed, the fact of nationalization initiated a transformation in labor-state relations. With nationalization came the direct participation of workers in the administration of public enterprises. While in the railway industry this entailed the installation of a worker administration (1938), in the petroleum industry the workers were given four of the nine positions on the PEMEX board of directors. With union participation in administration, workers gained access to previously unavailable resources and channels of upward mobility. In PEMEX, new superintendencies (regional administrative units) were created to give labor leaders good jobs.[27] While the use of violence in intraunion labor struggles had always been present, now labor leaders turned PEMEX officials were furnished with additional resources by which to control union sections. These new arrangements worked in concert with the new union-party relationship described above.

By 1940, it was clear that Cárdenas's honeymoon with the trade unions was coming to an end. Both the railway and petroleum enterprises were faced with serious economic difficulties, and Cárdenas therefore sought to restructure them in order to increase efficiency, an objective that continued to engender conflict with their trade unions. The economic difficulties of these enterprises stemmed from a variety of factors, including outdated equipment, increased costs due to increases in salaries and employment, and controlled prices.[28] The Cárdenas administration therefore decided that major reorganizations involving substantial layoffs (3,000 in the case of PEMEX) were unavoidable, a decision that engendered worker unrest.[29] By the close of the Cárdenas administration, the direction in which state-worker relations were evolving was clear: firm limits would have to be placed on worker mobilization and union autonomy.

The subsequent administration of Avila Camacho (1940–1946) was characterized by growing worker quiescence, particularly on the part of the CTM. The war effort became the justification for the abandonment of almost any manifestation of worker militancy. As salaries remained frozen and prices increased, purchasing power was seriously eroded during the period.[30] Worker unrest, generated by the deterioration of living standards, would soon pose a serious threat to the state. The formal structures of corporatism would not be sufficient to stem the tide of rising worker unrest. These structures would have to be fortified by institutionalized union corruption, known as *charrismo*.

Charrismo and the Taming of Labor

The administration of Miguel Alemán (1946–1952) is usually associated with the harsh repression of worker demands and with the imposition of *charrismo*. According to one author, the institution of *charrismo* represented a qualitatively different approach by the state toward labor, characterized by direct intervention in unions and the creation of a new kind of labor bureaucracy.[31] The term *charrismo* has its origins in the nickname (*el charro*) given to Jesús Díaz de Léon, a corrupt leader of the Railway Workers' Union (Sindicato de Trabajadores Ferrocarileros de la República Mexicana, STFRM), the word referring to his penchant for cowboy gear. The term originally referred to the deposition of democratically elected leaders and subsequent imposition of new leadership by the army or police. Over time, it has come to be applied to all corrupt union leaders supported by the government and management. *Charro* leadership is overwhelmingly characterized as an instrument used by the state to control the workers' movement.

The economic deterioration experienced by workers during the Second World War was further aggravated by the devaluation of 1948, which stimulated inflation and a further decline in purchasing power. Workers sought alternatives to the progovernment CTM, setting up no less than eight new worker centrals during the period.[32] The public enterprise unions grew particularly impatient with CTM passivity, a fact reflected in the CTM's inability to control their growing combativeness. In the face of this upsurge in worker insurgency, the state responded with direct intervention in the Railway Workers' Union in 1948, the Petroleum Workers' Union (Sindicato de Trabajadores Petroleros de la República Mexicana, STPRM) in 1946–1949, unions in the mining industry during 1951–1952,[33] and in one of the electricity unions (the SME) in 1952.

At the root of the fierce resistance of public enterprise unions to the incorporative pressures imposed by the CTM and the state—resistance that manifested itself in demands for union autonomy and democratization—was the failure to redress workers economic grievances. It was not long before these struggles caused serious divisions within the CTM.[34] The failure of the CTM to support a strike of petroleum workers had not only produced a serious division of opinion but had also resulted in the abandonment of the CTM by the Petroleum Workers' Union. But it was the CTM's decision supporting collective membership in the PRI through union membership that created the bitter 1947 leadership struggle pitting the progovernment candidate (supported by Fidel Velázquez) against Railway Workers' Union leader Luis Gómez Zepeda, who called for the democratization of worker organizations.[35]

Gómez Zepeda's defeat spurred a concerted effort on the part of public enterprise unions to form a new workers' central to replace the CTM. In 1947, the Single Confederation of Workers (Confederación Unica de Trabajadores, or CUT), with support from the miners and the railway, petroleum, electrical, and telephone workers, was established,[36] followed shortly thereafter by the signing of a solidarity pact by the mining, petroleum, and railway unions, calling for the ouster of the CTM leadership and a rejection of its antidemocratic methods. In 1949, the Peasants' and Workers' Union of Mexico (Union General de Obreros y Campesinos de México, or UGOCM) was established. The UGOCM was supported principally by the petroleum workers and miners—not by the Railway Workers' Union, since by this time it had been neutralized. The new union launched a campaign against the CTM and called for internal union democracy and independence from the state and political parties. Refused official registration by the government, while its most important supporters underwent intense state repression, the UGOCM soon disappeared.

This threat of independent union opposition lead by the public enterprise unions, along with the broader political threat posed by their refusal to be incorporated into the party apparatus, was to bring down the heavy arm of the state in the form of the charrification of union leadership. Although differing in details, the blows dealt the petroleum, railway, electricity (SME), and mine workers' unions between 1946 and 1952 shared a number of common features. Prior to the *charrazos,* each had experienced persistent labor unrest over salaries, layoffs, and labor contracts. The use of force against striking workers was routine: it was used against striking railway workers in 1945 and against striking miners in 1950, and troops occupied the petroleum installations during the 1946 strike and the installations of the Mexican Light and Power Company during a 1952 strike. But the repressive manipulation of union leadership by the state proved to be particularly effective.

State cultivation of progovernment, pro-CTM groups within each of these unions, including the fomentation of intraunion violence and the use of state repression, was probably the most important facet of the strategy to secure compliant unionism. This tactic was employed in the Petroleum Workers' Union between 1946 and 1947,[37] in the SME in 1952,[38] and in the Railway Workers' Union in 1948.[39] In the case of the railway union, the authorities finally arrested Gómez Zepeda, while police agents from the Federal Direction of Security took over union locals.[40]

The manipulation of union conventions in order to secure the imposition of cooperative leaderships was a less direct, but no less violent, method of achieving the same end. In response to the Petroleum Workers' Union's decision to stay out of the CTM, join the UGOCM, and sign a solidarity pact with the mining and railway unions, the Federal Direction of Security Forces and Ministry of Labor police were used to impose the new executive elected by a union convention (Sixth Ordinary) whose delegates had been imposed by the government.[41] Similarly, in 1950, police were used to impose government-selected delegates at the sixth National Mining Metallurgical Union convention, with the result that the convention elected a secretary general closely linked to the Ministry of Labor.[42] The secretary of labor then ordered authorities to force rebel union sections to recognize progovernment executive committees. When miners showed resistance to this *charrazo* in 1951 by means of a protest march from Nueva Rosita to Mexico City, the government responded with violence carried out by the police against workers[43] and rejected worker demands for the recognition of legitimately elected local executive committees.

Once *charro* leaders were installed in power, the government took measures to ensure their co-optation by facilitating their ability to amass wealth. After installing Jesús Díaz de León as head of the Railway Workers' Union, the government facilitated arrangements so that union dues would go directly to de León rather than to the legally recognized union treasury.[44] But it was in the petroleum industry where the greatest economic opportunities were created. Clause 36 of the 1947 collective agreement allowing the participation of private contractors in construction and transportation opened the way for union leaders to set up contracting companies to supply services to PEMEX.[45] The use of contracts by PEMEX, providing lucrative opportunities to labor leaders, opened a new stage in labor-state relations. It gave rise to a tightly knit network of clientelist relations, headed up by PEMEX superintendent Jaime Merino de la Peña and including corrupt labor leader Pedro Vivanco and private petroleum contractor Jorge Díaz Serrano (later director general of PEMEX) in what was then the richest petroleum region in the country, Poza Rica.[46]

There is no doubt that the *charrazos* were highly effective in breaking up the antigovernment alliances that these unions had created: all three left the opposition coalition. *Charrismo* worked well as a mechanism of labor control as long as a basic minimum of workers' demands could be met. The relatively high degree of labor peace during the López Mateos years, for example, was in large part due to increased public investment in such areas as electrification, petroleum extraction and refining, petrochemicals, and steel and to the security in employment and improved working conditions that the unions of strategic public enterprises had been able to achieve for their workers.[47] Deterioration of economic conditions, as occurred in the late 1950s and early 1970s, however, gave rise to renewed worker insurgency—demands for increased salaries and the removal of *charro* leaders who were unwilling to deliver on these demands. The government's harsh response in 1958 to the Railway Workers' Union illustrated its complete unwillingness to tolerate union insurgency with overtones of political opposition.[48]

Once again, continued deterioration in real wages was the impetus behind the Railway Workers' Union's demands for higher salaries and its attempt to remove *charro* leadership in 1958–1959. And once again, the progovernment CTM opposed these union demands. When union elections returned *charro* opponent Demetrio Vallejo to the general directorship of the Railway Workers' Union with an overwhelming majority, the government launched a campaign for his removal, involving anticommunist propaganda and the use of violent repression against his supporters. When the union went on strike, the police and the army quickly moved in, arresting thousands of workers, including Vallejo. Repression was also employed against petroleum and mining workers who were supporting the striking railway workers.[49] With the imprisonment of the union leadership and the imposition of a more quiescent one, the opposition movement quickly dissipated.[50] The union now agreed to join the PRI. The authorities justified their use of repression on the grounds that the movement was not simply a working class movement but a political movement of "grand proportions," which had as its objective the defeat of the government.[51]

Similarly, by the early 1970s, growing economic stagnation had given rise to renewed worker insurgency: both strike activity and the emergence of independent unions increased dramatically between 1974 and 1975.[52] The government's response was increased repression of worker demands.[53] Worker insurgency this time was led by dissident workers in the nationalized electricity sector, with important participation from the railway workers.[54] Growing opposition was also found among steel workers, faced with a worsening world market for steel and the failure of their *charro* leadership to satisfy wage demands.[55]

In both the steel and electrical industries, however, the expansion of the state signaled the reinforcement of *charrismo*. In the case of the dissident electrical workers, the 1960 nationalization of the industry had raised the specter of a loosening of government union control due to the necessity of incorporating companies with unions having strong independent and democratic traditions. Two currents existed within the electricity unions. One was the corrupt and unresponsive National Union of Electricity Workers (Sindicato Nacional de Electricistas) of the state-owned Federal Electricity Commission (CFE),[56] and the other, combative unions of the recently nationalized private sector companies, the Mexican Electrical Workers' Union (Sindicato Mexicano de Electricistas, or SME), representing the workers of Mexican Light and Power, and the National Federation of Workers of Industry and Electrical Communications (Federación Nacional de Trabajadores de la Industria y Communicaciones Electricas, or FNTICE), representing the workers of other nationalized private sector companies.[57] These unions are believed to have been less corrupt and highly combative in the defense of worker interests.[58]

The struggle involved the fierce resistance of these more combative unions, in particular the FNTICE, against incorporation and subjugation within the National Union.[59] The government could not allow the resistance, which came to be embodied in the Democratic Tendency within the National Union, to triumph—to do so would have meant the loss of control over this strategic industry, on which the operation of all other industry depended. The Democratic Tendency's supporters were dismissed, and the National Union offered money and other benefits to workers who would desert the resistance group. A strike declared by the Democratic Tendency in 1975 was confronted with further layoffs, and riot police were used against a demonstration in 1977.[60] By 1978, the movement had disappeared.

When the state decided to move into steel production with the establishment of its own steel plant, SICARTSA (Siderúrgica Lázaro Cárdenas–Las Truchas S.A.), in 1968, management fostered the formation of a malleable work force. Three years prior to the opening of the plant, to contain workers' demands and ensure timely completion of the project, management established its own "union" organization.[61] This union was encouraged to affiliate to the charrified National Mining Metallurgical Union by a promise of immediate recognition if it did so.[62]

It was only within the Telephone Workers' Union (Sindicato de Telefonistas de la República Mexicana, STRM) that labor acquiescence was achieved without much of a struggle, due to the union leadership's fear of a government-instigated *charrazo*. Here, a struggle against the *charro* leadership of Salustio Salgado resulted in the victory of democratic candidate Hector Hernández Juárez by an overwhelming majority. One of the union's first moves after this victory was to reject affiliation to the PRI. Government officials then began to apply various forms of pressure to ensure that the union did not leave the Congress of Labor (Congreso de Trabajo, or CT).[63] This produced a reversal in Hernández Juárez's earlier position: he now began to say that the best way to strive for union democracy was to remain within the CT and be assured of the protection of the government[64]—a thinly veiled allusion to the fear of charrification should the government lose patience.

Mechanisms of Control in the Public Enterprise Unions

While the state has employed violence to quell union dissidence and impose acquiescent leadership, control through *charrismo* became largely dependent on more subtle methods of persuasion and co-optation. The system depends on the exchange of largely material rewards (1) from the state (and indirectly, from the private sector) to the labor union leadership, and (2) from the labor union leadership (selectively) to the rank and file. Hence, *charrismo* is a form of patron clientelism that has served to reinforce and solidify the corporatist political structures that bind labor unions, particularly those of the public enterprise unions, to the officially sanctioned national labor organizations (the CTM and the CT) and these organizations to the party.

The way in which patron clientelism contributes to political quiescence and therefore to political stability in developing countries has been discussed in a substantial body of literature.[65] One key point is worth noting: while material rewards are distributed only selectively, the hope of future access to such rewards is instrumental in dampening radical political behavior among all those who may not at the moment benefit materially from patron clientelism. Such expectations induce potential clients to see their economic salvation in winning a patron's favor rather than in collective political action to overturn the status quo. Because the flow of resources to the government-owned petroleum company, PEMEX, was so great, especially between 1976 and 1982, the Petroleum Workers' Union became the archetype for patron-client *charro* political control.[66] But the sorts of mechanisms at work here have also been present in the labor-management relations of other public enterprises.

Both legal and informal structures have mitigated rank-and-file dissidence and potential dissidence. Probably the most important instrument of leadership control of the rank and file has been the clause of exclusion (closed-shop clause) found in virtually all collective contracts of public enterprise unions. This clause means that it is necessary to be a member of the union in order to keep one's job. The clause of exclusion is further reinforced by clauses of inclusion, which require management to hire exclusively from the union. Such clauses operate in conjunction with the Labor Code requirement that all unions must be registered with the Ministry of Labor to receive the benefits of that code. Since only one union is recognized in each enterprise, the authorities have the ability to empower cooperative unions over uncooperative ones, while the union leadership can easily rid itself of uncooperative workers by expelling them from the union.[67]

The vulnerability of workers' job tenure also increases the power of union leadership over the rank and file. By 1977–1982, temporary workers in the petroleum industry constituted 52.3 percent of all workers.[68] These workers were manipulated by the union leadership in an explicitly political way. An agreement reached between the union and management in 1947 provided that new positions must be filled either from union membership or from names proposed by the union. Those vying for even temporary contracts had either to pay for their jobs or somehow to curry favor with the union leadership. While active union members were given priority for permanent jobs, such jobs were to be distributed to temporary workers on the basis of distinctly political criteria. In the 1970s, union statutes established that half of all permanent jobs were to be given to temporary workers, on the basis of, first, their union militancy and, second, seniority. The other half of vacated positions were to go to the families of temporary workers (sons and brothers), using the same criteria. Union militancy was defined in terms of participation in the union and in its organized political activities. Union militancy, assessed by the union leadership, meant, in effect, loyalty and obedience. Temporary workers who wished to obtain additional contracts or permanent jobs had to obtain the support of the union leadership through such activities as working (for free) on union farms, providing sexual favors if they were women, and, of course, providing enthusiastic political support.

A similar system has operated in the National Mining Metallurgical Union, where, since the 1930s, union control over the distribution of temporary jobs to workers has resulted in manipulation for political support.[69] Likewise, *charro* control of the National Union (of the Federal Electricity Commission) was facilitated by the fact that at its inception, the majority of its workers were temporary (construction) workers and therefore vulnerable and in a position to be manipulated by the union leadership.[70]

The practice of voting by raised hand rather than by secret ballot is another powerful incentive against opposing union leadership. Given the power that union leaders have over the rank and file, these workers can be expected to try to further ingratiate themselves with union leaders by demonstrating their support when votes are taken.

While the Petroleum Workers' Union allows only permanent workers to be present at union assemblies, in fact the union leadership has encouraged temporary workers to attend and to vote, since it is thereby more readily able to manipulate them.[71]

In addition, the union leadership has at its disposal a variety of rewards to dispense or withhold according to the degree of worker cooperation. A large number of company benefits, for example, were channeled directly to the workers through the union. These included, most commonly, housing, scholarships, promotion based on seniority, appointments to new jobs, loans, vacations, and transfers between regions or departments.[72] Again, union militancy, loyalty, and payoffs to the union leadership constitute the criteria on which rewards are granted or withheld. At the same time, the ample resources afforded *charro* leaders enabled them to exercise violent repression should co-optative measures prove inadequate. Joaquín Hernández Galicia (nicknamed La Quina), the once powerful leader of the Petroleum Workers' Union, kept a paramilitary organization of 3,000 thugs for precisely this purpose.[73]

The union's exclusive ownership of the collective contract, combined with union statutes, facilitated the concentration of power in the hands of its national executive committees.[74] The national executive committee has exclusive power to call elections, accept or reject candidates, declare a strike, and apply the clause of exclusion, powers that enable it to deal effectively with troublesome grassroots opposition.[75] Even the leadership of the National Mining Metallurgical Union, the most decentralized of the big public enterprise unions, has the power to dismiss local leadership from their posts, totally revoke the union rights of a union section, and expel union members from the union and thereby ensure that they are fired from the enterprise.[76] Regional leaders of the Petroleum Workers' Union were kept in line through the selective distribution of funds for social works (for housing, schools, hospitals, company stores) only to those regional groups who cooperated.

Equally important has been the lucrative business opportunities afforded union leadership, opportunities that have successfully secured its loyalty to the political elite and guaranteed the delivery of rank-and-file support. The union administration of benefits, such as loans, the sale of jobs, and the collection of union dues, not only provides means by which to control rank-and-file workers but also provides ample opportunity for individual union leaders to accumulate wealth. Through such means, for example, the *charro* leader of the National Union (electricity), Francisco Peréz Rios, amassed a huge fortune, becoming the owner of considerable real estate and the principle shareholder in the Banca Azteca.[77]

Another source of wealth for union leadership has been the contributions made by public enterprises to the union for various social works. This has set public enterprise unions apart in the services they have been able to provide their membership. Unions in the telephone, railway, and petroleum industries have been able to operate their own hospitals, clinics, and recreational institutions, all subsidized by the state. In the early 1970s, the Federal Electricity Commission agreed to make an annual cash contribution to the union to provide loans to workers and for the construction of sports facilities.[78] In 1977, the Petroleum Workers' Union achieved management's agreement to pay to the union's social fund 2 percent of the value of contracts to third parties. Funds provided by the enterprise have also aided in the establishment of union-owned factories, stores, and ranches (the so-called social sector) and have become additional means of union leadership enrichment. The profits from such companies are not shared with workers.

Encouragement to labor leaders to become contractors to public enterprise has provided perhaps the most lucrative avenue for the accumulation of private wealth. In addition to agreements reached in earlier years, a number of agreements between PEMEX and the union during the 1970s and the 1980s stimulated the proliferation of a large number of contracting companies whose boards of directors included the top members of the Petroleum Workers' Union bureaucracy.[79] The union's contract committee acted as a subcontracting agent to provide work for these companies. La Quina, the country's most powerful labor leader until his arrest in 1989, has been linked to ownership of the Continental de Perforación y Construcción, a Texas contracting company that does work for PEMEX.[80] Ernesto Ramírez, secretary of local 36 of the Petroleum Workers' Union in the town of Reynosa, state of Chiapas, owns a construction company that has done work for PEMEX, while a truck fleet owned by brothers Felipe and Francisco Balderas of local 11 of the Petroleum Workers' Union in the town of Nanchital, state of Veracruz, has also done work for PEMEX.[81] Similarly, in the mining industry, labor leaders have been enriched by their ownership of enterprises having contracts with public enterprises.[82] In this way, the union leadership achieved an important economic stake in the existing order and became a staunch supporter of the political system. It has been able to join the capitalist class and has ceased, it has been argued, to belong either materially or ideologically to the working class.[83]

Besides material wealth, cooperative union leaders also have a variety of political rewards made available to them. They may be appointed to the board of directors of public enterprises (most reserved a number of positions to workers), to the executive committee of the CT, the CTM, or some other confederation within the CT, or to a position within the PRI bureaucracy. They may be given the opportunity to run for the senate or the Chamber of Deputies. At this level, the importance of the official union bureaucracy rose until 1985: while between 1964 and 1967 labor delegates in the Chamber of Deputies represented 15.3 percent of PRI delegates, during 1982–1985 this figure rose to 24.3 percent.[84] Among the public enterprise unions, the one with the greatest political clout has undoubtedly been the Petroleum Workers' Union. It has been the most important financial contributor to the CTM,[85] and, until 1983, had close and supportive ties with the political elite—La Quina had been very close to both presidents Luis Echeverría (1970–1976) and José López Portillo (1976–1982). The Petroleum Workers' Union itself was able to secure six seats in the Chamber of Deputies. In the words of Kevin Middlebrook, "the postrevolutionary political leadership and major elements of the organized labor movement forged a social pact . . . based on the revolutionary elite's acceptance of labor as a legitimate political force entitled to play a major role in national politics."[86] But as Middlebrook himself notes, it was a highly unequal arrangement, placing labor in a generally subordinate role on economic policy issues.

In return for a variety of benefits, then, the labor leadership was expected to keep labor demands in line, within the parameters of government policy, to provide support at critical times (for example, during an economic crisis), to provide money and votes at election time, and to organize marches and demonstrations in support of the PRI. The most charrified and powerful of Mexico's trade unions, the unions of the public enterprises, faithfully carried out these functions until 1988, although not without intermittent resistance from intra-union insurgent movements. In addition to the benefits obtained from a variety of lucrative opportunities, the behavior of labor leaders has also been determined by the sanctions brought to bear against uncooperative leaders. Strikes can be prohibited and violence can be used against workers if they do not return to work. Leaders and workers can be arrested, jailed, and deprived of their livelihood.

Conclusion

Historically, the most combative trade unions have been those in strategic sectors of the economy—mining, railways, petroleum, and electricity. Starting out as foreign enclaves, these industries have been the areas where worker revolutionary nationalism took root and the areas subject to either nationalization or growing state intervention. It was in the public enterprise sector, therefore, that the state had both the greatest need and the greatest opportunity to contain worker unrest. It is not surprising, therefore, that the corporatist and clientelist structures of popular control achieved their greatest expression in the largest and most important public sector enterprises.

Charrismo appears to have been an essential ingredient of the government's industrialization strategy. Indeed, the unions of those public enterprises independently created, not nationalized or expropriated by the state (such as SICARSTA and the CFE), were born charrified. A compliant labor force in industries providing essential inputs and transportation for industry was deemed essential. Due to the high degree of worker mobilization during the Cárdenas years, *charrazos* were necessary to achieve the restructuring in the petroleum and railway industries during the 1950s, industries on whose efficiency Mexico's expanding industrial base depended. The success of the system, however, was contingent upon the ability of union leaders to pass on some benefits to rank-and-file workers while holding out the promise of much greater rewards to selected clients. During those periods when the economic conditions of workers deteriorated (the mid to late 1950s and the early 1970s), union insurgency rose and the corporatist-*charro* structures were threatened. This corporatist-*charro* system played an important role in the government's ability to implement the post-1983 economic restructuring program—in particular, in its ability to restructure public enterprises in order to make them marketable to the private sector. However, in carrying out this role, the corporatist-clientelist system has set in motion its own disintegration. This process has had important implications for the social basis of the state and for its methods of political control.

4

Debt Negotiations and the Triumph of Economic Liberalism

Both the expansion of state enterprises and the wealth made available to the official labor movement during the petroleum boom years came to an abrupt halt with the 1982 economic crisis. As prices for Mexico's major export, petroleum, declined on the international market and interest rates rose, the Mexican economy fell into deep recession. When Miguel de la Madrid Hurtado took over the Mexican presidency in December 1982, inflation stood at 100 percent, the public deficit represented 16.9 percent of GDP, and the growth rate in GDP was negative (table 4.1). By the end of the year, Mexico's foreign exchange reserves were almost exhausted. Moreover, less than one month before President de la Madrid's inauguration, Mexico had been forced to sign a strict austerity agreement with the IMF.

However, in less than two years, Mexico was being praised in the international press not only for having implemented tough stabilization measures but also for having initiated economic reforms believed to be necessary for the resumption of economic growth. President de la Madrid's economic program entailed two stages: first, to stabilize the economy (reduce inflation and the balance of payments deficit) and second, to restructure it so as to reduce the country's dependence on petroleum exports, alter the nature and extent of the state's intervention in the economy, and make the economy

TABLE 4.1

Selected Economic Indicators, 1982–1993

Indicator	1982	1983	1984	1985	1986	1987	1988	1989	1990	1991	1992	1993
% Change in real GDP	−0.6	−4.2	3.6	2.6	−3.8	1.7	1.2	3.3	4.4	3.6	2.8	0.4
Change in real minimum wage	−12.6	−20.1	−1.6	−5.9	−2.9	−3.8	−15.7	6.1	−8.9	−4.7	−4.6	−0.8
Investment growth	−16.8	−26.6	4.3	7.9	−11.8	−0.1	5.8	6.4	13.1	8.1	10.8	−1.4
Trade balance[a] ($US billions)	7.0	14.1	13.2	8.4	5.0	8.8	2.6	0.4	−0.9	−7.2	−15.9	−13.5
Federal government deficit as % of GDP	16.9	8.6	8.5	9.6	14.9	15.0	10.9	5.0	2.8	0.3	−1.6	−0.7
Direct foreign investment flows ($US billions)	1.7	0.5	0.4	0.5	1.5	3.2	2.6	3.0	2.6	4.8	4.3	4.9
External debt as % of GDP	49.1	61.0	54.2	52.6	76.6	73.6	59.1	48.6	39.8	36.4	33.4	33.5

Sources: **GDP and federal deficit figures, 1982–1984:** Secretaría de Hacienda y Credito Público, *Mexico: A New Economic Profile,* 18; **for 1985–1993:** Banco de México, *The Mexican Economy, 1992,* 213, 242, 258; *The Mexican Economy, 1994,* 214–15; **trade balance, 1982–1990:** Salinas de Gortari, *Quarto Informe de Gobierno,* Anexo, 1992, 216; **for 1991–1993:** Banco de México, *The Mexican Economy, 1994,* 214; **minimum wage, 1982–1988:** González Aguilar, *La crisis y los trabajadores,* 18; **for 1989–1993:** Suárez and Pérez, "Caída y recuperación: Los Salarios en México, 1987–1883," 97; **investment growth, 1982–1984:** Brailovsky, Clarke, and Warman, *La política económica del desperdicio,* 390; **for 1985–1993:** Banco de México, *The Mexican Economy, 1992,* 213; *The Mexican Economy, 1994,* 215; **direct foreign investment flows:** Banco de México, *The Mexican Economy, 1992,* 263; *The Mexican Economy, 1994,* 263; **external debt: 1982–1990:** Secretaría de Hacienda y Credito Público, *Mexico: A New Economic Profile,* 40; **for 1990–1993:** Banco de México, *The Mexican Economy, 1994,* 275; and Salinas de Gortari, *Quarto Informe de Gobierno,* Anexo, 1992, 36.

a. Includes in bond industries (assembly plants).

export competitive in manufactured goods. The administration of President Carlos Salinas de Gortari (1989–1994) further deepened these structural reforms. And, with the currency crisis of December 1994, President Ernesto Zedillo announced additional measures of privatization and deregulation.

The reorientation of economic policy from the statist-protectionist model of the pre-1982 period involved a major alteration in the power structure within the state. This change involved the resurgence of the finance sector bureaucracy[1] and the imposition of its neoliberal economic vision—a vision that, although endogeneous, was strengthened by the process of reaching agreement with the IMF and obtaining World Bank loans. Ongoing economic crisis after 1982 and the pressing need to renegotiate the foreign debt on terms more favorable to Mexico narrowly defined Mexico's domestic economic policy options and influenced the redistribution of power within the state in the direction of those top-level political bureaucrats most amenable to economic stabilization and deep economic restructuring. Those cabinet secretaries directly responsible for negotiations with creditors and with the macroeconomic issues of greatest concern to Mexico's creditors (the public deficit and inflation) solidified their position within the state, while political bureaucrats who raised questions about the efficacy of the new economic model were increasingly marginalized.

The Return of the Finance Dominance of the State

The ongoing struggle of the Finance Ministry to retain control of public enterprises and, after 1970, to regain its previously dominant position within the state apparatus was outlined in chapter 2. The crucial importance of international factors in explaining the policy strength of finance bureaucrats and their allies (the Bankers' Alliance) has been pointed to in Sylvia Maxfield's work. She argues that as the leverage of international creditors increased in the 1980s, the interest of state finance bureaucrats (the Finance Ministry and the Central Bank) and their private sector allies reasserted itself due to the pressing need for good relations with international creditors.[2]

The Ministry of Finance's neoliberal ideological tendencies, however, predate Mexico's debt crisis, while its distinct institutional evolution sets it apart from other parts of the Mexican bureaucracy. Even those studies critical of the application of a bureaucratic politics approach to the analysis of Mexican policy making acknowledge the distinct policy predispositions of certain Mexican ministries of state, particularly the Ministry of Finance and the Central Bank. John H. Purcell and Susan Kaufman Purcell, whose work stresses the predominance of personal groupings in intrabureaucratic politics in Mexico, find clear policy consistencies in at least two ministries: the Finance Ministry is described as pro private sector and concerned with the level of government expenditure, while the Ministry of Natural Resources and Industrial Development (SEPAFIN, previously the Ministry of National Wealth), responsible for industrial public enterprises, is seen as statist in its policy orientation.[3] They argue that these ministries have the most clearly defined constituences (the Finance Ministry's being the private banking sector, SEPAFIN's the public enterprise sector) and are therefore the bureaucratic institutions demonstrating the greatest degree of policy consistency. Subsequent studies have confirmed the importance of institutional identities and constituency ties in the policy process. Dale Story's analysis of the 1980 decision not to join the GATT, for example, argues the importance of institutional actors and extrastate allies: the statist SEPAFIN, with close ties to small and medium industrialists who would have been the most adversely affected by entry into the GATT, and the Ministry of Foreign Relations, with close ties to the National College of Economists, led the assault against joining the GATT.[4]

A number of studies examining the administration of José López Portillo (1976–1982) describe a sharp division between those state managers favoring a high degree of state intervention in the economy (in the Ministry of Natural Resources and Industrial Development) and those concerned about inflation and the fiscal deficit (in the Ministry of Finance and the Central Bank) advocating state withdrawal from the economy. Policy has been explained as a consequence of the struggles between these two groups.[5] Hence, while a certain homogenization in the backgrounds of Mexico's political leaders occurred, especially from the 1970s (that is, the leaders came increasingly from within the state bureacracy),[6] this elite was far from cohesive, exhibiting marked differences in policy prescriptions through both the Echeverría and López Portillo *sexenios* (six-year terms).

While the ultimate decision-making authority rests in the hands of the president, the process of decision making generally allowed a variety of perspectives to come into play. The 1988 decision to nationalize the banks represented an important departure from this practice: it was taken in secret by the president and a few close advisors identified with the statist-expansionary group. Finance officials were informed only after the decision had been made. This decision-making style, involving the exclusion of one of the two traditional bureaucratic policy tendencies, would become increasingly the norm during the following two *sexenios* of Miguel de la Madrid and Carlos Salinas. But by that time, the finance sector bureaucrats excluded those with more statist-expansionary policy tendencies.

The neoliberal predisposition of the Finance Ministry and the Central Bank is rooted in its traditional contact and alliance with the private banking sector and has been reinforced by a process of institutional socialization that has created a homogeneity of views. The common outlook of middle- and upper-level technocrats in the Ministry of Finance and the Central Bank has been traced to an in-house training program developed by the bank.[7] Cohesiveness and attitudinal homogeneity are further reinforced in the Finance Ministry and the Central Bank by a high level of personnel continuity and a tight network measured by exchange of personnel. Moreover, it would appear that *camarillas* for finance sector bureaucrats are confined within their specific institutional setting and do not span a wide variety of government ministries and agencies. Roderic Camp found that President Salinas's personal *camarilla* shared his career background in national financial agencies and that most of its members were trained economists.[8] The Finance Ministry's monetarist views have been further reinforced by its long-standing relationship with the IMF dating back to the 1940s, when IMF-supported currency devaluations were carried out in response to balance of payments difficulties.[9]

With the election of Miguel de la Madrid in 1983, the intrabureaucratic struggles between statist and antistatist bureaucrats that had characterized the previous administrations were considerably muted. The top-level state managers under de la Madrid were more homogeneous in outlook than had been the case during the administration of his predecessor. Wishing to avoid the sharp conflicts of the previous administration, de la Madrid surrounded himself with cabinet secretaries whose views were not widely dissimilar from his own. President de la Madrid was, at heart, a fiscal conservative with an antistatist bent, despite the central role he had played as secretary of budget and planning in President López Portillo's expansionary program.[10] De la Madrid and the vast majority of his cabinet appointees had risen up through either through the Ministry of Finance or the Central Bank.[11] Indeed, the most common point of entry for Mexico's 1983 bureaucrats (from the director general level on up) was the Finance Ministry.[12]

Indeed, virtually all the top-level statist bureaucrats were purged and replaced by more antistatist de la Madrid appointees.[13] Cabinet responsibilities were immediately reorganized to reduce the power of the ministry that had been the power basis of the statist bureaucrats: the Ministry of Natural Resources and Industrial Development (SEPAFIN). SEPAFIN was stripped of its responsibility for industrial development, which was handed over to the Ministry of Commerce, renamed the Ministry of Commerce and Industrial Development (SECOFI). SEPAFIN (the Ministry of Natural Resources and Industrial Development) now became the Ministry of Energy, Mines, and Parastate Industry (SEMIP).

The Ministry of Finance increased its powers at the expense of SEMIP: it became responsible for the projection of revenue for the entire federal government, including public enterprises under SEMIP, and it now had ultimate responsibility for the setting of prices and tariffs of public sector goods and services, many of which were produced by public enterprises under SEMIP. The powers of the Ministry of Budget and Planning (SPP) were also enhanced, at SEMIP's expense, when it acquired responsibility for the budgeting, evaluation, and approval of all state investment, including that of public enterprises.[14] The SPP was also placed in charge of federal government subsidies to public enterprises. Finally, the pressing need to reduce the public deficit by instituting greater controls over public expenditure resulted in the creation of the Ministry of the Comptroller General of the Nation (Secretaría de Contraloría General de la Federación). This new ministry was responsible for the implementation of an auditing system and for regular audits of all government departments and agencies and of public enterprises.

Revenue collection and expenditures were now more tightly controlled from above. Although President de la Madrid set up four subcabinets (of economics, agriculture, health, and foreign trade), by far the most important was the economic cabinet. In fact, the other three rarely met. Composed of the Ministry of Finance and the Ministries of Budget and Planning (SPP), Energy, Mines, and Parastate Industry (SEMIP), Commerce and Industrial Development (SECOFI), the Comptroller General, and Labor, during the de la Madrid years the economic cabinet was dominated by the Ministry of Finance and the SPP.[15] The Office of Economic Advisors to the President (the president's personal advisory team) also played an important role in the formulation of economic policy.

The increasingly exclusionary nature of decision making and the minimization of conflict within the senior levels of the bureaucracy was further facilitated by the fact that cabinet meetings were now generally restricted to cabinet secretaries; subsecretaries and other officials were in attendance only if their presence was required for a specific matter. This practice, according to several senior-level officials, contrasted sharply with the López Portillo and Echeverría years, during which cabinet meetings were attended by a large cross section of upper-level officials and vigorous debate often ensued. Both Presidents Echeverría and López Portillo expected, and, indeed, encouraged statist and antistatist bureaucrats to express their views. And these presidents, according to my informants, expected ministers to advocate the interests of their various clienteles.

The frustration created by the now more closed policy process is reflected in the comment by one senior-level offical that "it was [now] impossible to know what was going on." Senior-level officials interviewed believed that this new decision-making style had been deliberately implemented to avoid the bureaucratic conflicts of earlier sexenios and to make policy change easier to achieve. The new situation gave the president and the most powerful members of the cabinet considerably greater leeway in policy making by reducing the opportunity for bureaucratic resistance. Ignorant of the policy issues at stake and excluded from the process, bureaucrats below the ministerial level no longer were afforded the opportunity to offer their opinions on the most important matters of public policy. The new arrangements now meant greater consensus at the cabinet level, since there were now far fewer participants in the policy-making process and those few participants did not span a variety of institutions and constituencies.

But while the statist/antistatist struggle was greatly subdued, it was not eliminated, and it resurfaced during the de la Madrid years as a debate over the timing and pace of economic restructuring. Institutional responsibilities likely played an important role in further reinforcing policy positions. The ministries most directly involved with debt negotiation and the formulation of macroeconomic policy, the Finance Ministry and the SPP, were understandably the most concerned with meeting IMF targets with regard to inflation and the public deficit. Although the SPP had demonstrated a tendency toward statism during the López Portillo years, the last vestiges of this attitude were swept away under Carlos Salinas, who demanded adherence to neoliberal policy prescriptions. The Finance Ministry and the SPP, therefore, supported a fairly swift and deep restructuring of the economy. The Ministries of Commerce and Industrial Development (SECOFI) and Energy, Mines, and Parastate Industry (SEMIP), although led by strong supporters of neoliberal economic reforms, had narrower, more sectoral concerns and therefore supported a slower-paced program. SECOFI was concerned about the negative impact of rapid trade liberalization on the private sector, while SEMIP resisted the dramatic reduction of government investment and expenditure and the divestiture of state enterprises.

Institutional responsibilities and identities, however, were not the only factors involved and must themselves be viewed within the context of the growing predominance of finance bureaucrats and the routing out of statist bureaucrats from the state apparatus—a factor that has no doubt facilitated a greater homogeneity of views than would otherwise have been the case.

While the implementation of economic restructuring during the

76

de la Madrid years involved the consolidation of power in the hands of the most powerful members of the economic cabinet, it also involved the growing influence of the IMF and the World Bank, especially through the Ministry of Finance, as debt negotiations took on an overriding importance. The administration of Carlos Salinas witnessed a further centralization of power in the hands of finance sector bureaucrats. Under Salinas, the coterie of political bureaucrats involved in the formulation of economic policy became even smaller: the powerful economic cabinet excluded SEMIP, consisting for most of the *sexenio* only of the secretary of finance and the secretaries of budget and planning, commerce and industrial development, labor, and the director of the Central Bank. Among Salinas's cabinet ministers, the secretary of finance, Pedro Aspe, became dominant, while the SPP receded in importance[16] until it was eliminated in 1992 and its functions handed over to the Finance Ministry, making Aspe, until the economic downturn in 1993, the front-runner in the presidential succession struggle.

In addition, a new superministry, the Office of the Presidency of the Republic (Oficina de la Presidencia de la República), was created to verify the implementation of programs and instructions spanning the responsibility of more than one ministry. Its purpose was also to coordinate and carry out decisions made by the various specialized cabinets. The man in charge of this new superministry, José Córdoba Montoya, is believed to have been President Salinas's closest advisor and was a critically important figure in the debt negotiations and also important in the privatization drive.[17] Under Carlos Salinas, the most powerful actors in economic policy making were a tightly knit group: the president, Córdoba, and Aspe. The director of the Central Bank, the secretary of commerce and industrial development, and the secretary of budget and planning (until the elimination of this ministry) were significant, though less important, players.[18] Again, this closed decision-making style was viewed by informants as an explicit arrangement intended to reduce the obstacles to presidential goals presented by protracted bureaucratic conflict.

The establishment of the Ministry of Social Development in 1992, from the former Ministry of Urban Development and Ecology, provided a certain decree of counterbalance to the power of the Finance

Ministry, although not in matters of economic policy. It centralized social policy in the hands of one of Salinas's most important cohorts: Luis Donaldo Colosio, the winner of the succession struggle and, later, the assasinated PRI candidate for the 1994 presidential election.[19] In addition to housing, ecology, and urban and regional development, the new Ministry of Social Development (SEDESO) also took over responsibility for social policy in general and for regional, state, and federal planning. Most important, it took over the administration of the National Solidarity Program (PRONASOL), a program that matched funds raised by local groups for projects providing infrastructure and services to local communities.

Those in charge of the formulation and implementation of economic policy under President Salinas were probably the most homogeneous superpolitical elite ever.[20] Their career backgrounds were in the finance sector. They were young and had graduate degrees from Ivy League American universities.[21] While it is true that Salinas made cabinet appointments from among people with some party experience (either in the policy or control functions), with the exception of the Ministry of Labor such people were entirely excluded from matters of economic policy.[22] This small group of finance sector political bureaucrats led the debt negotiations and defined the direction of economic policy. Although there was some initial bureaucratic resistance to the policy preferences of neoliberal bureaucrats and multilateral lending agencies in the early de la Madrid years, the difficulties presented by continued external shocks reinforced the power and commitment of the president and those responsible for macroeconomic policy and economic liberalization.

External Pressure and Initial Bureaucratic Resistance

While external pressures were instrumental in propelling Mexico's economic restructuring program, the viewpoint that a fundamental reorientation in economic policy was necessary had been present within the bureaucracy, especially within the Ministry of Finance, since the economic and political crises of the late 1960s. Indeed, the Finance Ministry had been a long-time opponent of both the expansion of state expenditure and public enterprise. It is doubtful, however, that even these officials contemplated the drastic changes that were eventually to occur. During the petroleum boom years (1976–1981), high economic growth rates and abundant foreign exchange earnings had made it possible to paper over the basic structural deficiencies of the Mexican economy: a chronic balance of payments deficit in the current account, an uncompetitive manufacturing sector, a decline in agricultural production and exports, and a burgeoning public sector deficit. Hence, officials critical of the government's interventionist free spending policies could be largely ignored.[23] During the period, even fiscal conservatives were prone to adopt free spending habits in the face of the bureaucratic imperatives of the petroleum bonanza.[24]

The shock of 1981–1982, however, stimulated the emergence of an invigorated neoliberal economic reformism within the Mexican state. The dramatic change in circumstances afforded by the 1981–1982 crisis offered instant legitimacy to critical voices that had been subdued during the petroleum boom years.[25] By 1982, circumstances made it imperative that Mexico arrive at an agreement with the IMF; its foreign exchange reserves were depleted, and banks were refusing to lend. Top officials of the incoming de la Madrid team negotiated the 1983 economic agreement with the IMF,[26] an agreement outlining the new economic direction.

At the same time, however, the de la Madrid administration did not see eye to eye with IMF officials: during 1983–1984, Mexico resisted the IMF's recommendations for economic liberalization and disputed its demands for public deficit reduction. Interviews with senior-level government officials suggested largely political reasons for this resistance. The most commonly cited reason was political opposition from labor, from the PRI, from the private sector, and from within the public bureaucracy itself. It took time to win over or neutralize outside political opponents and to root out or win over statist bureaucrats.[27] One senior-level official, however, while acknowledging the presence of enormous political resistance, felt that the slow start to Mexico's economic liberalization drive was also a consequence of a conscious government strategy that saw political as well as economic pitfalls in the too rapid implementation of economic liberalization.

The major dispute with the IMF during the early years of the de la Madrid administration revolved around the question of reduction of the public deficit. While Mexican government officials were willing to agree to only a modest reduction of the public deficit to 14–15 percent of the GDP, the IMF demanded 6 percent. The 1983 agreement, however, reiterated in Mexico's 1984 letter of intent to the IMF, clearly reflected the IMF's policy preferences, especially in the area of the public deficit. It aimed for a public deficit as percent of GDP of 8.5 percent in 1983, 5.5 percent in 1984, and 3.5 percent in 1985. It also pledged increases in the prices and tariffs of public enterprises, interest rate increases, and the rationalization of subsidies, along with a variety of measures designed to stimulate exports, including a flexible exchange rate policy and the rationalization of the tariff structure and import licence requirements.[28] Salary increases were to be tied to "the objectives of employment and . . . productivity."[29]

The government's domestic economic program, however, played down economic liberalization and focused instead on concern for inflation, employment, and the strict enforcement of price controls on items in the basic food basket. In fact, neither the National Development Plan (Plan Nacional de Desarrollo, or PND) nor the 1984 Plan Nacional de Fomento Industrial y Comercio Exterior (National Program for Industrial Development and Foreign Trade, or PRONAFICE) made any mention of entry into the GATT, a move that would be a reality by 1986. Indeed, there remained a considerable degree of foot-dragging on the question of economic liberalization during this initial period. A commitment to statist solutions was a salient feature of the early de la Madrid years. The National Development Plan asserts the state's economic leadership role, and constitutional reforms carried out in the early months of the de la Madrid administration reiterated the centrality of the state's role in the economy: article 25 was modified to give to the state "the rectory [leadership] role in national development." The state was given exclusive jurisdication over strategic areas defined by the constitution and shared responsibility (with the private and social sectors) in priority areas. Articles 27 and 28 enunciated specifically the strategic areas for which the state was responsible, while article 28 reserved public banking and credit services exclusively to the state.[30]

Of the policy goals agreed to with the IMF, only in the area of public sector deficit reduction did the administration move forward quickly during its first two years (see table 4.1).[31] Economic liberalization stalled; generalized subsidies were not removed; and while the prices of basic food items increased, new subsidies were instituted.[32] Both trade liberalization and privatization proceeded slowly. While in 1984, import licenses were eliminated from 2,844 of 8,000 product categories and tariffs were reduced on key imports,[33] the overvalued exchange rate continued to provide protection. In fact, a "real" trade liberalization program and membership in the GATT were rejected by the president as inappropriate at that time.[34] In the words of one senior-level government official involved in what he described as "very tough" negotiations with the World Bank during the early de la Madrid years, "the World Bank wanted trade liberalization done immediately . . . but the government rejected this. They don't have to be concerned with domestic responsibilities—we do. [We said] that we have to do it at our own pace."

Both SECOFI and Finance Ministry officials interviewed acknowledged that much of the opposition to a more rapid trade liberalization drive came from SECOFI, whose views reflected, to a certain extent, concerns present among much of the private sector with which it had ongoing dealings. As other researchers have noted, the Ministry of Commerce's policy positions have been more ambivalent than those of the Ministry of Finance and the Ministry of Natural Resources and Industrial Development (the Ministry of Energy, Mines, and Parastate Industry after 1983), although it has tended to be moderately statist (in light of the fact that it supervises some large public companies) and sensitive to domestic and foreign business interests.[35] SECOFI argued in favor of a gradual process of trade liberalization in order to give national industry the time to modernize, restructure, and become competitive.[36] Hence, this ministry now opposed Mexico's entry into the GATT, arguing that such a measure was not feasible without sufficient investment to achieve greater productivity.[37] This position apparently represents a departure from the Ministry of Commerce's 1980 position in favor of the GATT[38] and its post-1988 position in favor of a North American Free Trade Agreement (NAFTA). There may well have been division within the ministry on the issue, further complicated by the transfer of the industrial development function from the former Ministry of Natural Resources and Industrial Development, a known bastion of statist bureaucrats. Two senior officials interviewed said that Hector Hernández Cervantes, secretary of commerce during both the López Portillo and de la Madrid administrations, had never really been a strong supporter of trade liberalization, despite his public pronouncements in favor of the GATT. He had taken this public position because President López Portillo had wanted him to.

SEMIP took a similarly cautious position on the restructuring and divestiture in the public enterprise. But by early 1985, the more cautious approach expressed by these two ministries had been replaced by the decision to accelerate economic restructuring, particularly economic liberalization.

Renewed Economic Crisis and the Decision to Accelerate Restructuring

External pressures formed the context for the radical restructuring program implemented by the government after 1985. Without these external pressures, intrabureaucratic resistance could have been sustained, and the achievement of economic restructuring would undoubtedly have occurred much more slowly than it did.[39] Mexico's worsening economic circumstances (the further decline in petroleum prices and the increase in interest rates) made agreement with the IMF inescapable. Of particular importance was the commitment of finance sector political bureaucrats to the pursuit of policies they perceived as favored by multilateral lending agencies, coupled with the growing reticence of some to allow continued negative growth rates. The strategy on the Mexican side, therefore, was to support economic liberalization while standing firm on the demand for an alleviation of austerity. Hence, as time went on, the conflict with the IMF, and the source of severest intrabureaucratic struggle, was not so much over the question of economic liberalization (which everyone agreed on) as over the question of how much more austerity Mexico could be allowed to bear.

The deterioration of petroleum prices on the international market prompted the decision of the economic cabinet, taken in February of 1985, to accelerate economic liberalization, including privatization.[40] This decision was not made public until after the impending July elections. The government had originally assumed that economic growth would pick up after 1984: a stable to positive growth rate was predicted for 1984 and between 5 and 6 percent growth for 1985–1988. Faced with elections in July of 1985, government expenditure helped stimulate industrial production in late 1984 and early 1985.[41] While investment picked up, positive economic growth rates were realized in 1984 and 1985, and the drastic decline in the minimum wage abated somewhat (see table 4.1).

Renewed shocks beginning in late 1984 and continuing through 1986, however, derailed hopes for a resumption of economic growth. By the end of 1984, OPEC, fearing a price slide, agreed to reduce its production of crude. At the beginning of 1985, as the international price of crude began to decline, Mexican petroleum exports dropped by approximately two hundred barrels per day; at the beginning of February, PEMEX lowered its price for Isthmus crude, resulting in a loss of foreign exchange of some $330 million.[42] In 1985, as well, increases in the costs of production and U.S. import barriers discouraged manufacturing exports to that country. Faced with a major earthquake (September 19 and 20) in 1985, Mexico was unable to fulfill the performance criteria agreed to in its 1983–1984 agreement with the IMF. With Mexico's public deficit as a percent of GDP approaching 10 percent, the IMF suspended loan disbursements, while creditor banks refused to grant new credit. Mexico then unilaterally postponed repayment of $950 million due October 1 and November 4 and announced that a further $250 million due in 1986 would not be paid.[43]

The February decision to accelerate restructuring was followed shortly thereafter (in April) by a letter of intent to the IMF pledging to bring the public deficit to 5.1 percent of GDP and to accelerate a variety of neoliberal policy reforms including privatization.[44] Hence, some observers have claimed to see the strong arm of the IMF behind Mexico's neoliberal policy reforms.[45] The process, however, was rather more subtle than such assertions would imply: the marked deterioration in Mexico's economic circumstances strengthened the position of those bureaucrats who had all along supported such policies, since everyone, including those with a more statist bent, was now convinced that there was absolutely no alternative. The IMF did not have to dictate economic policy to Mexico; changed circumstances now made it easy for those wanting deeper restructuring to win their case. Their more cautious opponents could offer no viable alternative. By the time the decision was made public immediately following the elections, the continued deterioration in petroleum prices put an end to hopes for the resumption of economic growth and further reinforced the commitment to these drastic policy reforms.

Indeed, during 1985, even while negotiations with the IMF stalled, Mexico continued to pursue IMF-supported policies such as budget cutbacks and measures of economic liberalization. Cuts in government expenditure were announced in early 1985, and the July 1985 emergency package called for a further cut in government spending of 150 billion pesos.[46] The July emergency measures also included an acceleration in state divestiture and the replacement of import licenses by tariffs for over three thousand tariff categories. These measures were followed throughout 1986 by further budget cuts, tax increases, and tariff reductions, the elimination of quantitative controls, an export promotions program, and the withdrawal of many subsidies, including those on basic food.[47] Having initiated negotiations for entry into the GATT in 1985, Mexico formally joined in July of 1986.

Despite such moves toward economic liberalization, however, negotiation of a rescue package involving Mexico, the IMF, the World Bank, and fifteen creditor governments was difficult and protracted. Talks became deadlocked in May 1986 over the IMF's insistence that Mexico reduce the size of its public deficit even further.[48] As private bankers refused new money, Mexico was reported to be on the verge of suspending all debt payments over the weekend of June 7.[49] The size of the public deficit had been a major sticking point in the 1985 IMF agreement and continued to be so during negotiations in 1986. The IMF was reported to have demanded that the deficit be held to 5–6 percent of GDP, despite the drastic fall in oil prices, which accounted for half the government's official receipts; Mexico argued for a deficit of around 10–13 percent of GDP.[50] The IMF focused especially on sharp reductions in subsidies to public enterprises and drastic measures against inflation, such as major restrictions on salaries, consumption, and investment.[51] At this time, rumors of strong pressure for an acceleration of economic liberalization (relaxation of foreign investment rules, privatization, reduction of tariffs, and elimination of quota and tariff restrictions) from Mexico's creditors were so prevalent that de la Madrid felt compelled to reject such pressures publicly.[52]

The suggestion has been made that in view of the impossibility of Mexico meeting the IMF's public deficit demands, the IMF may well have focused conditionality on measures such as further liberalization of trade and investment regulations and an accelerated program of privatization.[53] Mexico refused to accept an economic program that would mean a growth rate of less than 3–4 percent in 1987–1988. Mexican officials also demanded interest rate concessions, debt payments linked to the price of oil, and incorporation of the inflationary component into the calculation of the budget deficit.[54]

The rescue package was negotiated under the terms of the Baker Plan (a scheme announced by then U.S. Treasury Secretary James Baker), which offered new commercial and multilateral credit to debtors who would commit themselves to economic reforms designed to boost the role of the private sector. The resulting agreement was hailed as a landmark agreement: the IMF agreed to a 3–4 percent economic expansion for 1987 (as opposed to a 4–5 percent negative growth rate) and a commitment to adjust lending to changes in international oil prices. Mexico would receive additional loans from the banks should the average price fall below $9.00 per barrel, while the level of financing would be similarly reduced if oil prices should rise above $14.00 per barrel.

It was agreed that the fiscal deficit would be reduced by 3 percent, from an expected 13 percent of GDP in 1986. However, the IMF accepted the notion of operational deficit, which excludes the inflationary component of the service on the internal debt, a change in calculation that was expected to reduce the public deficit estimate by 2–3 percent of GDP. The agreement also sealed Mexico's commitment to an intensification of economic liberalization: there would be further tariff reductions and the substitution of permits by tariffs, prices of public sector goods and services would be "adjusted," divestiture would be accelerated, "unjustified" subsidies eliminated, and state enterprises such as CONASUPO restructured, and there were to be measures to stimulate foreign investment and increase exports.[55] The World Bank supported the rescue package with a $1 billion loan in 1986 to promote exports and ease entry into the GATT.[56]

The discussion within the economic cabinet that produced both the Mexican negotiating position and an invigorated restructuring program (from early 1986 to May) focused on the question of continued austerity. The debate brought about a brief alliance between the SPP, SECOFI, and SEMIP, all pushing for an alleviation of strict austerity and measures to stimulate economic growth, against the Ministry of Finance and the Central Bank officials, whose major concern was inflation and the fulfillment of IMF conditions. The then secretary for budget and planning (SPP), Carlos Salinas de Gortari, a strong proponent of economic liberalization, emerged as the major protagonist to the Finance Ministry's willingness to buckle under to more IMF-prescribed austerity. Many of his concerns were further bolstered by a hard-hitting report presented to the economic cabinet in May of 1986 by the head of the Committee of Economic Advisors to the President, Leopoldo Solís.[57] Indeed, the Solís report formed the core of Mexico's negotiating stance with the IMF.

The clash between the secretary of finance, Jesús Silva Herzog, and the budget and planning secretary, Carlos Salinas, culminated in the resignation of Silva Herzog in June of 1986 and his replacement by Gustavo Petricioli. Silva Herzog, heading up negotiations with the IMF, was increasingly perceived both within the government and outside of it as an internal advocate of IMF demands. Although there have been conflicting interpretations regarding the reasons behind Silva Herzog's resignation, the most plausible suggests he was forced to resign after the economic cabinet refused his recommendation that Mexico try to meet the IMF's demands for public deficit reduction in return for a mutually agreed on ninety-day suspension of interest payments on the debt.[58]

But the Salinas victory for a tougher negotiating stance with the IMF and an alleviation of austerity had tremendous political and economic implications over the longer term. Until his resignation, Silva Herzog had been a front-runner for the PRI presidential candidacy. His apparent inability to handle the debt negotiations and his subsequent resignation removed him from the contest and immediately thrust forward economic liberal Carlos Salinas as the dominant figure in the economic cabinet and as the front-runner for the PRI candidacy and, therefore, for the presidency.[59] Middle- and senior-level bureaucrats interviewed for this book overwelmingly saw the resignation of Silva Herzog and the consequent rise of Carlos Salinas's dominance of the cabinet as the turning point in Mexico's economic liberalization drive. Salinas's strong support for economic liberalization was attested to by all; hence, after 1986, there was no turning back. Salinas's victory over Silva Herzog, followed by his designation as the PRI presidential candidate in 1987, sealed the fate of those cabinet members, the secretaries of SECOFI and SEMIP, who had resisted an accelerated economic liberalization campaign. By 1986, their gradualist ideas had lost force in the economic cabinet as the belief in the necessity of accelerated economic liberalization, propagated by Salinas, became dominant.

The Triumph of Economic Liberalism and Export Promotion

While during the first six months of 1987, oil export revenues rose, nonoil export revenues began to suffer as a consequence of U.S. protectionism.[60] Average per barrel petroleum prices then fell once again, anticipated loans failed to materialize, and inflation hit 130 percent.[61] Two objectives, linked in the minds of Mexico's top policy makers, now governed economic decision making: the control of inflation and economic liberalization. Trade liberalization, according to the official view, would not only help reduce inflation (by allowing cheaper products to enter the domestic market) but would also stimulate greater efficiency. Both the reduction of inflation and economic liberalization would produce economic growth and increased employment in the long run, since both were conducive, it was argued, to private investment and export competitiveness.

The government's response to inflation was the economic solidarity pact (Pacto de Solidaridad Económica). Signed by government, business, worker, and peasant representatives, it committed the government to further expenditure reductions, a restrictive credit policy, privatizations, tax and price increases, and further trade liberalization while guaranteeing the maintenance of prices of basic products at their 1987 price levels. Labor agreed to restrict wage increases, and business to keep prices down.

The overriding concern with inflation and trade liberalization was not, however, accepted by SECOFI and SEMIP; both protested the immediate recessionary impact of the government's anti-inflation measures as inhibiting the investment necessary to become truly export competitive. Both, therefore, had lobbied heavily for the application of IMF contingency funds.[62] SECOFI continued to argue that export competitiveness based on modernization of the productive plant was impossible as long as high interest rates and a tight money supply were in effect. SEMIP made a similar argument for public sector industry: plant modernization was dangerously imperiled by the severe restrictions on public investment. The views of the financial ministries prevailed, however, and Mexico did not apply for the extra funds from the IMF, despite the fact that the sharp fall in GDP and fixed investment during the first quarter of 1987 entitled it to such funds.[63] Instead, it opted for the pact and further restriction on growth. Low investment rates, therefore, remained a feature of the last years of the administration (see table 4.1). Meanwhile, trade liberalization went forward, as did various export promotion measures such as credits, tax relief, and drawbacks.[64] By 1988, 96 percent of imports did not require an import permit.[65]

The alternatives discussed within the economic cabinet between 1983 and 1988 excluded any strategies other than economic liberalization. The debate was over the pace of economic liberalization, never over the wisdom of the policy itself. Not only did the diminishment of state resources preclude a statist response, but those state managers with the strongest nationalist-statist bent, who would have most vigorously opposed economic liberalization, had been largely excluded from the highest reaches of political power by 1983. More-over, the resumption of Mexico's economic crisis—the suddenness and depth of the 1985 external shocks, after severe adjustments had already been made—constricted policy options within narrow limits. Domestic political pressures demanded a resumption of economic growth, while international lenders demanded austerity and accel-erated economic liberalization. Mexico's negotiators, already predis-posed to most of the policy recommendations of the major lending institutions, therefore decided to accelerate economic liberalization while demanding an alleviation of strict austerity.[66]

Once the struggle within the state over how much austerity Mex-ico could bear was resolved in favor of an alleviation of austerity compatible with control of inflation, a stimulus for future economic growth had to be vigorously pursued. Indeed, when both economic stagnation and inflation continued into 1987, the pursuit of the eco-nomic liberalization strategy became even more important. Full com-mitment to the new motor force of economic growth, the exportation of manufactured goods, was now mandatory. Moreover, it was be-lieved to be preferable to move toward trade liberalization without any further hesitation. As a consequence of the 1983–1984 experi-ence, bureaucratic supporters of trade liberalization believed that further delay would only serve to give opposition forces, especially from the business sector, time to mobilize to thwart trade liberali-zation.[67] In any case, as has already been suggested, intrabureaucratic resistance was not to the policy itself but to the pace of change.[68] It might have been possible to slow down this strategy had an alter-native means for the achievement of economic growth been pre-sented—but none was.

Carlos Salinas and the Deepening of Economic Restructuring

While the essential ingredients of a thorough economic liberalization program had been set in motion by 1987, the debt negotiation process continued to ensure that policy did not deviate from the chosen path. Indeed, while Carlos Salinas was certainly committed to economic liberalization, the debt negotiations reinforced the economic liberalization drive of Mexico's rulers and blocked the emergence of intra-state resistance. Mexico's 1989 agreement was negotiated under the auspices of the Brady Plan proposed by U.S. Secretary of the Treasury, Nicholas Brady, in March 1989. This plan offered the reduction of debt (interest and principal) in return for reforms deemed necessary to encourage investment and internal savings and promote the return of capital. Such reforms were to include new regulations facilitating foreign investment, privatization of public enterprises, increased reductions in public expenditures, and trade liberalization.[69] "Voluntary" debt reduction was to be stimulated on a case-by-case basis and backed by the IMF and the World Bank. It is estimated that between 1989 and 1994, the Brady Plan reduced Mexico's net transfers abroad by $4 billion.[70]

As Mexico's economic difficulties persisted, the pressures on Mexico's political leaders to find a way to jump-start the economy were becoming overwhelming. Calls from the opposition parties for a moratorium on the debt mounted, while the official labor movement balked at any further wage restraints—a development that threatened to unravel the government's anti-inflation program. More important, debt repudiation had become a major economic theme in the 1988 presidential campaign in which Salinas's leftist rival, Cuauhtémoc Cárdenas, posed a serious political threat.[71] It was becoming increasingly clear that steps would have to be taken to stem the outflow of capital for debt payments if economic growth were to occur. Once elected, the Salinas administration, therefore, began to declare that its priority would no longer be to pay off the debt but to provide for a resumption of economic growth. Growth, it was declared, was not possible as long as 5 percent of the national product was transferred out of the country. Public statements made by President Carlos Salinas now repeatedly reiterated his commitment to seek new terms from the country's creditors to reduce the transfer abroad of resources from 6 percent to 2 percent of GDP.[72]

In return for a reversal in the outflow of capital, which would make possible the resumption of economic growth, the administration further committed itself to the restructuring program. Negotiations were carried out between multilateral lending agencies, Mexico's creditor banks, and the Mexican negotiating team headed up by Pedro Aspe and José Córdoba Montoya. In its negotiations with the

IMF, the Mexican team is reported to have told the IMF that further austerity would have grave social and political consequences.[73]

Agreement was reached with the IMF in 1989. The 1989 letter of intent stressed Mexico's achievements in opening the economy and in reducing the size of the public sector, particularly through divestitures. It emphasized the importance of achieving growth of up to 6 percent along with a permanent reduction in the transfer of resources abroad. Moreover, the letter pledged to continue trade liberalization, divestitures, and efforts to make the public sector more efficient and to recognize the important role of foreign capital.[74] The IMF specifically provided funds for debt reduction, while the World Bank provided three separate policy loans (of US$500 million each) for assistance with structural change in the industrial, public utility, and financial sectors. One of these was to be channeled through NAFINSA to stimulate improvements in efficiency in the public enterprise sector, including the carrying out of studies to identify possible enterprises to be divested.[75] Indeed, according to a leaked confidential World Bank Report, the Bank had been pressuring Mexico to accelerate and extend its economic liberalization drive.[76]

To reverse the outflow of capital, Mexico presented a menu of debt reduction options to its private creditors, arguing for its preference of a reduction of principal or interest rates over capitalization of interest and new lending. Negotiations with the private sector were arduous. The banks' counterproposal was allegedly less than one-half of the US$4.5 billion a year Mexico had been seeking from them over the coming three years. At one point, Mexico broke off the talks while the United States put intense pressure on the banks to come up with an acceptable proposal. An agreement was finally reached, narrowly averting a suspension in debt payments. The agreement signed with the Bank Advisory Committee, covering only the public sector debt, gave banks the choice of three options: (1) a 35 percent reduction of principal, (2) reduction and stabilization of interest rates at 6.25 percent, and (3) new credits, equivalent to 25 percent of the outstanding exposure.[77]

Throughout the difficult negotiation process, the administration continued to pursue policies it knew would help convince creditors of the country's economic stability. The anti-inflation pacts, continued into the Salinas administration, reflected a commitment to economic liberalization: tariffs were to be further reduced, public finances watched carefully, government regulations further decreased and divestitures accelerated.[78] Moreover, just a few short months after the Brady Plan was announced, Mexico modified its foreign investment legislation through its 1989 Reglamento de la Ley para Promover la Inversión Mexicana y Regular la Inversión Extranjera (Regulation for the Law Promoting Mexican Investment and Regulating Foreign Investment). This regulation removed the 49 percent restriction on foreign investment for all industries not reserved exclusively to the state or to Mexican nationals under certain specific conditions.[79] No longer was permission required for foreign investors to take over Mexican firms, and neither *maquiladoras* (assembly plants) nor export companies would require official authorization for their establishment. Furthermore, the new regulations effectively opened up to foreign investment even in those areas legally restricted to Mexican nationals or the state. With these changes, foreign capital could own up to 100 percent of the shares of companies through temporary trust companies (established for a maximum of twenty years and nonrenewable) in activities exclusively reserved for Mexicans (domestic air and maritime transportation and forestry) and in sectors where foreign investment was otherwise restricted to 40 percent (mining, petrochemicals, and automotive components).[80] Other resolutions passed in 1989 sought to reduce the red tape and simplify bureaucratic procedures for foreign investors.

These measures were no doubt important in gaining the confidence of Mexico's creditors. When agreement was finally reached between Mexico and the Banking Advisory Committee negotiating for Mexico's private banking creditors, the committee announced its enthusiasm for Mexico's measures of structural adjustment, particularly for the new foreign investment law.[81] Indeed, there was considerable justification for this initial enthusiasm: until mid-1993, and with the exception of the worsening trade deficit, economic indicators suggested that the Mexican economy was on an upswing: growth resumed, investment rates picked up, the federal deficit was considerably reduced, the external debt situation improved, and the flow of foreign investment increased (see table 4.1). But by December 1994, Mexico once again faced economic crisis—a crisis rivaling the 1982 one in its severity. Presidential pronouncements promising stabilization and even more structural reforms signaled the opening up of some of the last areas of exclusive state responsibility to private capital.

Ernesto Zedillo and the 1994 Currency Crisis

The 1994 financial crisis, set in motion by a 15 percent devaluation on December 20 and the subsequent float of the peso, has further solidified the regime's commitment to liberalizing reforms. While this most recent economic crisis seemed to burst forth suddenly and unexpectedly, its origins had been evident over the previous year. The economic cause of the crisis was Mexico's chronic and increasingly heavy current account deficit that was being financed by unreliable short-term capital inflows, especially portfolio investment in the form of *tesebonos*, government bonds guaranteeing payment in dollars.[82] By 1994, Mexico's external debt had risen to $130 billion, $30 billion more than when the debt was restructured in 1990.[83] Enthusiasm of financial institutions for Mexico's liberalization policies fueled an inflow of short-term capital. In a scenario reminiscent of the 1982 crisis, Mexico once again took on more credit than it could handle.

Between January and September 1994, the current account deficit increased by $7.8 billion, while capital inflows declined.[84] Political factors played an important role in this decline: the pace of portfolio investment declined notably after the Chiapas uprising and again after the political assassinations in 1994 of Luis Donaldo Colosio, PRI presidential candidate, and José Francisco Ruiz Massieu, secretary general of the PRI.[85] These developments put increasingly strong pressure on the exchange rate. Faced with an election in 1994, the Salinas administration resisted devaluation.[86] Defense of the peso during the final year of the Salinas administration resulted in a dramatic decline in the country's reserves, which stood at $5.5 billion by January 1995, down from over $25 billion at the beginning of 1994.[87] By March 1995, the peso had dropped 50 percent against the dollar. Squeezed by both the increase in the foreign current debt due to devaluation and a growing number of bad debts due to the recession, the country's banks teetered on the verge of failure.[88] Faced with a dramatic rise in imported inputs, big industry laid off workers and small firms closed down.[89] Portfolio investment declined even further and foreign investors, such as Walmart, abandoned their investment plans.[90]

With $10.2 billion of short-term debt coming due in March 1995, Mexico sought desperately for support from international creditors. Once again, regaining the confidence of international creditors became the pressing issue. In this way, economic crisis continued to propel the state's privatization drive forward—a policy drive to which the country's homogeneous neoliberal policy leaders were already committed. A rescue package was quickly put together involving $20 billion from the United States, another $5 billion from the Bank for International Settlements and $3 billion from a group of U.S. banks.[91] Under intense U.S. pressure, the IMF granted Mexico the largest loan ever granted: $7.8 billion.[92] In addition to agreeing to strict IMF supervision, Mexico promised a tight monetary and restrictive fiscal policy and cuts in government spending. It also pledged to raise $12–14 billion from privatizations.[93] The country's oil revenues were put up as collateral for the U.S. loan, and the government pledged to remove the remaining restrictions on foreign-owned banks.[94]

With the economic crisis of 1994–1995, Mexico's policy elite has been forced to abandon its plans for economic growth. A further drop in living standards is unavoidable. Economic growth is predicted at −2 percent for 1995 and inflation at 42 percent.[95] According to the private sector, the number of jobs lost in January and February 1995 was on the order of 200,000 to 250,000, while the Labor Ministry has admitted that the adjustment process will probably involve a loss of 500,000 jobs.[96]

Conclusion

In less than ten years, Mexico's economy was transformed from a highly statist and protected economy to one open to foreign competition and investment. The context for this policy reversal was a deteriorating international economic situation and growing pressure from international lenders to make these policy adjustments. The interaction of this international context and these external pressures with domestic political processes determined the timing and depth of Mexico's economic liberalization drive. Bureaucratic resistance could not survive the shocks of 1985–1986; those shocks strengthened the antistatist bureaucrats responsible for macroeconomic policy who had long supported the policy reforms now being called for. Hence, Mexico's process of policy reform was not, until after 1986, the product of a fixed strategy carried out by a cohesive technocratic elite. Rather, it evolved incrementally in response to intensifying international pressures.[97] While pressures from international lending institutions for policy reform were ongoing from 1982 through 1989, the turning point in Mexico's pursuit of economic liberalization came with the external economic shocks of 1985–1986 and the rise of Carlos Salinas to the predominant position in economic policy making. After that date, Mexico's economic liberalization program, particularly its privatization drive, acquired its own internal momentum.

During the process of debt negotiation and economic restructuring, the economic policy-making process became increasingly exclusionary: by 1992, it was in the hands of a homogeneous superelite dedicated to economic liberalization. No longer did a variety of bureaucratic groups and policy tendencies have the opportunity to influence the policy process. Most important, statist bureaucrats were now totally excluded. Privatization, particularly divestitures, was a critical component of the government's economic restructuring program and became closely tied to the goal of export competitiveness. Like trade liberalization, privatization met stiff resistance, and, like trade liberalization, that resistance was largely defeated with the rise of Carlos Salinas to political ascendency.

5

Power and Public Enterprise Reform

The plan to restructure the state's mammoth public enterprise sector was officially announced in 1983 and, along with trade liberalization, became the cornerstone of the government's economic program after 1985. Official explanations of public enterprise restructuring closely linked the program to the government's manufacturing export promotion strategy. State firms directly involved in exports could not be export competitive if inefficiencies were tolerated, and those providing inputs for the private sector, if allowed to remain inefficient, would hurt the export competitiveness of the private sector by increasing their costs. While the most publicized aspect of public enterprise restructuring has been divestitures, the reform of state enterprises that remained in state hands was an integral part of the process. Indeed, divestiture and public enterprise reform were at times indistinguishable, as public enterprise reform was a prerequisite to eventual divestiture—although the intrabureaucratic struggle over whether or not divestiture would occur often obscured the question of exactly what areas the state would move out of. Even for firms remaining in state hands, reforms sought to open up public company activities to market forces. In the process of reforming the public enterprise sector, finance officials subjected public enterprises to tightly centralized control.

Reform was to involve a number of related changes: investment in plant modernization, alterations in labor-management relations, financial restructuring, and administrative reorganization. The objective of all these changes was to increase efficiency, reduce costs, and increase profits. While industrial reconversion, as it came to be called, was originally to include both plant modernization and basic changes in labor-management relations, the absence of investment capital meant a decided emphasis on the latter—a situation that deeply alienated the public enterprise trade unions. The alterations sought after involved an assault on the collective contracts and privileges of the official labor hierarchy of the public enterprise unions. As such, a struggle for power was at the core of the process of restructuring labor relations: for the finance sector, the influence of official labor leaders on the policy process had to be completely and irrevocably removed. This objective was particularly marked in the petroleum sector, where the aim of asserting control actually increased inefficiency.

While the relations between labor and the state deteriorated, the state used its public enterprise restructuring program to court business support. Both public enterprise reform and divestiture were strongly supported by the private sector, and, while the initiative for public enterprise restructuring did not come from it, business enthusiasm helped to propel the program forward once it was under way. Indeed, both public enterprise reform and divestiture helped restore business confidence and did much to solidify business support for the regime during the Salinas administration.

As we saw in the previous chapter, as the debt issue rose to overwhelming importance, the finance sector became predominant within the state apparatus. Public enterprise reform involved a further redistribution of power: it meant a marked decline in the power and autonomy of public enterprises, a growth in the influence of the private sector, and a decline in the influence and status of the official labor leadership of the public enterprise unions.

Business-State Relations and Public Enterprise Reform

Although business expansion occurred largely under the aegis of the state, it was not long before the private sector became a political force to be reckoned with. Both neo-Marxist and traditional social science literature have grappled with the question of the extent of the Mexican state's independence from domestic and foreign capitalist interests. Drawing their inspiration from neo-Marxist structuralism,[1] a number of authors have explained reforms instituted during the Cárdenas years in terms of conjunctural circumstances that allowed the Mexican state to institute policies against the short-term interests of capitalists. The autonomy of the state from domestic and foreign business was, however, only relative, in that the capitalist context within which policy makers operated established the outside boundaries of their actions and ensured that they would act in the long-term interests of capitalism.[2] In this way, it was possible to explain the radical and transitory nature of policy as integral to the long-term enhancement of regime legitimacy and to capitalist reproduction. Others, examining the post-Cárdenas years, have adopted an instrumentalist Marxist perspective, arguing the presence of a "power elite" (often referred to as the "revolutionary family") of business and political leaders at the helm of economic and political power in Mexico.[3] According to this view, policy stems from the coincidence of the interests of a cohesive ruling elite. Business's direct and informal channels to the highest reaches of political power have ensured that its interests are those guiding the direction of public policy.

Mainstream social science literature on Mexico has also explored the relative strengths of business and the state and, in contradistinction to neo-Marxist approaches, has argued the *absolute* autonomy of the state. This literature emphasizes the distinction between the state and the private sector and points to the state as the initiator of state policy.[4] Some have emphasized the ways in which capital has been dominated and controlled by the state through the allocation of credit, import licenses, cheap inputs, and other business requirements.[5] And while business influence over policy as a consequence of its representation on various boards, agencies, and commissions is acknowledged, it is argued that business is always in a minority in a process that is one of consultation rather than bargaining.[6] This viewpoint has been challenged, however, by those who see business and the state as separate, autonomous, and evenly matched power contenders. The absolute autonomy of the Mexican state was demonstrated, according to this viewpoint, by the 1982 bank nationalization decision.[7]

State-business relations in Mexico are further complicated by the fact that the Mexican private sector is not homogeneous. It has been historically split between the proregime small and medium industrialists of the Valley of Mexico and the more politically hostile business leaders of Monterrey. The former group, emerging with the depression and the Second World War, has been represented by an organization known as the National Chamber of Transformation Industry (Cámara Nacional de la Industria de Transformación, or CANACINTRA),[8] a group that has been strongly supportive of the state and of state intervention in the economy.

The Monterrey group originated in prerevolutionary Mexico, during which time it assiduously strove to manipulate the state in order to ensure market monopolies and high profits.[9] The group is a network of powerful financial and industrial conglomerates. Geographically isolated from the Mexican state, it has been characterized by fierce resistance to state incursions into its economic realm and strong antilabor sentiments. Its firm resolve to limit the authority of the state was precipitated by the 1931 Labor Code, which it regarded as overly generous.[10] Its ties to the state have been personal, rather than bureaucratic.[11] Despite such ties, the Monterrey group has experienced periods of extreme tension, if not conflict, with the state. The most notable conflicts occurred during the last years of the Echeverría administration and as a consequence of the bank nationalization under President López Portillo in 1982.

The economic importance of the Monterrey business group has been reinforced by increasing economic concentration since the 1960s, briefly interrupted by the bank nationalization. Powerful industrial and financial interests became linked through holding companies and connected to one of the major banks through bank ownership of shares and financial ties. By the late 1970s, these economic groups had become highly concentrated, with the biggest banks, BANAMEX and BANCOMER, acquiring ever larger numbers of industrial shares. The country's most powerful industrial and financial interests, thirty-seven businessmen controlling some seventy economic groups, are represented by the Mexican Council of Businessmen (Consejo Mexicano de Hombres de Negocios, or CMHN), an organization founded in 1964 to oppose the "mixed economy."[12] CMHN members interviewed by Roderic Camp agreed that their organization had favored access to the state, especially to the president, and stressed the importance of personal contact with the president and other members of the cabinet as the primary means by which their economic interests are communicated.[13]

The CMHN was largely responsible for the creation of the Business Coordinating Council (Consejo Coordinador Empresarial, or CCE) and continues to control it.[14] Established in the wake of President Echeverría's populist-statist drive, the CCE propounds an ideology based on individualism and private property and has repeatedly called for an end to state expansionism. Its international affairs arm, the Mexican Business Council for International Affairs (Consejo Empresarial Mexicano para Asuntos Internacionales, or CEMAI), promotes foreign trade and maintains close contacts with the National Association of Importers and Exporters (Associación Nacional de Importadores y Exportadores, or ANIERM), an organization representing the foreign companies (many with Mexican junior partners) that control the exportation of manufactured goods.[15] Other organizations in which the businessmen of Monterrey play an important role include the Employers' Confederation of the Mexican Republic (Confederación Patronal de la República Mexicana, or COPARMEX), an organization of industrialists, merchants, and agriculturalists; the officially recognized CONCAMIN and CONCANACO;[16] and the Mexican Bankers' Association (Associación Mexicano de Banqueros, or AMB), control of which stems from the group's control over major banking institutions.

For a brief period (roughly from the early 1970s until 1982), it was believed that the ideological and political distinctions dividing Mexico's entrepreneurs had begun to fade.[17] In particular, a homogenization of entrepreneurial views opposing state intervention in the economy appeared to be emerging with the views of the majority of entrepreneurs, including small and medium business, highly critical of the state's intervention in the economy.[18] The benefits that accrued to the private sector as a result of the state's participation in the economy make this hostility to the state's activist role difficult to grasp. The roots of this attitude are probably both pragmatic and ideological.[19] The massive expansion of the state and its ever increasing impact on the economy has resulted in state incursion into areas where it competes with domestic capital. In the 1970s, for example, two state investment projects in petrochemicals competed with plants set up by members of the Monterrey group.[20] A similar case occurred in 1985, when CONASUPO set up a biscuit factory in Monterrey.[21] The private sector has argued that such state enterprises constitute unfair competition, since public enterprises do not have to cover their costs in the way that the private sector must.

At the same time, growing private sector demands for privatization have gone hand in hand with an explicit ideologicial position: a doctrinal commitment to free market ideology and a firm belief in the unproductive nature of statist policies. The tension between business and state over the question of state intervention in the economy climaxed during the last few years of the Echeverría administration, when government expropriation of large landholdings in northern Mexico precipitated massive capital flight. The administration of President López Portillo, therefore, made a concerted effort to restore business confidence. In addition, the prosperity of the petroleum boom years appears to have undermined the growing radicalism of the hard-line antistatism of the private sector, allowing more moderate business leaders to gain the upper hand.[22]

The 1982 bank nationalization, however, was a major setback for state-business relations. All business associations, except CANACINTRA, which represented small and medium firms, vigorously opposed the measure. As business confidence plummeted, massive amounts of capital left the country. For Mexican business, the failure of the government to negotiate with the private sector prior to the execution of this policy represented a gross violation of the traditional rules of government-business relations.[23] As a consequence, the bank nationalization ushered in a reinvigorated antistatism on the part of business. By 1982, radical antistatists had won the presidency of both the CCE and CONCANACO and had retained control of COPARMEX.[24] The private sector mobilized against the government, holding assemblies and demanding "government by law."[25]

Reaffirming its commitment to neoliberalism, the private sector was highly critical of what it believed to be overly statist measures taken by the de la Madrid administration. CONCANACO condemned de la Madrid's 1983 constitutional reforms, which enshrined the state's leadership role in the economy and spelled out those strategic areas in which its role would be exclusive to the state. These measures were characterized as opening the way for the "centralization of productive power."[26] COPARMEX, the most antistatist of the entrepreneurial organizations, accused the state of seeking to "control the minds of children in favour of statization";[27] it feared that the state wished to replace the private sector as the driving force of the national economy and also charged that the state wanted to "control everything" and that the only beneficiary of state enterprises "is a privileged bureaucratic class which does not produce."[28] Even CANACINTRA, traditionally in favor of strong state intervention in the economy, now spoke out against excessive state controls. The true cause of the economic crisis, according to the president of that organization, Pizzuto Zamanillo, was "the desire to institute obligatory planning and to do away with the existing vestiges of the free and social economy of the market." Furthermore, he claimed, too much protection of public enterprises had hurt investment and production.[29]

The government's failure to consult the private sector prior to the bank nationalization convinced business leaders that the current political system excluded them from influence on major policy decisions. COPARMEX demanded that the political system be democratized.[30] The most radical business leaders began to participate in electoral politics by supporting opposition parties, particularly the National Action Party (Partido de Acción Nacional, or PAN), becoming heavily involved in local elections in 1983 in Chihuahua and in two races in that state in 1986.[31] In 1983, Fernando Canales Clarion, a prominent businessman, ran for the PAN in the race for the state governorship of Nuevo León, and in 1985 four former business leaders ran for the Chamber of Deputies on the PAN ticket.[32] In 1986, Manuel J. Cloutier, former national leader of the CCE and COPARMEX, was the PAN candidate for governor of Sinaloa.

The state responded to this new entrepreneurial political activism by pressuring important Monterrey businessmen to refrain from active participation in politics and from open opposition to its economic policies.[33] COPARMEX answered with the accusation that the government was violating the human rights of businessmen in exercising such pressure. Other entrepreneurial organizations, most notably CANACINTRA, called for reforms within the existing party state arrangements that would give the private sector greater influence. The establishment of a business sector within the PRI was advocated as a means of providing for business input.[34]

Most of those entrepreneurs who had actively opposed the government remained politically inactive in the 1988, 1989, and 1991 elections.[35] And, while the Carlos Salinas administration brought most business interests back into the political fold, many small and medium entrepreneuerial interests gave active support to the PAN in the 1992 elections.[36]

The political alienation of the business community during the de la Madrid years was further aggravated by the combination of an anti-inflation program that controlled prices and restricted credit and a trade liberalization drive that reduced industrial protection. The private sector disputed the state's contention that its restriction of credit was part of its anti-inflation program. Rather, this policy was believed to reflect the substantial resources required to finance the public deficit. The public deficit, according to the private sector, was absorbing the legal reserve requirement (set at 90 percent of bank reserves), leaving little credit available for the private sector.[37] Hence, as economic restructuring accelerated and business survival was threatened by the combined factors of loss of protection and inadequate credit, the private sector placed the blame on what it believed to be a bloated and unproductive state—public enterprise being the most obvious manifestation of the absence of spending restraint. Indeed, some business associations went so far as to suggest that public enterprise was the major cause of Mexico's ongoing economic crisis.[38]

The nationalized banking sector was one of the private sector's major targets: all business groups complained bitterly about the insufficient credit available to the private sector, declaring that the credit restrictions imposed by the nationalized banking sector were producing massive bankruptcies.[39] Moreover, the state's selective dispersement of this scarce resource[40] deepened private sector hostility even further. In addition, the private sector complained that more than 65 percent of industry was unable to take advantage of bank loans, due to high interest rates and red tape that delayed disbursements for up to six months.[41] By 1986, the industrialists of Monterrey threatened a moratorium on their payments to Mexican banks if more credit was not made available, as did the small and medium industrialists of CANACINTRA.[42]

The problem of insufficient credit was exacerbated by the commercial opening business claimed: Mexican industry could not compete if it lacked capital with which to modernize its productive plant.[43] Business complained that the amount of credit the nationalized banking sector was able to supply to the private sector was woefully insufficient and its interests rates too high. Foreign competitors, on the other hand, had access to cheaper interest rates. Mexican industry could only be competitive if it had access to competitive interest rates, and this would only be possible if the state got out of the banking business and allowed market forces to take over. As one owner of a large petrochemical firm declared in an interview, "with interest rates at 22 percent, we cannot compete with U.S. companies, for which the cost of money is much lower. If we are going to have trade liberalization, we must also have financial liberalization."

Public enterprises contributed to the country's economic difficulties in other ways, as well, according to the private sector. In general, inefficiencies in public enterprises translated into higher costs for the private sector, thereby contributing to the uncompetitiveness of Mexican business. Private business in the petrochemical industry was especially critical of PEMEX, as indicated by the following remarks made by another petrochemical executive: "PEMEX is big and unwieldy and impossible to deal with. Its inefficiencies translate into higher costs for us. We took the position that if the government is going to institute trade liberalization, then it must correct the inefficiencies of public enterprises." CANACINTRA was quite explicit on this point, demanding that since the commercial opening had resulted in the massive inflow of foreign products, the government was now obliged to allow the private sector to replace the inefficient public sector in the provision of goods and services.[44]

One of the major sources of inefficiency and increased costs in public enterprises was, according to Mexican businessmen, labor. Labor in general, but especially in the public enterprises, was regarded as having too much power and as providing an inappropriate model for labor relations in other sectors of the economy. COPARMEX and CONCANACO were vehement on this point, arguing that the "corruption of the unions in the strategic public enterprises—PEMEX, CFE, SIDERMEX and FERTIMEX—damaged the process of productivity and had negative repercussions for the labor relations of all state enterprises . . . the consequence being grave economic, political and social problems."[45] Business argued that the excessive concessions found in the collective contracts of public firms contributed to the deficits of these firms, raised costs to the private sector, and thereby contributed to the economic difficulties of the country.[46]

Trade liberalization was another policy that brought increasing criticism from business. Although big business organizations usually publicly supported trade liberalization, enterpreneurs and public officials interviewed in the course of research for this book declared that the private sector, even big business, opposed trade liberalization. In the words of one senior executive in one of Mexico's largest private companies: "None of the businessmen wanted trade liberalization—even the most powerful groups were against it. They had a safe and protected market. Why get into difficulties if you don't have to?" Senior-level government officials reported stiff opposition to trade liberalization from both small-to-medium and large industrialists.

Owners of small and medium-sized businesses, particularly those represented by CANACINTRA, were the earliest and most publicly vociferous opponents of trade liberalization. However, as the program got under way, even large industrialists (CCE) began to publicly express their unease, protesting that the economic opening was too rapid.[47] By 1988, the research arm of the CCE, the Center for Economic Studies of the Private Sector (Centro de Estudios Económicos de Sector Privado, or CEESP), was calling for a more gradual removal of industrial protection.[48]

With business opposed to so many aspects of its economic program, the restoration of business confidence was a major challenge for the de la Madrid administration. The restoration of that confidence was now more important than ever, since the government's depleted resources meant that it could no longer play the economic leadership role it once had. Private sector investment would now have to lead economic growth. However, business confidence remained low well into the de la Madrid administration: during the first six months of 1985, capital flight was conservatively estimated at US$25 billion.[49] The private sector declared that private investment would not be forthcoming until the government made further reductions in public expenditures (seen as the best remedy for inflation) and slowed down the commercial opening.[50] Firmly committed to trade liberalization, the government's desire to restore business confidence therefore focused on the reduction of government expenditures through restructuring the public enterprise sector, a policy to which it was already firmly committed.

But the public enterprise restructuring program never went far enough fast enough for most members of the business community. Business associations, especially those representing the country's largest enterprises, continued to pressure for an acceleration of the program—for complete government withdrawal from the financial system, the sale of the shares of strategic public enterprises (such as PEMEX and the CFE) to private investors, including foreign capital, and the elimination of CONASUPO.[51] Indeed, according to the CCE, flight capital would only return with the privatization of eight or nine public enterprises, among them CONASUPO, PEMEX, and the CFE.[52] Hence, the pressing need to reestablish business confidence was yet another factor reinforcing the government's commitment to public enterprise reform. However, as intense as pressure from the business community was, it was the operation of bureaucratic imperatives that directly shaped the nature of the changes in the public enterprise sector.

Bureaucratic Imperatives in Public Enterprise Reform

As the previous chapter pointed out, Mexican government institutions, particularly the Ministry of Finance and the Ministry of Natural Resources and Industrial Development (from 1983, the Ministry of Energy, Mines, and Parastate Industry), have pursued distinct institutional goals, reflective of their responsibilities and constituency ties. In the case of the Finance Ministry, a socialization process has ensured a homogeneity of views, while the Ministry of Natural Resources and Public Enterprises has tended to recruit statist-minded individuals. Institutional goals are further reinforced by the appointment by bureaucrats, themselves appointed by the heads of each of these ministries, of loyal *equipos* (employees bound to them by ties of personal loyalty) who pursue personal career advancement by identifying with and contributing toward the achievement of the goals of their superiors.[53]

Before 1982, the Ministry of Budget and Planning (SPP), originally set up in 1977 to oversee state investment and expenditure, demonstrated a statist and expansionary bent coincident with its responsibility to plan and administrate the country's wealth.[54] However, after 1982 a radical change in circumstances altered the responsibilities of the SPP: it was now charged with achieving a radical reduction in both investment and expenditure. Headed up by Carlos Salinas, the ministry was deluged with finance sector recruits dedicated to fiscal restraint and the reduction of inflation.[55]

The commitment of the Finance Ministry and the Central Bank to spending restraint, the control of inflation, and foreign debt reduction is linked to their revenue collection and monetary policy functions. These concerns were reinforced not only by a tendency to recruit bureaucrats with neoliberal views but also by the constant contact senior-level officials of these agencies have had with the most powerful faction of the Mexican business class, the private sector bankers. Prior to the bank nationalization of 1982, a direct and close relationship had developed between finance officials and private bankers. Close relations between finance officials and private bankers go back to the 1920s, when the two groups collaborated in the reconstruction of the financial system. These ties continued through subsequent years as a consequence of banking sector appointments to various financial regulatory agencies. In addition, their representation on the board of directors of the Bank of Mexico afforded the private sector an ongoing opportunity to present its views to finance officials, a situation highly conducive to a certain convergence of opinion between the private sector and public officials.[56] Indeed, the

107

interchange between this business group and the public sector has been greater than for any other private sector group.[57]

As argued in chapter 4, the overriding concern of the finance sector has continued to be reduction in the public deficit, a reflection of its macroeconomic responsibilities reinforced by ongoing and tough negotiations with the IMF. As the economic situation deteriorated through 1986, streamlining and reducing the public enterprise sector was perceived as unavoidable and as necessary to the achievement of the finance sector's macroeconomic responsibilities. Indeed, the most important reason given for privatization by finance officials was the pressing need to reduce the public deficit. At the same time, historical ties to the most powerful elements of the private sector bolstered the belief that the private sector operated more efficiently.

While finance officials focused on improvement of the financial situation and divestiture of public firms, the Ministry of Energy, Mines, and Parastate Industry (SEMIP) concentrated on the survival of the enterprises for which it was responsible—a survival now seriously threatened by both Mexico's economic crisis and the economic strategy adopted to confront it. Interviews of middle- and senior-level officials revealed that a major concern of SEMIP was that a minimum of investment be maintained in public firms, a requirement placed in jeopardy by de la Madrid's tough stabilization programs. SEMIP officials claimed to be supportive of the objectives of profitability and efficiency, but they also pointed out that public companies tended to have a variety of responsibilities, only one of which was profitability. The major complaint voiced by SEMIP officials was the woefully inadequate investment in plant modernization, which would inhibit public firms from becoming internationally competitive. However, as SEMIP's influence within the economic cabinet waned rapidly after 1986 and as the bureaucratic imperatives of the financial sector ministries, reinforced by Mexico's deteriorating economic circumstances, came to the fore, public enterprise reform came to focus almost exclusively on changes that would reduce the drain of public enterprises on the public purse. Within a context of deteriorating economic circumstances, plant modernization was viewed by finance sector officials as an impossibility.

For finance sector officials, a necessary first step was the establishment of tight budget control over public firms. The financial debacle of the López Portillo years, and the fact that the public companies bore such a high proportion of the public deficit and debt, focused attention on them. The ability of their directors to go over the heads of secretaries to the president for approval of extrabudget expenditures was widely believed to have been an important source of the problem.[58] In particular, the ability of PEMEX to avoid centralized financial and policy control was of special concern, due to its general economic importance and its contribution to the public treasury.

The establishment of a system of audit control in public firms occurred with the creation of the Comptroller General as a ministry of state in 1983. Greater control and coordination of public enterprises at the helm of economic decision making was established through the increased role given to the Intersecretarial Commission for Expenditure and Financing (Comisión Intersecretarial Gasto-Financiamento). In addition to its responsibility for the financial situation of public firms, it now became involved in the divestiture process.

One of the most important areas of concern was the negative financial consequences of contracts granted by public firms that did not go to public tender. With the 1984 Law of Public Works (Ley de Obras), a law pushed by the then SPP secretary, Carlos Salinas, industrial public companies were prohibited from adjudicating any contract without tender. In addition, the SPP established new norms stipulating that public projects that had been contracted out could only be carried out by the original contractor; that is, they could not be subcontracted out. This inhibited unions or any other contractor from providing lucrative subcontracts for kickbacks.

Dispositions passed in 1983 attempted to strengthen executive control over public enterprises, explicitly requiring the approval of the Ministry of Finance and the SPP for all public enterprise revenue collection and expenditures. Control of public firms through the appropriate cabinet secretary was ensured through the mandatory appointment of the responsible cabinet secretary to the chair of the boards of directors of all firms for which his ministry was responsible. These boards were responsible for the day-to-day operations of the firms.[59]

The policy governing public enterprises was brought together and passed as one piece of legislation in 1986 as the Federal Law of Public Enterprise Entities (Ley Federal de las Entidades Parastatales).[60] The law details the obligations of public enterprises to the financial ministries and represents a clear assault on the autonomy of these firms in reducing the independence of their senior-level administrations. Public firms were now required to provide information on demand. The director general of every public company was responsible to the board but could not sit on it. He was required by the law to have all revenues and expenditures of the company approved by the board, including external credit requirements.

More specific administrative responsibilities that could not be delegated to the director were given by law to the board of directors (or administrative councils). These included production priorities, program and budget approval, prices and tariffs of goods and services, loans from national or international creditors, approval of annual auditor's reports, approval of all programs' contracts with other entities, and administrative appointments (at the top two levels).[61]

In addition, agreements for financial rehabilitation and structural change, signed by the federal government and individual public companies beginning in 1985, committed public companies to production, investment, and export goals, to the elimination of transfers, particularly subsidies, to price increases, and to "the rationalization of the labor force," in return for federal government assumption of all or a portion of the enterprise's debt. By 1987, the government had entered into eight such agreements, including ones with FERRONALES, CFE, SIDERMEX (Siderúrgica Mexicana), and CONASUPO.[62] Another type of agreement, the surplus-deficit agreements, ensured against budget overruns in public firms under federal budget control. The first budget surplus agreements were signed with fifteen companies in the first quarter of 1985; ninety were signed in 1986.[63]

Financial reforms of the public enterprises, particularly sharp cutbacks in expenditure and investment, were resisted by SEMIP and those firms hardest hit by austerity. Always careful to place their criticisms within the context of the officially sanctioned economic strategy, the intrabureaucratic opponents of reform argued that the achievement of export competitiveness required greater, not less, investment in public companies and that the protection of the productive plant required an alleviation, if not the abandonment, of strict austerity. Even official documents contained thinly disguised criticisms of government policy: SEMIP warned of the risks of reduced investment for productivity over the long term.[64]

However, the severity of the economic crisis faced by Mexico and its deepening after 1985 precluded the resumption of economic growth and reinforced the concern with the public deficit. While public sector spending declined drastically, public enterprise spending declined even more precipitously: total public enterprise expenditure as a proportion of all public sector spending decreased after 1985, as did federal government transfers and subsidies to public companies (see table 5.1). Public enterprise investment as a proportion of total public expenditure also declined (table 5.2). Government transfers accounted for a declining share of the income of the most important public firms during the period, and most were forced to rely increasingly on their own resources (table 5.3). The economic situations of the most important industrial public firms remained tenuous in 1988–1989: while federal transfers continued, most of the most important public firms faced deficits in 1989 (table 5.4).

It was therefore necessary to reduce labor costs and alter collective agreements in order to permanently weaken labor's ability to press for increased wages and benefits. Interviews revealed two additional reasons for the desire to reduce labor costs—both linked to economic liberalization. One was the recognition that public companies would never be marketable with the current "generous" labor contracts. The other was an explicit link between the reduction of labor costs and export competitiveness. According to one senior-level SECOFI official, "with the economic opening, there was now the problem of national enterprises being competitive. Therefore, the government now had to be tough with labor. It had to keep wages and benefits down." Although the economic cabinet in general supported the drive to alter collective agreements, it was the finance sector, in particular the secretary of budget and planning, Carlos Salinas de Gortari, who would become the driving force behind important changes in labor-management relations in public companies.

111

TABLE 5.1

Public Enterprise Expenditure and Transfer Payments
(as percentage of total federal government expenditures)

	Public Enterprises Under Budget Control	Transfers to Public Enterprises Under Budget Control	Transfers to Public Enterprises Outside Budget Control
1982	40.9	7.6	10.8
1983	45.2	9.8	9.5
1984	50.0	9.2	8.9
1985	42.8	8.8	8.7
1986	38.6	6.8	7.5
1987	33.9	4.9	6.6
1988	34.1	3.6	6.2
1989	35.3	4.4	7.7
1990	37.2	4.3	8.8
1991	37.9	3.2	10.4
1992	34.2	3.2	12.3

Source: Carlos Salinas de Gortari, *Segundo Informe de Gobierno*, Anexo, 155–57; Carlos Salinas de Gortari, *Quinto Informe de Gobierno*, Anexo, 274, 276–77.

Note: Federal government expenditures include operating subsidies, capital transfers, and support for the payment on interest and commissions on the debt.

Making Public Enterprise Labor Contracts Flexible

Labor-management relations in the public enterprises had long been seen by both the private sector and elements in the political bureaucracy as one of the most important causes of inefficiency and rising costs. The fiscal impact of labor's privileges became especially important with the economic crunch of 1985. Strikes, demands for improvements in wages and benefits, the privileges granted unions with regard to government contracts, and the interference of unions in areas believed to be the exclusive purview of administration were all seen as eroding the financial situation of enterprises. Moreover, as interest in selling public enterprises increased, changes in collective contracts were perceived as necessary for successful sale. As the economic situation deteriorated and as the government resisted the wage and other demands from public enterprise unions and tried to dis-

TABLE 5.2

Employment and Investment in the Public Enterprise Sector

	Public Enterprise Employment as % of State Employment	Manufacturing as % of State Employment	Public Enterprise Investment as % of Total Public Expenditure	Public Enterprise Investment as % of GDP	Manufacturing as % of GDP
1983	25.4	5.7	14.7	6.0	4.8
1984	24.9	5.7	15.1	5.9	4.9
1985	24.6	5.4	13.0	4.9	4.7
1986	23.7	4.9	11.5	4.8	4.9
1987	23.6	4.2	10.2	4.5	4.5
1988	23.2	3.7	10.1	4.0	3.2
1989	23.1	2.9	10.6	2.9	3.6
1990	20.8	2.4	10.8	2.1	0.4
1991	17.7	1.7	12.6	2.0	0.2
1992	—	—	12.9	3.1	—

Source: Carlos Salinas de Gortari, Segundo Informe de Gobierno, Anexo, 138, 145–47, 155, 157, 166; Carlos Salinas de Gortari, Quinto Informe de Gobierno, Anexo, 242, 251, 254, 274.

mantle past privileges, these unions, traditionally the most highly organized, resisted.

Both the de la Madrid and Salinas administrations ruthlessly crushed labor resistance, although the Salinas administration was the bolder in this regard. The de la Madrid administration made frequent use of the *requisa,* a constitutional provision (article 112) allowing the government to intervene in a strike, annulling the collective agreement, and forcing workers back to work. It is supposed to be used only in very unusual circumstances, such as when the security of the country is endangered, but its frequent use is indicated in table 5.5. The other mechanism used by both administrations to quell worker unrest was rulings, or threatened rulings, by the Board of Conciliation and Arbitration as to the legality of strikes. The legality of strike activity is ruled on in accordance with the 1931 Labor Code. Strikes may be declared illegal (permitting employers to discharge workers at will or call for the armed intervention of the police or armed forces if workers continue to strike), nonexistent (which

Table 5.3

Selected Public Enterprises: Income from Transfers and Own Resources
(as percentage of total income)

	CFE		CONASUPO		FERRONALES		FERTIMEX		SICARTSA	
	Transfers	Own Resources	Transfers	Own Resources	Transfers	Own Resources	Transfers	Own Resources	Transfers	Own Resources
1982	50.8	26.2	42.6	49.1	48.7	44.4	45.0	53.1	23.0	44.0
1983	62.3	23.4	28.9	41.9	52.7	44.8	62.3	37.7	16.0	41.0
1984	45.3	33.3	48.2	44.3	30.4	64.7	47.1	46.9	22.3	48.0
1985	49.5	36.3	53.7	46.3	31.1	68.8	46.5	42.8	21.6	27.6
1986	35.9	46.9	53.7	42.2	31.0	68.5	47.4	46.2	28.5	41.7
1987	33.8	54.8	43.0	40.6	34.7	65.6	41.5	46.3	25.4	42.5
1988	16.2	71.2	34.8	50.2	23.8	75.4	41.0	59.0	30.7	38.8
1989	19.5	77.8	46.0	38.3	24.8	75.2	25.6	61.7	36.2	50.7
1990	13.2	86.8	50.2	39.9	26.6	73.4	26.9	72.2	—	—
1991	7.2	93.8	47.0	52.9	36.1	59.8	27.0	72.9	—	—
1992	—	100.0	49.5	50.4	43.4	56.6	22.4	77.5	—	—

Source: Carlos Salinas de Gortari, *Segundo Informe de Gobierno,* Anexo, 153–54, 171, 173, 176; Carlos Salinas de Gortari, *Quinto Informe de Gobierno,* Anexo, 272–73.

Note: The balance is from external and internal financing.

TABLE 5.4

Major Public Enterprises: Deficit/Surplus
(in billions of pesos)

	CFE	PEMEX	FERRONALES	IMSS	ISSSTE	FERTIMEX	CONCARRIL	SICARTSA	AHMSA	AZUCAR[a]	CONASUPO
1982	−51.9	−9.7	−5.1	3.7	−1.4	−1.0	−1.3	−10.5	—	—	−2.5
1983	−61.7	176.9	−1.0	1.0	4.0	5.9	2.8	−26.6	−26.7	—	−119.5
1984	−176.7	542.3	−2.1	1.5	17.0	−2.5	2.6	−32.9	−36.8	−35.7	−24.4
1985	−179.4	447.7	8.5	29.2	−10.6	−21.0	0.7	−95.7	−88.7	6.5	112.8
1986	−172.4	12.5	45.3	−2.4	−1.7	−10.4	0.2	−79.9	−2.3	−43.5	45.2
1987	−289.4	271.7	87.5	72.1	91.2	−112.4	−0.5	−278.8	69.6	−64.5	1.2
1988	−880.4	603.2	−11.0	290.9	490.2	104.9	27.7	−403.7	371.9	512.1	−620.5
1989	−588.9	−1,269.9	81.0	219.9	235.8	−284.9	−15.4	−143.6	−223.8	202.0	−871.6
1990	−955.2	3,023.0	74.4	421.5	267.7	−30.2	—	—	—	−269.9	−821.9
1991	−2,331.3	−1,039.9	−30.7	336.3	−370.8	182.8	—	—	—	−400.6	651.9
1992	−2,191.4	−2,084.4	−112.7	800.0	119.9	69.6	—	—	—	518.9	130.9

Source: Carlos Salinas de Gortari, *Segundo Informe de Gobierno,* Anexo, 171–79; Carlos Salinas de Gortari, *Quinto Informe de Gobierno,* Anexo, 292–93, 295, 297–99.

a. Under budget control after 1985.

means workers must return to work within forty-eight hours), or legal.[65] While in theory decisions are supposed to be based on a union's adherence to certain procedures, in practice there is wide discretion in the interpretation of the labor code—most often pliant government appointees interpret the law according to the government's wishes. During the de la Madrid administration, many of the strikes of public enterprise workers were declared nonexistent (see table 5.5). In a couple of notable cases, the military occupied public enterprise installations (Fundidora Monterrey, Cananea), and recalcitrant labor leaders were removed through various means from both their employment and their official union positions (AEROMEXICO, SICARTSA, PEMEX).

Contract negotiations with the public enterprise unions involved the direct participation of the economic cabinet. During the de la Madrid administration, Carlos Salinas, along with the secretary of labor, played a prominent role in salary negotiations, and Salinas was appointed to the special commission charged with negotiating settlements with the public enterprise unions.[66] Negotiations after 1985, however, involved considerably more than just wages, as management began to demand significant changes in the clauses of collective contracts involving sharp reductions in the numbers of workers employed.

The changes demanded in collective agreements were geared toward the achievement of greater flexibility in the use of labor; the proposed changes, it was believed, would improve productivity and reduce costs. *Flexibility* has been defined as "the elimination, attenuation or adaptation of the norms of collective labor law with the objective of increasing investment and international competitiveness."[67] "Flexibilization" required an enormous reduction in the power of labor unions: it called for such changes as the removal of requirements to consult labor before the introduction of new technology, the replacement of union labor by "confidence" (nonunion) employees, the ability to move labor between company departments and between regions of the country without union approval, the use of private contractors in areas previously reserved for unionized labor, and the elimination of worker involvement in matters considered to be administrative, such as promotions and movement through the ranks.

While in some cases restructuring labor relations was clearly a

116

prelude to the sale of state companies (Companía Mexicana de Aviación, Teléfonos de México [TELMEX], DINA), in others, changes in collective contracts were perceived as necessary for reasons of fiscal health and efficiency, initially assuming that these firms would remain in state hands (steel, railway, electricity, and petroleum industries). The impact of these changes on employment was devastating, even leaving aside public firms that were closed down. In the steel industry, for example, an additional 9,000 steelworkers were laid off from various state steel plants following the closure of Fundidora Monterrey. Between 1984 and 1988, employment in Altos Hornos alone declined by 4,000.[68]

From 1986, an extremely hard line was taken to ensure the alteration in collective contracts. The strategy was to first attempt to convince labor leaders that such changes were both necessary and inevitable. When, as was usually the case at the beginning, such an attempt failed, the administration would threaten bankruptcy and closure of the firm. The cases of Fundidora Monterrey and AEROMEXICO were test cases in the evolution of this hard-line strategy. One senior-level government official was particularly candid about the administration's handling of the AEROMEXICO affair: "The AEROMEXICO contract was so favorable to the workers that the company could not make a profit and could not compete. We said we would close it if this was not changed, but the workers would not believe us, so we closed it." According to the same source, the union of Fundidora Monterrey was warned three times that if it did not accept changes in its collective agreement and structural changes in the company, the plant would be closed, "but they didn't believe us and we closed it."

Officials claim that following these cases, in which threats to close public firms were carried out, unions became much more amenable to alterations in their collective contracts. In short, the threat of bankruptcy and closure of public enterprises and liquidation of their unions was the explicit strategy used to obtain worker acquiescence in obtaining labor contract changes. Such threats are known to have been used in the cases of DINA, CONCARRIL, and SICARTSA, and compliance was obtained. Only in the case of Cananea did the tactic of bankruptcy and closure actually have to be implemented after 1988. Such threats were implied or explicit in all other cases.[69]

117

TABLE 5.5

Public Enterprises: Major Labor Conflicts and Responses

Company	Year	Issue	Union Response	Government Response
AEROMEXICO	1988	Contract changes, layoffs	Strike (ground workers)	Bankruptcy threatened, bankruptcy declared; strike declared nonexistent; union leaders jailed
Compañía Mexicana de Aviación	1983	Contract changes, salary dispute	Strike (flight attendants)	*Requisa*, strike declared nonexistent
	1988	Layoffs, participation in administration	Strike	*Requisa*
Fundidora Monterrey	1986	Contract changes, layoffs	Strike	Bankruptcy threatened, bankruptcy declared, troops sent in
DINA	1983	Contract changes, increase of confidence workers, layoffs	Strike	Agreement enforced, heavy layoffs
	1986	Contract changes, layoffs	Strike	Strike declared nonexistent, union leaders jailed
	1988	Violation of contract	Strike	Bankruptcy threatened, agreement reached
TELMEX	1984	Salary dispute	Strike	*Requisa*
	1987	Contract changes, salary dispute	Strike	*Requisa*, strike declared nonexistent
	1989	Contract changes	Talks suspended	Agreement reached

CLFC	1987	Salary dispute	Strike	*Requisa*, strike declared nonexistent
URAMEX	1983	Salary dispute	Strike	Strike declared nonexistent, plant closed
Cananea	1988	Contract changes	Strike	——
	1989	Contract changes	Strike	Bankruptcy declared, troops occupy installations
FERRONALES	1984	Contract changes	Sporadic protest	Modifications imposed
	1986	Contract changes, layoffs	Strike	Request that strike be declared illegal
	1988–1990	Contract changes	Sabotage, sporadic protest	Agreement imposed
CONCARRIL	1990	Salary dispute	Strike	Request that strike be declared illegal
	1991	Contract changes	Resistance	Bankruptcy threatened
SICARTSA	1985	Salary dispute, layoffs	Strike	Agreement reached, layoffs
	1989	Contract changes	Strike	Strike declared nonexistent, union leaders dismissed
	1991	Contract changes, four separate contracts	Resistance	Bankruptcy threatened
AHMSA	1989	Contract changes, contracting out, salary dispute (plant 1)	Rank-and-file revolts	Agreement imposed
	1989	Contracting out, layoffs	Strike	Agreement imposed
PEMEX	1989	Contract changes, layoffs, loss of benefits, privatization	Resistance	Leaders arrested, new leaders imposed, new agreement reached

Source: Author.

On the other hand, the Union of Telephone Workers and one of the electrical workers' unions (the SME) were the only public enterprise unions that adopted a strategy of negotiating modernization rather than opposing it outright. They may well have been influenced by the experience of AEROMEXICO and Fundidora Monterrey and were certainly aware that the government was not reluctant to use tough measures, since the *requisa* had been used against both by the de la Madrid administration (see table 5.5). Furthermore, the SME was rewarded for its compliance with management's contract demands (and for its political support for Salinas) by the return of full legal status to its company (Cía de Luz y Fuerza del Centro, or CLFC), which had been in the precarious legal status of liquidation since 1974.[70] There had been more leeway in the negotiations with the telephone industry, as this industry was slated to expand (unlike steel, which was faced with permanent contraction for a variety of reasons, including technological changes), and the protection of jobs in the sector was therefore possible. In 1986, the TELMEX union was successful in obtaining a clause in the collective agreement that allowed for worker participation in technological change through the participation of workers' representatives on a labor-management commission. However, in 1987, the TELMEX union's modernization program was rejected by management, and the union was forced to agree that a "profound modification" of its collective agreement was necessary.[71] By 1990, it had lost its right to participate in technological change.

The impact of public enterprise restructuring on employment as a consequence of divestitures, organizational changes, and alteration in the labor contracts of firms remaining in state hands is illustrated in table 5.2. In addition, employment in the state manufacturing sector (largely the responsibility of SEMIP) declined by 44 percent between 1983 and 1989. Public enterprise restructuring was clearly directed at the enterprises held by SEMIP.

While state managers subjugated unruly labor leaders and dismantled collective contracts with relative ease in most cases, fundamental changes in the country's most important industry and most powerful labor union, the Petroleum Workers' Union, proved considerably more intractable and required daring and tough tactics to bring about. In fact, reforms introduced during the administration of President de la Madrid were quite counterproductive: the immediate affect of the government's reforms was increased inefficiency. But if the changes set in motion did not contribute to the finance sector's economic goals, they did initiate the unraveling of the close and supportive alliance that the union leadership had enjoyed with the state. It would be left to President Salinas to deal the final blow; in doing so, he not only reduced the enormous power of the Petroleum Workers' Union's official leadership but also redefined the relationship between the union and the state.

Restructuring PEMEX

The administration's assault on the Petroleum Worker's Union had a fiscal motivation, the desire to reduce inefficiencies and increase productivity, but it also had an explicit political goal: to reduce the power of the trade union. These motivating factors were closely linked, because it was the weight of various interests tied to PEMEX—business, bureaucratic, and trade union—that had helped to propel PEMEX's expansionist drive and the flagrant borrowing and spending of the 1976–1982 period. The company's enormous importance in the economy and its consequent ability to skirt centralized policy control was now of greater concern than ever. Policymakers targeted the union influence over policy as especially reprehensible. In the words of one senior-level finance official: "The labor union had an equal relationship with the top administrators—they would march into their offices and make demands. . . . We had created a monster over which we had lost all control." Finance officials were highly critical of past PEMEX administrators, particularly its former director general, Jorge Díaz Serrano (1976–1981), for contributing to this problem by cultivating support from the union leadership.[72]

The driving force behind the government's new hard line against the Petroleum Workers' Union during the de la Madrid years was widely believed to have been the then secretary of budget and planning, Carlos Salinas. Salinas's very tough handling of the union at the beginning of his own presidential term would seem to support such a view. Indeed, parts of an unauthorized plan to deal with the

Petroleum Workers' Union attributed to Salinas were published in *Novedades* in 1984.[73] Characterizing La Quina's power over the economic policy of the country as "without parallel" in national history and the Petroleum Workers' Union as representing a serious threat to the state, the plan called for military protection of petroleum installations, legal action against the union leadership, and pressure on the CTM to support the government's restructuring of PEMEX and its labor relations.

The conflict with the Petroleum Workers' Union during the de la Madrid years revolved around two major issues: (1) the state's attempt to reduce or eliminate various sources of union power entrenched in the collective contract, and (2) the attempt to reduce lucrative business advantages afforded labor leaders by the company. Each of these issues touched directly on the amount of resources flowing to the union leadership and to the rank and file. These issues therefore vitally affected the union's power base, founded as it was on the distribution of patronage. The government's tactics involved a coercive manipulation of the traditional system of state-labor relations rather than an attempt to alter that system in any fundamental way. Although some success was achieved in reducing the power of the union over PEMEX, it was clear that union resistance was going to present a formidable obstacle to the kind of tight centralized control envisioned by finance sector officials. It was also apparent that the de la Madrid administration was reluctant to risk a full break with the union.

A report published by the Ministry of Finance on financial management in both PEMEX and the CFE for 1979–1982 pointed to both bad management and fraudulent practices as sources of budget overruns. In particular, the report noted untendered contracts, which resulted in personal enrichment at the expense of the financial health of enterprises.[74] Consequent measures to eliminate such practices were felt particularly acutely by the Petroleum Workers' Union. The 1984 Law of Public Works (Ley de Obras), requiring all government contracts to go to tender and preventing contractors from subcontracting, eliminated the lucrative arrangements that had allowed contracts to go to the powerful Petroleum Workers' Union for drilling and transportation.[75] The effect of this law was to force union-owned companies and firms owned privately by union leaders to compete openly for petroleum contracts. In addition to their unhappiness at the loss of these privileges, the union also complained bitterly about the administrative chaos and dangerous situations it claimed had been produced by severe cutbacks in maintenance expenditures. De la Madrid's pledge to end the union practice of selling jobs—a lucrative source of funds for the union—also caused resentment. At the same time, management pushed for a reduction in the number of temporary workers, a move designed to reduce union power, as it would reduce the number of economically vulnerable people subject to union manipulation and therefore reduce worker acquiescence in union leadership domination.[76]

One of the first tactics to reduce the union's power was the massive appointment of nonunion or confidence personnel.[77] The objective of the appointment of such personnel was to inhibit unionized workers from interfering with the management of the petroleum industry, a measure believed necessary to stimulate productivity. The administration wanted people at the middle levels, who were not compromised or co-opted by the union, to act as a barrier against the union bureaucracy's attempt to influence decisions.[78] Hence, after 1983, it was no longer just the top levels of administration and service branches that were expanding employment; operating branches in exploration, exportation, refining, and petrochemicals also grew. Confidence personnel increased 23 percent between 1983 and 1985 alone.[79] Indeed, between 1982 and 1988, the growth of the petroleum bureaucracy (union and confidence) was greater than at any other historical period. The result was a decline in productivity—between 1983 and 1987, the level of productivity of manual labor declined by 18 percent, increasing the firm's vulnerability in international markets.[80]

The influx of confidence personnel aroused the intense antagonism of the union, manifested in demonstrations and marches that were fairly successful in securing the temporary reversal of the policy. An agreement between PEMEX and the union in December of 1986 involved PEMEX's commitment to cancel vacant confidence positions, to refrain from hiring new confidence employees, and to liquidate 3,000 confidence employee jobs.[81]

By 1986, the issue of hiring massive numbers of confidence employees, combined with the union's loss of income due to the diverting of contracts away from union companies, brought tensions between the government and the Petroleum Workers' Union to new levels. These issues came to a head when PEMEX refused to consider contracting tankers belonging to a company partially owned by the Petroleum Workers' Union, while renting tankers from foreign and domestic companies that had not had to bid for the contract.[82] Such an obvious contravention of the government's own principles produced demands for official investigation into the matter and charges that government officials were using PEMEX to line their own pockets. While an investigation carried out by the comptroller general's office found no illegal conduct on the part of PEMEX Director General Ramón Beteta, a finding subsequently upheld by the Chamber of Deputies, union opposition ultimately forced Beteta's resignation and his replacement by a director general much more amenable to labor demands, Francisco Rojas.[83]

With Rojas's appointment in 1987, the union was victorious. Rojas immediately announced a US$15 million investment program. An agreement signed between PEMEX and the union in 1987 reduced the number of confidence employees (381 vacant jobs and 900 layoffs), put more funds into maintenance, and stipulated that 30 percent of PEMEX tanker requirements were to be rented from the social sector of the Petroleum Workers' Union. Moreover, the 1987–1989 collective agreement provided for increased benefits, a 25 percent salary increase (the third that year), and the promise that by 1992 PEMEX would own its own tanker fleet.[84]

The Petroleum Workers' Union's victory, however, was short-lived. In January of 1989, newly elected President Salinas and his closest collaborators orchestrated the boldest measure ever carried out against the country's most powerful labor union leader, La Quina, and more than forty of his closest cohorts. With military backing, the government arrested and imprisoned these top petroleum union officials. La Quina was charged with homicide and the illegal possession of arms. The move against the union appears to have been precipitated by the union's intense opposition not just to changes in the labor contract but also to the privatization of PEMEX activities, in particular to the opening up of basic petrochemicals (an area reserved to the state) to the private sector through their reclassification to secondary petrochemicals.[85]

With the removal of the old *charro* leadership, the administration installed an equally corrupt, though compliant, replacement. The administration resurrected an old enemy of La Quina's, Sebastián Guzmán Cabrera, whom it imposed as secretary general of the Petroleum Workers' Union over the opposition of the CTM.[86] Traditional *charro* methods were used to impose Cabrera: the assembly "electing" Cabrera was manipulated and participation by the rank and file excluded, and government-planted *porros*[87] supported by temporary workers prevented opponents from speaking and ensured the endorsement of the government's hand-picked candidates in union assemblies. During the following year, a concerted effort was made to root out Quinistas from union ranks: the leader of union local 30, Emérico Rodríquez, was removed as the secretary general of the CTM in Veracruz, the Quinista leader of local 26 was deposed by Cabrera, as was the leader of local 22, and loyal leaders were imposed on locals 45 and 47. Union dissidents, both Quinistas and those advocating greater union democracy, were forcefully pensioned off, and further arrests were carried out to dismantle La Quina's power base in Madero.[88]

While the power base of the new leadership was appreciably reduced due to subsequent alterations made in the collective contract, access to the personal enrichment of labor leaders through contracts with the company was not entirely eliminated. Cabrera was no less averse than former leaders to using PEMEX to advance his own personal wealth, and the administration did little to discourage this. In 1989, a petroleum contracting company involved in a variety of petroleum related activities, Proyectos y Construcciones Sociales "18 de Marzo" S.A. de C.V., was registered with Cabrera as one of its major shareholders. It quickly became one of PEMEX's most important contractors in the southern petroleum-producing region.[89] As PEMEX cut back employment and increasingly contracted out, Cabrera's company expanded. Cabrera's critics charged that contracts awarded to his company were his reward for having presided over the mutilation of the petroleum workers' collective agreement.

Guzmán Cabrera proved to be a most cooperative choice. He did not press for "unrealistic" salary increases, nor did he oppose government's attempts to modify important clauses of the collective agreement. Among the privileges lost in the 1989 agreement were PEMEX's obligation to subsidize union stores; the union's exclusive right to perform contract work in land drilling, plant maintenance, industrial installations, and infrastructure; the abolition of the requirement that PEMEX pay to the union 2 percent of the value of all outside contracts (for social works); and the obligation of contracting companies to employ union personnel. The 10 percent restriction of the employment of confidence personnel disappeared, and an estimated 9,000 technical and professional employees became confidence, rather than union, personnel. Furthermore, the agreement stipulated that no longer was union approval required for the institution of measures to increase productivity, such as decisions involving the reduction of jobs, transfer of personnel, or elimination of departments.[90] The 1989 agreement produced the layoff of some 30,000 temporary workers.[91]

The 1991 agreement brought about further substantial revisions. Union participation in the allocation of jobs and promotions was eliminated, the importance of seniority in deciding promotions was reduced (aptitude now counted for 80 percent), union interference in the organization of the enterprise was eliminated, and the number of confidence employees was increased.[92] Between 1989 and 1992, PEMEX's labor force was reduced from 212,000 to 150,000.[93] Such dramatic changes produced mounting labor unrest, and Cabrera's loss of control of his rank and file ultimately resulted in the government forcing his resignation in 1993.[94]

The reduction of union power facilitated the reorganization of the company, which has weakened the union still further. In 1992, PEMEX became the holding company for four subsidiaries: in production, refining, and processing of gas and the distribution and marketing of hydrocarbons and petrochemicals. Each company was expected to sign a separate agreement with its workers, a development that has further weakened the national strength of the union.[95]

What happened in the Petroleum Workers' Union is typical of the way in which labor-state relations have altered in public companies.

Since 1983, the traditional alliance between official unionism and the state has been severely tested at two levels: (1) the relationship between official union leaders and the state, and (2) the relationship between official labor leaders and their rank and file. Heavy-handed measures were employed against uncooperative labor leaders; their opportunities for the accumulation of wealth were restricted, although not eliminated. At the same time, drastic revisions in collective agreements entailing the elimination of union distribution of a variety of benefits to workers, combined with substantial declines in wages and benefits, have seriously undermined the ability of labor leaders to maintain the quiescence, if not the loyalty, of the rank and file. In short, a substantial part of the patronage system, which formed the basis of *charrismo,* has been dismantled. And while the most powerful of Mexico's labor unions have lost power, the time-honored methods by which they have been controlled remains largely intact. The difference is that while the rewards for cooperation are no longer so generous, the punishment for resistance is now more harsh.

Conclusion

Domestically, the strongest proponents of public enterprise restructuring have been the private sector and, within the state, the finance sector bureaucrats. The views of these officials have been shaped by their historic ties with powerful private banking interests, their ongoing relationship with international financial institutions, and the bureaucratic imperatives of their macroeconomic concerns, particularly the public deficit. To restore business confidence, they were encouraged to move ahead rapidly with public enterprise restructuring. In the face of such overwhelming pressure, combined with the deterioration in Mexico's economic circumstances, bureaucratic supporters of public enterprise were powerless to stem the flow of the new policy direction.

Fundamental alterations in labor relations within public enterprises was an objective agreed on by both government officials and the private sector. Both sought a substantial reduction in the power and influence of official labor leaders, especially those in the public enterprise sector. Both also sought a reduction in the cost of labor and increases in labor productivity, goals essential to export competitiveness. By 1992, the country's most powerful labor unions had been severely disciplined and the patronage mechanisms afforded by labor contracts largely dismantled. But it was the divestiture (shedding) of state companies that put a definitive end to the special relationship that public enterprise unions had enjoyed with the state.

6

Dismantling the State

Although the objective of Mexico's divestiture program was to diminish the state's role in the economy while increasing the role of private capital, the term *privatization* was never used by Mexican government officials—a reflection of the politically sensitive nature of the issue. Rather, the terms *redimensionamiento* (literally, to redetermine the size of the public enterprise sector) and *disincorporación* (to liquidate, transfer, merge, or sell state enterprises) were used in official statements on the subject. Moreover, public officials continually stressed that with the restructuring of the public enterprise sector, not only would the state continue in its economic leadership role, but the restructuring would strengthen that role through the concentration of resources in "strategic" and "priority" areas.[1] But despite this implicit recognition of the politically sensitive nature of divestiture, consideration of the political role of public enterprises and of the political implications of divestiture did not enter into the deliberations of those who formulated the country's divestiture program.

Throughout the de la Madrid years, the criteria for divestiture remained in flux, reflective of the ongoing struggle within the political bureaucracy over what should be divested. Disagreement focused on the question of what economic activities were to be defined as "priority." While strategic economic sectors were clearly defined in articles 27 and 28 of the constitution and are exclusive to the state, the constitution is vague on priority areas, stipulating only that the state may participate in such areas either alone or with the private and social sectors. The government's 1984 program stimulating trade, the National Program for Industrial Development and External Trade (Programa Nacional de Fomento Industrial y Comercio Exterior, or PRONAFICE), provided a more precise definition, identifying as priority areas iron and steel, fertilizer, tractors, transport equipment, diesel motors for buses and trucks, and the manufacture of nonferrous metals. The document also states, however, that the state's participation in priority areas will be constantly reevaluated and its participation withdrawn under certain circumstances.[2]

The disagreement over what exactly should be divested reflected the ongoing power struggle between finance officials and bureaucrats in charge of state enterprises. The dismantling of the state enterprise sector, a program that would appreciably reduce the power of the Ministry of Energy, Mines, and Parastate Industry (SEMIP), was an objective long cherished by the Ministry of Finance, with its penchant for fiscal restraint. As we have seen, by the time Carlos Salinas took over as president, finance sector officials had clearly triumphed. In the early 1990s, announcement was made of the privatization of a variety of state firms the de la Madrid administration had pledged would remain in state hands. By early 1993, the state sector comprised a reduced core of firms, and even some of the most important of these had been opened up to private investment. With the 1994 currency crisis, strategic areas reserved to the state by the Constitution have been formally opened up to private, including foreign, capital. The dismantling of the state featured a closed decision-making process that excluded statist bureaucrats, a process discussed in earlier chapters with reference to public deficit reduction and public enterprise reform. Divestiture also increased the economic importance of the country's most powerful private sector economic groups.

The Pace of Divestitures

During the first two years of the de la Madrid administration, there was no indication that the government would seek divestiture in

TABLE 6.1

Creation and Divestiture of Public Enterprises

	Divestitures Completed	Divestitures in Progress	Divestitures Authorized	No. of Companies Created	No. of Companies in Existence at Year's End
1983	75	32	107	10	1,058
1984	32	7	39	18	1,037
1985	89	23	112	7	932
1986	132	75	207	7	732
1987	86	49	135	15	612
1988	76	89	165	2	449
1989	69	170	239	2	386
1990	82	190	272	2	286
1991	95	87	—	5	241
1992	66	53	—	8	217
1993	15	—	—	4	209

Source: 1983–1989: Carlos Salinas de Gortari, *Segundo Informe de Gobierno,* Anexo, 209; 1990–1991: Salinas de Gortari, *Quinto Informe de Gobierno,* Anexo, 308.

Note: Banks are not included in public enterprise divestitures.

areas in which state enterprises accounted for an important portion of production. Aside from the privatization of enterprises held by the nationalized banking sector, divestiture was to occur only on a small scale. President de la Madrid reported that while state ownership was "under review," the state would withdraw only from "small and medium enterprises [with] . . . scarce influence on the behaviour of productive branches."[3]

During 1983–1984, therefore, divestiture proceeded slowly (see table 6.1). While between 1983 and 1984 the state divested itself of over one hundred state companies, these either were paper companies or were in areas considered neither strategic nor priority by most of Mexican society. The most important divestitures were the sales of Renault de México and Vehículos Automotores Mexicanos (VAM).

A second stage in the divestiture program occurred between early 1985 and May 1986, when the closing of the government-owned steel plant Fundidora Monterrey was announced. In early

131

1985, the economic cabinet had decided to accelerate both the liberalization of trade and the divestiture program. At this time, it was decided to divest of eighty-two additional entities (of which thirty-one were to be liquidated, forty-four sold, and seven transferred) and to study divestiture of another sixteen.[4] During this period, the state continued to divest itself of areas where state firms did not account for an important proportion of production. Of the thirty-one firms to be liquidated, fourteen existed only on paper. Among those put up for sale were enterprises in textiles, soft drinks, electrical domestic products, paper, cement, autoparts, secondary petrochemical industries, electromechanical products, and mining metallurgy.[5]

The third stage of divestiture was initiated with the closure of Fundidora Monterrey in 1986 and ended in late 1989 with the decision of the Salinas administration to privatize all state enterprises in areas not specifically mentioned in the constitution as "strategic." While it was clear that state managers did not agree on what should be divested, this phase featured a marked acceleration of the process and a movement into economic sectors hitherto considered priority—that is, legitimate areas of state enterprise participation, such as steel mining, petrochemicals, fertilizer, and capital goods.

The state steel sector, supplying three-quarters of total steel demand,[6] had been hard hit by both the contraction of the domestic market and the protectionist measures of the United States and Europe. The restructuring of the government-owned steel sector was initiated in 1986 with the announcement of the restructuring of SIDERMEX, the holding company set up to administrate the state's involvement in steel, especially its three major steel plants, Altos Hornos (AHMSA), Siderúrgica Lázaro Cárdenas–Las Truchas (SICARTSA), and Fundidora Monterrey. The restructuring was to involve the reorganization of SIDERMEX's affiliates as well as their fusion, liquidation, or sale. Divestiture was to focus largely on those affiliates not directly involved in steel production. However, by far the most important divestiture was the bankruptcy and closure of Latin America's oldest steel company, Fundidora Monterrey.

By 1987, however, an even more ambitious divestiture program had been put forward for the steel sector: SIDERMEX affiliates were to be reduced to twenty-eight, from ninety-one, and down to twenty-four by 1988.[7] Serious consideration appears also to have been given at this time to the sale or partial sale of other important state steel companies. Negotiations were reportedly under way with a group of Japanese interests for the sale of one-half of the SICARTSA steel complex.[8] Consideration was also given to the sale of AHMSA shares to Japanese capital.[9] The lack of consensus over what was to be privatized in the state steel sector was reflected in the government's denial that the privatization of AHMSA was being considered, while rumors spread that both AHMSA and SICARTSA were to disappear.[10] Meanwhile, the divestiture of four enterprises of the SIDERMEX group were suspended.[11]

Only days after Fundidora Monterrey was declared bankrupt, the government announced the divestiture of a further 123 public enterprises. At the same time, it declared its intent to move out of air transportation with the announced sale of Compañía Mexicana de Aviación, one of the country's two principal airlines. This was followed in 1988 by the declaration of the bankruptcy of the other government-owned airline, AEROMEXICO, following a four-day strike. After the sale of 65 percent of the shares of AEROMEXICO to the private sector, the company was reopened under a new name, Aerovías de México. With the announced sale of DINA, the government signaled the state's withdrawal from the capital goods industry.

Indeed, the last two years of the de la Madrid administration witnessed a marked acceleration in announcements of divestitures (table 6.2). In addition to withdrawal from mining-metallurgical (seventeen firms), the government declared its intent to sell its remaining sugar refineries, its silver and gold mines, which accounted for 50 percent of national production, and its major copper producer (Cananea) and to reduce the number of enterprises in the fishing industry from twenty-six to five.[12]

By the end of the de la Madrid *sexenio,* the criteria for what enterprises should remain in state hands had narrowed considerably. In general, public enterprises with social responsibilities were to remain. The industrial public enterprise sector had been pared down: according to official pronouncements made in 1988, the state would retain only PEMEX, the CFE, FERTIMEX, Azucar S.A., and some producers of capital goods such as Astilleros Unidos, SIDERMEX, and

Table 6.2

Major Divestitures: Nonfinancial Public Enterprises

Year of Announcement	Year of Divestiture	Company	Purchaser	Purchase Price ($U.S. millions)
1983	1983	Renault de Mexico and Renault/VAM	Renault France	30
1986	1990	Compañía Mexicana de Aviación	Grupo Xabre and U.S. and British investors	40
1986	1986	Fundidora Monterrey	Closed down	—
1986	1986	SOMEX companies	Electro-Domestic Group to Grupo VITRO (Garza Lagüera[a] and Garza Sada)[a]	—
1988	1987–1990	64 sugar refineries	Grupo Escorpión, FOMEX (Grupo Visa, Garza Lagüera),[a] and others	—
1988	1988	AEROMEXICO	Pilots Association, Grupo M. Alemán Velasco,[a] and BANCOMER	230
1988	1989	DINA	Consorcio G. S.A. de C.V.	810
1988	1990	Cananea	Mexicana de Cananea (Jorge Larrea)[a] and Belgian mining groups	475
1988	1989	Compañía Mexicana de Cobre	Minera Mexico (Larrea)[a]	430
1989	1989	CONASUPO plants	6 companies, the largest to Unilever	—
1990	1990	TELMEX	Grupo Carso (C. Slim Helú,[a] and French capital (21% of shares)	4,028.5
1990	1992	AHMSA	Acero Norte	145
1990	1992	SICARTSA	Villacero	170
1990	1992	FERTIMEX (12 plants)	8 different companies	—
1991	1992	CONCARRIL	Bombardier (Canadian)	70
1992	1993	Media package (TV, cinemas)	Radio Televisora del Centro (RTC)	640

Source: Latin American Weekly Report, 1983–1993; La Jornada, Proceso, Excelsior, 1983–1993.
a. Members of the CMHN.

TABLE 6.3

Divestitures by Administrative Unit, 1983–1993

Administrative Unit	1983	1993
SEMIP (Mines & Public Enterprises)	378	13
Fishing	29	0
SEDUE (Environment & Urban Development)[a]	72	19
SHCP (Finance and Public Credit)	142	40
SARH (Agriculture & Hydraulic Resources)	89	6
SCT (Communications & Transportation)	62	20
SPP (Budget & Planning)[b]	23	—
SEP (Education)	48	45
SECOFI (Commerce & Industry)	29	25

Source: Salinas de Gortari, *Segundo Informe de Gobierno*, Anexo, 206–09; Salinas de Gortari, *Quinto Informe de Gobierno*, Anexo, 305–08.

a. SEDUE became SEDESOL (Ministry of Social Development) in 1992.

b. SPP was eliminated in 1992.

CONCARRIL.[13] SEMIP's Subsecretariat of Basic Transformation Industry was slated to disappear, and it was even rumored that SEMIP itself was to be abolished.[14] By the end of the de la Madrid years, the state had divested itself of 706 enterprises. SEMIP accounted for the bulk of state divestitures (see table 6.3)—331 of which were completed between 1983 and 1989. SEMIP's public enterprise holdings had been reduced by more than 80 percent.

By 1988, the impact of the divestitures measured as percent of GDP does not appear to have been great. If PEMEX is included in the calculation, the enterprises subject to divestitures accounted for only 2.9 percent of the GDP of the total public enterprise sector.[15] However, at the sectoral level, the divestiture program was significant: by early 1988, the state's presence in nonpetroleum manufacturing had been reduced by at least 25 percent of the value of production and 30 percent of employment.[16] By the end of 1988, the state had substantially reduced its participation in the production of capital goods and had withdrawn totally from the production of consumer durables and from five branches producing intermediate inputs: thread and fabric of soft fibers, thread and fabric of hard fibers,

135

basic chemicals, synthetic resins and artificial fibers, and basic industries of nonferrous metals. In the area of nondurable consumer goods, the state withdrew totally from the preparation of fruits and vegetables, the production of bottled soft drinks, and the manufacture of clothing and medicines.[17] The bankruptcy of Fundidora Monterrey reduced the state's presence in integrated steel production to 50 percent of national production from the more than two-thirds it had been in 1985.[18] The government had reduced its participation in industry from twenty-eight to twelve branches.[19]

A fourth stage in the divestiture process was initiated with the presidency of Carlos Salinas. The results of this stage of divestiture would be startlingly significant. In late 1989, the economic cabinet agreed to divest of all public enterprises in sectors not specifically named in the constitution as strategic; that is, the state would retain PEMEX (petroleum), CFE (electrical energy), FERRONALES (railways), and the Central Bank, along with agencies involved in mail delivery, radio telegraph, and communications via satellite.[20]

The most important announcements were of the sales of the two state steel companies, the state's shares in the telephone company (TELMEX) and the privatization of the banks, nationalized by President López Portillo in 1982. While the announcement that the state's steel companies would be sold caused considerable uproar in the Chamber of Deputies, the privatization of the banks generated the greatest political difficulties. Since the state's exclusive role in the provision of bank services had been enshrined in the constitution by President de la Madrid, a constitutional amendment was required before the bank privatization could go forward. The North American Free Trade Agreement (NAFTA) further stimulated the opening up of Mexican financial services to foreign capital: Mexico agreed to allow U.S. registered banks access to the Mexican market, with the proviso that Mexico could impose restrictions if foreign institutions took a disproportionate share of that market.[21] This was followed by new regulations allowing foreign financial institutions to set up shop in Mexico, although they were initially allowed no more than 8 percent of the market.[22]

Divestitures announced by the previous government were completed under President Salinas, some with considerable difficulty. Cananea, for example, was sold only after three earlier deals had fallen through,[23] while the state was able to divest itself of DINA after one failed deal and after the holding company had been pared down to its four most viable companies. Later, the sales of FERTIMEX and CONCARRIL were announced, and both companies were subsequently sold.

On top of all this, the Salinas administration privatized functions carried out by state enterprises in areas exclusively reserved by the constitution to the state; that is, in the so-called strategic areas of petroleum, basic petrochemicals, railways, and certain areas of mining. Privatization of a variety of PEMEX functions has probably been the most politically difficult change. The reclassification of petrochemical products from "basic" (for which the state is exclusively responsible) to "secondary" has opened such products up to private, including foreign, investment. President de la Madrid had reclassified thirty-six basic petrochemicals as secondary. Under Carlos Salinas, fifteen more were reclassified in 1989, twenty in 1990, and fourteen more in 1992.[24] Sixty-six secondary petrochemical products were reclassified as tertiary, thereby opening these sectors to 100 percent foreign participation.[25] The reclassification of petrochemical products is one area that appears to have been opened up to private capital as a consequence of the intense pressure exerted by the private sector petrochemical industrialists, who felt that with trade liberalization they must have access to the cheaper inputs that would be afforded as a consequence of private sector competition.[26]

Moreover, foreign investors could now participate in the construction of basic petrochemical plants, which the government would rent and eventually purchase. With the establishment of Grupo PMI (Petróleos Mexicanos Internacionales) under de la Madrid, international trade (the marketing of crude and petroleum derivatives) was removed from PEMEX's Gerencia de Comercio Internacional and its representatives abroad and handed over to six foreign subsidiaries.[27] President Salinas continued this trend with the establishment, in 1989, of Mexpetrol S.A. de C.V., with 25 percent of its shares in the hands of PEMEX and the rest in the hands of national capital. Replacing PEMEX's Subdirección de Proyectos y Construcción de Obras, its responsibility is to promote and market goods, services, and technology linked to the petroleum industry.[28] The 1992 reorganization of PEMEX into a holding company with four affiliates allows the affiliate responsible for secondary petrochemicals to establish joint ventures with private firms, including foreign ones.[29] And a number of companies in which PEMEX holds shares have been slated for privatization, as have thirty service stations.[30] In early 1993, PEMEX announced that the sale of some of its sixty petrochemical plants would be open to domestic and foreign purchasers, while three or four of its smaller plants would be closed.[31]

Mining has also been opened up to private capital. The 1989 foreign investment regulations began the process of opening mining up to foreign capital: through the creation of trusts, 100 percent foreign ownership of mining companies, hitherto limited to 49 percent, became possible.[32] Since 1990, significant alterations have occurred in the laws regulating most of Mexico's mining activities. The state eliminated its control over mining reserves, opening these up to foreign and domestic capital investment; and with the 1992 Mining Law, foreign investors were allowed to purchase up to 100 percent of the full voting shares of mining companies, even for those mining sectors that had been exclusively reserved to the state (sulphur, potassium, iron, and phosphorous).[33]

Electrical energy is another strategic economic sector that was opened up to private capital under Salinas. A new set of regulations was established allowing groups of enterprises and industrial parks to supply their own electrical energy needs, with the stipulation that any excess electrical energy must be sold to the public electrical company, CFE.[34] With the signing of the Free Trade Agreement, a further commitment was made to open up electricity to outside capital: the agreement states that private investment in the electrical industry in Mexico would be allowed for (1) production for self-consumption, with any excess going to the CFE, (2) production for industrial use, with the excess going to the CFE, and (3) independent production for sale to the CFE. In addition, the private sector is now encouraged to construct electrical generating plants, which the CFE would then rent.[35] The CFE's research arm is also to be privatized.

Other measures opened up the postal system to private capital, allowed the state to grant concessions for the construction of roads, opened the railways to private investment, and allowed for the sale of concessions for management of services in the country's airports and seaports.[36] The state withdrew from urban transportation, granting route concessions to private operators of buses and minibuses. Public firms having exclusively social functions have also been subject to the current privatization drive. Much of the cleaning and garbage collection for the IMSS is now contracted out, while pension management has been placed in the hands of private insurance companies.[37] Once a sacred symbol of revolutionary nationalism, CONASUPO, the state marketing agency, shed 9 industrial plants, 589 Conasupers, and 25 supermarkets.[38] The government's two television networks and numerous cinemas were also shed.

Of special note during the presidency of Carlos Salinas has been the opening up of the agricultural sector to market forces. State companies providing technological and marketing services to farmers have been privatized. And reform to article 27 of the constitution privatizing *ejidal* (communal Indian) lands gives peasants the legal right to own land, and therefore the right to sell it, rent it, or form joint ventures with agribusiness. The primary objective of all these policies has been to stimulate investment in the agricultural sector and to raise export competitiveness.

By 1990, 286 public enterprises remained, and the public enterprise sector had been reduced to 11.8 percent of GDP. Table 6.4 shows the decline in its share of GDP.[39]

TABLE 6.4

Public Enterprise Sector % of GDP

1983	15.8
1984	15.0
1985	13.9
1986	12.1
1987	13.9
1988	11.9
1989	11.1
1990	11.8
1991	10.4

The Salinas years (1988–1994) witnessed a dramatic reduction in the public enterprise sector, particularly when the size and importance of the firms divested is considered. Furthermore, 75.6 percent of the value of all funds received from the sale of public firms sold between 1982 and 1992 was realized in 1991—some $9.5 billion.[40]

A fifth and final stage in Mexico's privatization saga occurred with the December 1994 financial crisis during the current presidency of Ernesto Zedillo. The Emergency Plan announced on 3 January 1995 called for the outright privatization of sectors hitherto under the exclusive jurisdication of the state: the railways, electrical generating plants, and the satellite communication system. In addition, other remaining state holdings were to be quickly shed: toll roads, ports, and petrochemical plants. The remaining restrictions on foreign bank ownership were to be eliminated, thereby allowing 100 percent foreign ownership of subsidiary financial institutions, including banks.[41] Thus far, the government has denied rumors that it plans formally to privatize PEMEX.

Bureaucratic Resistance to Divestiture

Among the ministries, the strongest opponent of rapid divestiture, not surprisingly, was SEMIP, the ministry in charge of the largest block of industrial public companies and the ministry that bore the brunt of the divestiture program. Senior- and middle-ranking officials in both the Ministry of Finance and SEMIP all admitted that SEMIP had supported a slower-paced divestiture program than that advocated by Finance Ministry officials. All agreed also that even stiffer resistance came from the bureaucrats of the public firms under SEMIP. Officials interviewed reported that resistance also came from other ministries (such as agriculture and communications and transports) that administered public enterprises.

As in restructuring in general, SEMIP bureaucrats, and this was especially the case for the secretary himself, did not take a directly oppositional position—no one wanted to be seen as going against what was understood to be approved presidential policy. Opposition was only to the pace of divestiture, just as it had been to the pace of public enterprise reform—never to the principle of the policy. Although the protection of bureaucratic turf was at least partly responsible for SEMIP's opposition, its officials couched their objections in considerably less self-interested terms. SEMIP officials, for example, claim to have argued for a slower-paced divestiture process in order to provide more time to modernize public enterprises, to improve their productivity and financial situations, and to make them profitable, in order to sell them at a good price. As we saw in the previous chapter, SEMIP officials, in line with their institutional interests, saw their major responsibility as ensuring the survival of state enterprises. The sale of state firms was acceptable, they claimed, as long as the price was right. They believed their efforts to improve public enterprise efficiency had brought in better sale prices for state firms than would otherwise have been the case. Several officials suggested, for example, that SEMIP's improvements in the efficiency of the state sugar refineries, while delaying their sale, produced a better deal for the state than would have occurred had the companies been sold immediately. SEMIP officials also claim to have been concerned about the impact of divestitures on employment and regional disparity. One middle-ranking official explained SEMIP's struggle against the divestiture of FERTIMEX during the de la Madrid years in terms of its impact on agricultural production:

> We were concerned with the fact that if it [FERTIMEX] were privatized and prices for its products reached market levels, the agricultural producers would no longer be able to buy fertilizer, and production in the countryside would decline. We therefore argued that the government must hold off selling FERTIMEX until credit and other arrangements are made to enable producers to buy fertilizer. FERTIMEX would be sold, but not until these problems were solved.

Several SEMIP officials claimed responsibility for the inclusion of conditions with the sale of some enterprises, especially regarding future investments by the purchaser. Such conditions, they argued, were important in ensuring the continuity and economic health of former state firms over the long term.

SEMIP officials characterized the push for rapid divestiture as a consequence of the finance sector's overriding concern with getting the public deficit down. In the words of one senior ranking respondent: "Their attitude was very short term—to sell the public companies quickly, to get the money and reduce the deficit and debt." Opposition to the pace of divestiture may have been a strategy adopted by SEMIP to prevent the divestiture of its most important state firms. The hope was that with the achievement of a financial turnaround and increases in productivity, divestiture could be avoided, as the firm in question would no longer be inefficient or a fiscal drain on the state—conditions making divestiture necessary, according to the finance sector. A number of bureaucratic insiders, both sympathetic and unsympathetic to SEMIP, expressed views similar to the following: "SEMIP's strategy was to make its industries more efficient, so that it could justify hanging on to them—that is, if the government runs them efficiently, it should be allowed to keep them."

Certainly, SEMIP's official documents stressed the success of restructuring and reconversion (modernization) programs in achieving the financial viability of enterprises, in increasing productivity, and in stimulating exports.[42] Moreover, official documents blamed financial difficulties on factors outside the control of management: SIDERMEX blamed its difficulties on the contraction of the domestic steel market and increased protectionism, while FERTIMEX stressed the negative financial impact of its controlled prices. Both complained bitterly of the negative impact of the drastic decline in investment and expenditure each had been experiencing.[43]

Between 1985 and 1989, SEMIP's view of the spectrum of economic activities in which the state should retain its enterprises remained considerably broader than that agreed to by the Ministry of Finance, the Ministry of Budget and Planning, and the presidency. It was in these areas—steel, mining, petrochemicals, sugar, fertilizer, and capital goods—where the greatest degree of conflict over the pace of divestiture occurred. While the secretary of SEMIP between 1983 and 1986, Francisco Labastida Ochoa, readily agreed that the state should get out of such fringe activities as bakeries and laundries, it must, at the same time, he argued, take a more active role in "the production of goods that fortify our independence" and even expand its role in sectors where it was previously absent.[44] Indeed, Labastida Ochoa is said to have opposed pressure from finance sector officials for a number of divestitures, especially in mining, and to have clashed with Salinas over the closing of Fundidora Monterrey.[45] Indeed, SEMIP's definition of "priority" activities where state ownership was justified included not only those listed in PRONAFICE, the industrial development and export promotion program, but also sugar, all capital goods, some secondary petrochemicals, pharmaceuticals, and high technology sectors such as biotechnology and electronics.[46] Both SIDERMEX and FERTIMEX described their economic sectors as "strategic," a term that suggested that even though neither steel nor fertilizer were mentioned among the list of strategic sectors in the constitution, their importance was equivalent.[47]

Although Labastida Ochoa's successor, Alfredo del Mazo (1986–1988), was more amenable to divestitures, he too favored the retention of enterprises in sectors where there were growing pressures from the finance sector for divestiture. Speaking before the Chamber of Deputies, del Mazo defined the "nucleus of state activities" where the role of the state should be strengthened as petroleum, petrochemicals, fertilizer, mining, sugar, and transportation equipment[48]—divestitures in the latter three sectors were set in motion before the end of the *sexenio*. Del Mazo opposed strong pressure from the finance sector for divestitures in the steel industry.[49]

While SEMIP's spokesmen were somewhat circumspect in their public opposition to divestiture, the same cannot be said of the bureaucrats of public enterprises. Public enterprise administrators put up strong resistance to divestiture.[50] Opposition was particularly sharp from such sectors as mining and steel.[51] Moreover, directors of public firms were not averse to making their opposition public. The de la Madrid–appointed head of SIDERMEX, Guillermo Becker, warned against "the conservative tendencies of the country," which, under the guise of economic liberty and international competitiveness, were "demanding the state's withdrawal from all public enterprises in the sector of industrial transformation."[52] While FERTIMEX's annual report warned that modernization and increased productivity could not be achieved if "the closing of obsolete plants is not combined with a program of investment," its director, Alfredo Acle, called for greater autonomy for public enterprises and declared that "privatization in the case of Mexico is an expression of reaganomics."[53] Even Francisco Rojas, secretary of the comptroller general's office (1983–1987) and director of PEMEX (1987–1988), denounced policies that sought to reduce the role of the state to a "mere supervisor of economic activity" and "hand over the destiny of the nation to the free flow of market forces." The public enterprise, he declared, was "inalienable public property."[54] Public enterprise bureaucrats resisted divestitures through a variety of subversive tactics, such as failing to provide information necessary for the consideration of divestiture or necessary for an enterprise to be put up for sale, and even by providing misinformation. This type of sabotage of the government's objectives was apparently severe enough to force the government to withdraw a number of offers to sell in 1984.[55]

While SEMIP and its various firms were the major source of intrabureacratic resistance to divestiture, they were by no means the only source. All secretaries with public enterprise holdings, outside of the Ministries of Finance and Budget and Planning, resisted any diminishment of state enterprises under their control. The Ministry of the Comptroller General was also apparently an ally of SEMIP in its struggle to hang onto various public enterprises in the short term, attesting to SEMIP's improvements in their efficiency and financial situations. SECOFI, the Ministry of Commerce and Industrial Development, joined SEMIP in its demands for a slower-paced restructuring program. From outside the government, there was fierce opposition from the public enterprise unions, from opposition leftist political parties, and from within the PRI itself—some government officials interviewed suggested that this latter group presented the most difficult challenge to the government. While business in general was highly supportive of the divestiture program, those dependent on public enterprise contracts (especially small and medium firms) began to express reservations.

While initially President de la Madrid did not appear to support divestiture in "priority" areas such as steel, mining, and fertilizers, by the end of his administration those finance sector bureaucrats close to Carlos Salinas were winning the divestiture struggle. In fact, interviews revealed that these bureaucrats favored state withdrawal not only from all "priority" areas but also from the strategic sectors (such as petroleum) specifically mentioned in the constitution. According to one senior-level finance official interviewed: "It would be preferable if PEMEX, or part of it, were privatized, but there are noneconomic reasons why this cannot be done." By 1993, the Sal-

inista vision of the Mexican state was a reality. While it was undoubtedly true that the NAFTA negotiations put pressure on Mexico
to open up its energy sector,[56] particularly petroleum, and that therefore Mexico's elite were encouraged to find ways of doing this that
did not involve an amendment to the constitution, opening up of
such strategic sectors to private capital was also a goal close to the
hearts of the most Salinista of Mexico's government officials. By 1994,
the severity of the financial crisis now made it possible to move ahead
with the formal privatization of strategic areas such as railways, satellite communications, and electrical power plants.

Desire to protect bureaucratic turf—to ensure the continuity and
even expansion of organizations under their control—drove bureaucrats to oppose divestiture, or at least the pace of it. The homogeneity
of de la Madrid's economic team—that is, the fact that statist officials
had been pretty well routed from the highest levels of political power
and replaced by neoliberals—suggests that the top administration of
SEMIP may well have been subject to a certain degree of institutional
socialization that predisposed its top ranks to policy positions defending what was regarded as the ministry's institutional interests.
In other words, while Labastida Ochoa and del Mazo were both
trained economists who had held positions in the finance sector, their
attitudes were likely influenced heavily by their interactions with
the officials in the public companies for which their ministry was
responsible. Although the directors of public firms could be dismissed, it was not feasible to replace large numbers of technocrats
with specialized knowledge[57]—and these bureaucrats remained
fiercely opposed to divestiture.

All bureaucrats interviewed felt that stiff bureaucratic resistance
had been an important factor slowing down the pace of divestiture.
By 1987, with the emergence of Salinas as the PRI presidential candidate, voices of opposition to the pace of divestiture within the state
were reduced to a murmur. By 1989, the uncertainty as to what was
to be divested had been resolved. Although rumblings from the bureaucrats of state enterprises could still be heard—as late as 1991
former secretary of natural resources and industrial development
(1976–1982), José Andrés de Oteyza, head of Aeropuertos y Servicios
Auxiliares, publicly declared the strategic importance of the enter-

prise[58]—the accelerated pace of divestiture was quickly removing opponents. As two middle-ranking informants explained, once the divestiture process was under way, it rapidly gained momentum—since as privatization proceeded there were fewer and fewer statist bureaucrats around to resist the policy.

Given the intensity and extensiveness of opposition to divestiture during 1983–1986, both from within and from outside the government, a highly centralized and closed policy process, one that excluded statist bureaucrats, was the only one able to ensure that divestitures would go forward.

The Process

The essential backdrop to the divestiture program was Mexico's debt situation and the tough negotiations with the country's creditors. Given the financial sector's institutional history and its role in the debt negotiation process, the intrabureacratic push for public enterprise restructuring in general and divestiture in particular came from the financial ministries—the Ministry of Finance and the SPP—and from the presidency. As was the case for public enterprise reform, the pressing need to reduce the fiscal deficit and the belief that public enterprises were the most important contributor to that deficit appears to have been the primary motivating factor behind divestiture.[59] This explanation was not only the official one but the one overwhelmingly cited by finance sector officials interviewed in the course of this research. With the crunch of 1985, finance officials concluded that the selling off of public enterprises was by then the only way left to reduce the deficit. Indeed, revenue from the sale of public enterprises (largely TELMEX and a few of the banks) had, by 1991, turned the public deficit into a surplus.[60] By 1992, resources obtained from the sale of public enterprises represented the most important source of government income.[61] Ninety percent of the funds from privatization went for the amortization of the external and internal public debt (of a total of $16 billion generated by the sales of state companies during the Salinas administration). Indeed, it became possible for the government to trim nearly $7.2 billion from the nation's foreign debt in 1992 as a consequence of its privatization program.[62]

The severe economic difficulties experienced by particular sectors, such as steel, combined with the grave fiscal crisis faced by the state rendered divestiture almost the only policy choice. But motivations were not entirely pragmatic: there was also an important ideological element, especially after 1986. Some senior officials, the most notable being divestiture's most ardent proponent, Carlos Salinas (who came to dominate economic policy after 1986), believed firmly that most of the economic activities in which the state was involved were better carried out by the private sector. Salinas and those closest to him agreed with the World Bank's preference for direct subsidies to the most needy members of the population rather than the use of what was deemed to be inefficient instruments, such as public companies. The state, according to this view, should focus its attention on areas of great need, which were more appropriately its domain—health, education, and infrastructure—and leave the rest for the private sector.

Political bureaucratic proponents of divestiture came to believe that important organizational changes were necessary to carry through on this growing commitment to divestiture. The apparent lack of commitment to a divestiture program during 1983–1984 was accompanied by a policy process that gave the opponents of divestiture the edge. During this period, secretaries were asked to present to the Intersecretarial Expenditure and Financing Committee (Comisión Intersecretarial Gasto-Financiamento) recommendations as to which of their public enterprises should be divested.[63] Recommendations would then go on to the economic cabinet for approval and to the Ministry of Finance for implementation. This procedure yielded little in the way of results. Due to bureaucratic resistance to divestiture, few proposals for divestiture ever came forward.

Officials supporting divestiture also explained the slow start to the program as a consequence of their initial need to bring over opponents of the program (especially labor leaders, politicos within the PRI) and to expel or win over bureaucratic opponents. They also claimed that time was required to learn how best to privatize, since this was not something that Mexico had had much experience in.

With the 1985 announcement that the divestiture program was to be accelerated, an important change in policy procedure was implemented. All secretaries were now required to present to the commission a list of public enterprises for which they were responsible and to fully justify those they wished to retain. By this method a list of enterprises to be divested was to be drawn up. Once approved by the commission, the SPP took the list of proposed divestitures before the economic cabinet for approval. The Ministry of Finance continued to be responsible for the implementation of divestiture decisions. In 1986, this procedure was enshrined in the Law of Public Enterprises (Ley Federal de Parastatales). Also in 1985, a committee of subsecretaries from SECOFI, the Ministry of Finance, and SEMIP was established to define the criteria for divestiture. Although the committee wrote reports for the economic cabinet suggesting areas from which the state should withdraw (such as textiles) and areas where it should remain (such as steel), in the words of one official, "we were not the ones making the decision." Decisions on divestitures, especially the more important ones, rested squarely in the hands of the most powerful government secretaries—heads of the Ministries of Finance and of Budget and Planning—and the president.

While affected ministries might be asked for their opinions about what should be divested, the final decision was made by the two most powerful financial secretaries and the president after 1985. In some cases, decisions were made without prior consultation of the secretary concerned.[64] As noted earlier, particularly after 1986, SEMIP's influence in the economic cabinet declined. The secretary of labor, as a member of the economic cabinet, was closely involved in divestiture decisions, but not as an advocate of even the interests of official labor leaders. His role was to ensure labor's quiescence. Some negotiations with labor occurred during the de la Madrid years, in contrast with the following administration of Carlos Salinas, in which all pretext of negotiation was abandoned.[65] During the de la Madrid years, an attempt had been made to persuade labor leaders that divestiture was the only means by which companies could be saved. Government officials also told labor that changes aimed at greater efficiency, which would involve the alteration of collective agreements, would have to be made, whether or not companies were privatized. In general, the secretary of labor was expected to take a hard line toward labor, and the incumbent during these years, Arsenio Farell Cubillas, was widely praised by divestiture supporters for having done so.[66]

In short, Mexico possessed what John Waterbury has described as one of the essential ingredients for successful privatization: a tech-nocratic "change team" dedicated to the goal of privatization and isolated (at least, for the moment) from the political arena. But while Waterbury suggests the importance of presidential support for the "change team" in explaining the success of Mexico's privatization drive, this analysis situates Salinas as the driving force behind that team and calls attention to the added ingredient of President Salinas's doctrinal commitment to economic liberalization.[67]

But even before Salinas's rise to predominance, economic circum-stances were increasingly circumscribing debate on the divestiture issue. Although Mexico's divestiture program got under way prior to its actual inclusion in various IMF-related documents, the insis-tence that the public deficit be drastically reduced, along with Mex-ican government officials' understanding of what sort of program would be viewed favorably by the IMF, constricted the choices avail-able and strengthened the prodivestiture advocates.

The divestiture issue, along with other economic liberalization issues, formed a part of the tough 1986 negotiations. While the coterie of finance officials closest to Carlos Salinas clearly favored privati-zation, international circumstances, especially the pressing need to demonstrate a commitment to sound economic policies in the face of IMF negotiations, reinforced and helped to carry forward their vi-sion. It is pertinent to note that the closures of both Fundidora Mon-terrey and AEROMEXICO occurred in May 1986—a crucial time in IMF negotiations, which went on from January to July. It is perhaps no mere coincidence either that the third stage of the divestiture program, which featured a movement into previously legitimate ("priority") areas of state enterprise activity, occurred during the final months of negotiation with the IMF before signing the 1986 agreement stipulating that divestitures would be accelerated and state enterprises restructured.

Furthermore, reduction of the public deficit continued to be a contentious issue during the 1986 negotiations, with Mexican gov-ernment officials resisting further drastic reductions. Insofar as deficit reduction was a requirement imposed by the IMF, the divestiture program was a response to this external pressure: as mentioned, most Mexican bureaucrats regarded divestiture as the best, perhaps the

149

only, way to achieve further reductions. After the 1986 IMF agreement was reached, Mexico continued to have difficulty in reaching an agreement with the private banking sector, a problem that delayed the resumption of credit. The de la Madrid administration was therefore under considerable pressure to intensify its reform program, including its divestiture program, in order to convince the banking community that his administration was capable of making the promised structural reforms. By 1990–1992, a new external pressure had entered the picture: the desire to realize the North American Free Trade Agreement was yet another factor in encouraging the government to open up the energy sector to private investors, including foreign investors.

It appears that a number of factors influenced which of the public companies were removed from state control during the de la Madrid years. The combination of an extremely poor financial situation, a recalcitrant labor union with what was regarded as an overly generous collective agreement, and the pressing need for investment capital compelled decisions to liquidate such public companies as Fundidora Monterrey, AEROMEXICO, and Mexicana de Autobuses (MASA) of the DINA group.[68] Although mining could be classified as "basic" to industrial development, the state lacked the resources to develop the sector and therefore had to turn to private sector investment. In such cases, government officials believed they had no choice but to divest. The strong position taken by SEMIP bureaucrats that certain firms must remain in state hands, at least in the near future, and the effectiveness of their arguments appears to have delayed the divestiture of some public enterprises, such as SICARTSA, AHMSA (steel), and FERTIMEX. Both steel and fertilizer were seen as strategic by SEMIP: steel because it produced essential inputs for industry and fertilizer because of its importance in agricultural production. Sectors such as sugar and fishing clearly had a weaker claim in this regard. On the other hand, proponents of divestiture agreed that manufacturing in general was something that ought to be left to the private sector. State involvement in both consumer and capital goods industries was therefore seen as expendable.

Accelerated divestiture during 1987 and 1988 and the numerous announcements of divestitures in 1988 were a reflection of the predominance of Carlos Salinas in the policy process, given that by this time he was the PRI's presidential candidate. Hence, despite the fact that the pressure to arrive at an agreement with the IMF (and therefore the external incentive to privatize) had been lifted somewhat, the program was now propelled forward by a domestic political determinant: the predominance of Carlos Salinas in the economic policy process, as the PRI candidate and as the president from 1989. Salinas was firmly committed to the view that the state should divest itself of all but constitutionally declared strategic firms. Once Carlos Salinas assumed the presidency, his vision of the small state was vigorously pursued. Organizational changes now further expedited the process. From 1989 onward, the minister of finance was appointed chair of the board of directors of any public enterprise slated for divestiture. This was done in order to facilitate the Finance Ministry's acquisition of information from the enterprise necessary for its successful sale. In this way, Finance Ministry officials sought to quell attempts by public enterprise bureaucrats to block the sale of their firm by failing to provide information or providing misinformation. In 1989, those finance officials in charge of implementing divestitures were formally constituted as the Unit Responsible for Divestitures (Unidad de Disincorporación), in charge of arranging sales of public firms through the banks, calling for bids, and drawing up conditions of sale.

Consideration of the political impact of divestiture, of its impact on labor unrest and on the PRI's support from some of the country's most powerful labor unions, was not an important part of the divestiture decision-making process. If anything, divestiture was used as a weapon against labor when it proved to be in the way of the government's restructuring objectives. Officials interviewed involved in the divestiture process maintained that whatever negative fallout from labor occurred as a consequence of divestiture would simply have to be borne by the government. They pointed out that attempts were made to persuade labor leaders that divestiture was the best way to maintain employment. Several suggested that generous settlement packages had been worked out in order to reduce discontent at the plant level. All claimed that PRONASOL was the major government strategy for reducing political discontent. But as one senior official observed, "there was not much sympathy for the labor question." Government officials were committed to divestiture, whether or not labor supported it.

The confrontation and defeat of corrupt and demanding labor union leaders was seen as a necessary component of economic policy in general and divestiture policy in particular. However, there was a clear attempt by Salinas, once he became president, to make privatization politically palatable: he declared that money from the sale of public enterprises would be used to attend to the poor.[69] With the acceleration of divestitures, it was argued, more funds could be put into PRONASOL, the National Solidarity Program: in 1991, funds from privatization would contribute US$1 billion to that program.[70] However, the use of funds obtained by the privatization of public firms to attend to the needs of the poor was not a consideration when divestitures were discussed at senior policy-making levels.

The Beneficiaries of Privatization

Perhaps the most striking consequence of Mexico's privatization program was its implications for economic concentration: a small number of entrepreneurs were purchasers of the state's largest companies. Occasionally, these investors made their purchases in association with foreign capital. Table 6.2 (above) notes those purchasers of state companies who were members of the Mexican Council of Businessmen (Consejo Mexicano de Hombres de Negocios, or CMHN), an organization of thirty-seven top businessmen who control the country's principal industrial, commercial, and financial groups.[71] By 1992, nine purchasers accounted for 38 percent of nonbanking public enterprise purchases—28 percent if TELMEX and affiliates are excluded (see table 6.5). The sales of BANAMEX, BANCOMER, SERFIN, and COMERMEX accounted for 70 percent of the total monies received from the government in payment for the banks (table 6.6).

BANCOMER and BANAMEX together account for 50 percent of all banking assets in the country.[72] The principal shareholders of investment groups purchasing the four major banks are all prominent members of the CMHN; all have extensive nonfinancial holdings, and most have links with the purchases of other public firms: Alfred Harp Helú, purchaser of BANAMEX, is cousin to Carlos Slim Helú, the major shareholder of Frisco and the Carso Group (purchasers of mining com-

TABLE 6.5

Major Purchasers of Nonfinancial State Companies
(Salinas Administration)

Purchaser	No. of State Companies Purchased
Grupo Xabre	9
Peñoles	5
Frisco	5
Grupo Carso	19[a]
Concorcio G.	4
FOMEX	4
Siderúrgica del Pacifico	6
Grupo Acero del Norte	13
Ispat Mexicana	5
Trade unions	8

Source: Excelsior, 13 April 1992, 28-A.

Note: Out of a total of 184 state companies sold to the private and social sectors.

a. TELMEX and affiliates.

panies and TELMEX shares); Eugenio Garza Lagüera is a major share-holder in thirteen conglomerates, including VAMSA, and Probursa (purchasers of BANCOMER and Mercantil), and VISA (purchaser of various state sugar refineries); Adrián Garza Sada, related to Eugenio Garza Lagüera, is himself a major shareholder in four conglomerates, including VITRO (purchaser of state electro-domestic firms) and VISA; Augustín Legorreta Chauvet, the former owner of BANAMEX, is a principal shareholder in fourteen groups, including ALFA. In mining, economic concentration as a consequence of privatization is particularly marked. The state copper companies, Compañía Mexicana de Cobre and Cananea, were acquired by Jorge Larrea, giving him control of over 90 percent of the nation's copper production.[73] Larrea is a principal shareholder in nine of the country's industrial conglomerates. Two consortia that dominate the soft-drink market, Fomento Económico Mexicana (of the VISA group) and Grupo Excorpión (Pepsi-Cola) acquired state sugar refineries, giving them control of 55 percent of national production.[74] And while originally the two state airlines fell into separate hands, subsequent investment by insurance investor Gerardo de Prevoisin left AEROMEXICO with a 55 percent stake in Mexicana.[75] Although some of the trade unions bought state compa-

TABLE 6.6

Bank Privatization, 1991–1992

Bank	Principal Buyer	Principal Shareholders	Amount Paid ($U.S. millions)
Multibanco Mercantil	Probursa	J. Madariaga Lomelín	203.7
BANPAIS	Mexival	Adrian Sada[a]	181.7
CREMI	Multivalores	Jalisco Investment Group	294.4
CONFIA	Abaco	D.F. & Nuevo León Invest't Gp.	299.4
BANORIENTE	Margen	Marcelo and Ricardo Margaín Berlanga	77.7
BANCRESER	R. Alcántara, C. Mendoza Guadorrama, & R. Goldberg[b]		141.1
BANAMEX	Accival	A. Harp Helú,[a] R. Hernández	3,233.3
BANCOMER	VAMSA	A. Bailleres,[a] E. G. Lagüera,[a] E. Hernández Pons[a]	2,853.2
BCH	Cabal Peniche	C. Cabal Peniche et al.	292.7
SERFIN	Operadora	Adrian Sada,[a] G. Ballesteros,[a] B. Garza Sada[a]	918.0
COMERMEX	Inverlat	A. Legorreta Chauvet,[a] G. Sottil Achutequi	872.0
SOMEX	Inverméxico	C. Gómez & G. M. Somoza Alonso	611.2
Atlántico	GBM	Alonso de Garay Gutiérrez, J. Rojas Velasco	482.5
PROMEX	FINAMEX	E. Carrillo et al.	351.0
BANORO	Estrategia Bursátil	R. Esquer et al.	370.7
BANORTE	Maseca	González Barrera	514.6
Internacional	GF Prime	A. del Valle Ruiz, Villareal Elizondo et al.	430.0
BANACEN	Multivalores	Hugo Villa et al.	252.0

Source: Banco de México, *The Mexican Economy, 1992*, 99; *El Día*, 20 April 1991, 10; *El Financiero*, 24 August 1992, 5; Ortiz Martínez, *La reforma financiera*, 331–36.

a. Members of the CMHN.

b. Both principal buyers and principal shareholders.

nies, thereby giving a veneer of popular capitalism to the process of divestiture, most of these companies were later resold to the private sector.[76] The purchasers of state companies are those industrial financial groups that have benefited inordinately from other aspects of state economic policy, as well.

While many of the pre-1982 industrial and financial magnates remain, economic restructuring has brought some new faces to Mexico's economic elite. Carlos Slim Helú, for example, acquired his wealth in the 1960s with construction, furniture, and stock brokerage companies and, with depressed prices in the early 1980s, was able to expand rapidly.[77] Roberto Hernández, another example of new money, founded a stock brokerage house in 1971 and made his fortune during the stock market boom of the late 1980s, following investments in the depressed market of the early 1980s. Carlos Efraín de Jesús Cabal Peniche (purchaser of banks Cremi and BCH) rose from being the owner of a modest fruit farm to banker and industrialist in less than ten years.[78]

The closure of state enterprises benefited large domestic and foreign capital by leaving them with a greater share of the market. The closure of Fundidora Monterrey, for example, gave a greater market share to the steel producer Hysla, of the Alfa group, leaving as it did a production gap of some 1 million tons a year,[79] while U.S. airlines took over AEROMEXICO's international routes following its restructuring and sale.[80] Clearly, the reclassification of basic petrochemicals has benefited Mexico's largest industrial economic groups: a large number of companies that manufacture secondary petrochemicals are subsidiaries of Mexico's eight major groups: ALFA, Celanese, CYDSA, IDESA, IRSA, Penwalt, Oxy, and PIMEX.[81] Moreover, those national companies with foreign associates, controlling 40 percent of the Mexican secondary petrochemical market, have been in a position to move into production and to take advantage of the new opportunities created by the reclassification of basic petrochemical products.[82]

The acquisition of privatized companies by a relatively small number of industrial and financial conglomerates has lead to charges, particularly by opposition parties, that Mexico's political elite have benefited financially by privatization. Rumors have circulated, for example, that Carlos Slim Helú acted as a straw man for investors personally close to Salinas in the TELMEX privatization.[83] Cabal Peniche is accused of having been de la Madrid's front man.[84] Whether or not this is true, it was inevitable that privatized public companies would fall into the hands of the country's most powerful industrial and financial conglomerates: only they and their foreign allies were capable of obtaining the financing necessary to purchase such firms. Indeed, in a number of cases (Cananea, DINA), there was a serious dearth of acceptable purchasers. Some early consideration may have been given to an attempt to avoid concentration of ownership, but such objectives were abandoned in the belief that a policy of this type would inhibit international competitiveness.[85]

While the country's most powerful business interests were able to take advantage of the opportunities offered by divestitures, small and medium firms began to express reservations. CANACINTRA has complained that small and medium firms have not been able to participate in privatization.[86] Although supporting private participation in the petroleum industry, CANACINTRA has come out against state divestiture of PEMEX, which it describes as "national patrimony," and was also opposed to the reclassification of basic petrochemicals that, it argued, must remain in government hands.[87] And economic stagnation, according to CANACINTRA, was due, in part, to the decline in goods and services provided by the state, a consequence of privatization.[88]

Conclusion

The dismantling of the state signifies a permanent alteration in the nature of Mexico's political elite: it has left the finance sector bureaucracy as the dominant intrastate force and has eliminated the most important institutional basis for statist bureaucrats. While the de la Madrid presidency witnessed the removal of statist bureaucrats at the highest levels, the public companies themselves remained strong proponents of state-led growth, while the secretaries in charge of these companies put up some resistance to at least the pace of divestiture. With the divestiture of these companies, however, bureaucratic statism has been permanently reduced, if not removed, as a force within the Mexican public bureaucracy.

During the de la Madrid years, the divestiture debate within the political bureaucracy was largely molded by bureaucratic imperatives, although there was a concerted effort to present those imperatives as broader concerns. By 1986, international circumstances and the difficulties of IMF negotiations interacted with the dynamics of the presidential succession struggle to bring about the rise to political ascendancy of Carlos Salinas de Gortari, who was personally committed to a dramatic reduction of the state enterprise sector. Divestiture went forward with decision-making authority in the hands of a homogeneous neoliberal political bureaucratic superelite, for whom the issues of public deficit reduction, productivity, and export competitiveness were of paramount importance. The complete exclusion of the statist bureaucrats after 1986 was reflected in the split within the ruling PRI. The emerging PRI dissident group was headed up by such former statist bureaucrats as Carlos Tello, former secretary of budget and planning and director of the Central Bank, and Porfirio Muñoz Ledo, former cabinet minister and PRI chairman.

The decision-making process on divestiture was as revealing for what was discussed as for what was not. Although there was initially some attempt to win over opponents of divestiture, and there have been some attempts in public pronouncements to link privatization with improved public welfare, matters of a political nature do not appear to have entered, in any important way, into cabinet-level discussions when divestiture decisions were made. The negative implications of privatization (and the alteration in the collective contracts that preceded privatization) were accepted as unavoidable, and no global strategy was devised to stem the political fallout from organized labor. Indeed, it was assumed by members of the de la Madrid administration that there would be no major negative political impact. Nor was there consideration given to measures to inhibit the concentration of ownership that results from public firms falling into the hands of the country's most powerful financial industrial interests.[89] The difficulty in finding buyers for public firms combined with the goal of export competitiveness induced policy makers to accept this result as inevitable.

In their dismantling of the state, Mexico's rulers appear to have been carried forward by economic difficulties and external pressures;

they responded to such exigencies by strengthening their commitment to economic liberalization. Desperately short of investment capital, state managers have ceded important economic activities to the private sector. In doing so, they have divested themselves not only of their economic leadership capabilities but also of important sources of patronage and, therefore, important mechanisms of political control. More than ever, the new economic model is dependent on the confidence of the private sector. In opening up strategic areas to private investment, including foreign investment, state enterprises have become more permeable to private capitalist interests. The dismantling of the state, therefore, assumes both a greater dependency on and a greater integration with the country's most powerful capitalist interests.

7

The Politics of Privatization

Mexico's economic crisis of the 1980s set in motion an economic restructuring program, including a privatization drive, that accelerated the transformation of the political system, a process that had been under way since the late 1960s. Much of the recent literature on Mexico has been preoccupied with the nature and direction of this transition. One common approach links political liberalization and democratization with the emergence of the institutions and cultural attributes of liberal democracy. Clean elections, a competitive party system, independent interest group activity (pluralism), and individual democratic freedoms are viewed as especially important.

As well, much of the literature takes the position that policies such as trade liberalization, investment deregulation, privatization, and severe fiscal austerity, including policies to create greater efficiency in the public sector and eliminate corrupt practices, are undermining the two pillars of Mexican authoritarianism—corporatism and patron clientelism.[1] An increasing number of observers argue that the post-1982 economic policy changes are strengthening the forces for democracy in producing an ever growing diversity of social and political actors, suggesting the emergence of the political pluralism believed to characterize liberal democracies. Leopoldo Gómez and John Bailey, for example, argue that the economic crisis and the attendant changes in the economic model have severely undermined regime legitimacy. This loss of legitimacy has resulted in a growing public clamor for a clean electoral process, a development that has coincided with the regime's search for a new source of legitimacy by allowing more competitive elections.

These changes have in turn precipitated pressures within the PRI for greater responsiveness to the voter—all in all leading to "growing pluralism and electoral competitiveness."[2] At the same time, the dramatic decline in resources available to the state has severely undermined the ability of the state to maintain support from corrupt labor leaders, a development that has undermined state support from the official union bureaucracy.[3] Privatization, in particular, is seen as having cut into vested union interests: as patronage is replaced by market forces, there has been a decisive decline in worker clout. M. Delal Baer argues that the long-term impact is a more automomous labor movement.[4]

Further facilitating the demise of the old corporatist and clientelist authoritarian political forms has been the rise of new social movements combined with the emergence of broad fronts uniting such organizations.[5] Arising in the early 1980s in response to economic crisis, these movements increased in importance with the 1985 earthquake. They acquired political importance during the 1988 election, playing an important role, some believe, in the electoral successs of the Cardenista coalition in 1988.[6] Since these new groups are often viewed as rejecting clientelism and subordination to the state, they are seen as representing a social and political force capable of challenging the PRI's corporatist and clientelistic practices.[7] Furthermore, a number of observers have argued that President Salinas's solidarity program (PRONASOL) has actually contributed to the empowerment of local groups, which are now engaged in a process of pluralist bargaining with the state.[8] In sum, according to this viewpoint, the combined impact of the state's neoliberal economic project and the emergence of new groups that question the traditional forms of mediation is dismantling both corporatism and clientelism.

The emergence of business as a more independent social and political actor is another result of the dramatic changes that have occurred in the Mexican economy since the early 1980s. The old economic model, which featured a closed economy conducive to economic monopolies and political repression, curtailed the evolution of business as an independent political force.[9] Peter Smith has argued that traditional Mexican authoritarianism will now be moderated by the fact that business is currently demanding more open decision making and constraints on presidentialism: the president's ability to take unilateral action that can harm the private sector is now considerably more restricted.[10] Indeed, the dramatic reduction in patronage due to the commitment to fiscal austerity is said to have been instrumental in producing a rupture in the state elite and an acceleration in the long-term decline in the credibility and authority of the presidency, producing a fragile democratic breakthrough.[11] In short, for perhaps the majority of observers, the sum of all of the changes outlined above indicates an evolution toward political liberalization, if not democratization.

Despite this general optimism, however, a variety of reservations have been expressed about the process of political liberalization in Mexico—even by those with a generally positive outlook regarding Mexico's political prospects. Reservations have been expressed about the prospects for autonomous and democratic labor union activity, given the logic of an economic model that requires workers to be squeezed economically: wage increases must be restricted in order to increase the country's export competitiveness.[12] At the same time, the ability of new social movements to push the political system toward greater political liberalization and their abilty to resist the co-optative power of state clientelism has been questioned.[13] PRONASOL, for example, may tie such new groups to the state in a new form of clientelism.[14] Hence, even if social movements are challenging clientelism, the emergence of a new pluralism is not inevitable. The PRI project could well be, in one observer's words, "to refurbish and rationalize corporatism and not dismantle it."[15] And, although generally hopeful about Mexico's transition toward democracy, Wayne Cornelius, Judith Gentleman, and Peter Smith caution that economic liberalization may foster closer business-government relations and that business "may be satisfied with a very restricted form of democracy."[16]

Some have suggested a transition entailing not less but more political centralization. Joe Foweraker, for example, argues the presence of a bureaucratic commitment to centralized forms of political mediation, a development he sees as counter to democracy.[17] Roderic Camp offers evidence suggesting the rising abuse of presidential authority: from the political assassinations of opposition PRD (Partido de la Revolución Democrática) supporters to Salinas's record for the removal of state governors.[18] And John Bailey argues that while PRONASOL entails a delegation of administration, decision-making authority remains highly concentrated.[19] This chapter, examining the impact of Mexico's privatization program, points to trends that question Mexico's evolution toward political liberalization and democracy. But while evolution in this direction remains problematic, it is clear that important alterations have occurred in the bases of regime support and in the traditional authoritarian system of control.

Although the de la Madrid years laid the foundation for later economic and political transformations, it was during the administration of President Carlos Salinas that a fundamental alteration in state-societal relations began to take place. The sharp erosion in the alliance between the official labor movement and the state became an explicit objective of policy. In place of the old corporatist-clientelist arrangements, in which public enterprise trade unions had a pivotal role, Mexico's rulers moved in the direction of a segmented neocorporatist structure in combination with a new clientelism. This new clientelism sought to tie the homogeneous bureaucratic political elite to a politically weak and fragmented mass base. At the same time, this bureaucratic political elite deepened its dependence on the country's most powerful business interests.

Labor and the Crisis of Corporatism

There is no question that the impact of the 1982 economic crisis on Mexico's corporatist structures has been profound. While some scholars claim that the demise of the traditional corporatist system, which bound labor to the state, is under way (in view of its incompatibility with economic restructuring),[20] others emphasize the evolution of traditional corporatist arrangements toward a form of neocorporatism.[21] Mexico's post-1983 economic restructuring program affected the traditional system of labor incorporation in three ways:

(1) at the confederation and union levels, it deepened divisions within the labor movement, thereby making control through a single national labor organization virtually impossible; (2) it undermined the loyalty of *charro* union leadership to the state; and (3) it eroded rank-and-file support for both *charro* leadership and the PRI.

The harshness of the adjustment program, particularly its firm commitment to hold down the cost of labor, propelled the official labor organizations, the Congreso de Trabajo (Labor Congress, or CT) and its most important affiliate, the CTM (Confederación de Trabajadores de México),[22] into increased criticism of government economic policy. The CTM had become accustomed to the lion's share of privileges afforded by the state—the highest representation in congress, the right to represent labor on a variety of boards and commissions, and the status of official worker sector within the PRI. Under the new conditions of economic restructuring, such privileges were not sufficient to keep labor in line. From the outset, both the CT and the CTM complained bitterly about government austerity measures, the deterioration in salaries and employment, and the government's acquiesence to international credit institutions.[23] By 1985, veteran labor leader Fidel Velázquez (head of the CTM) was suggesting that the alliance between the workers and the state be redefined.[24] In a strongly worded document presented at its fiftieth anniversary banquet, the CTM announced its rejection of "policies that attempt to impose sacrifices only on the workers and their families and result in their marginalization below the minimum of human dignity."[25]

But while the official labor movement may have been united in its opposition to the government's economic program, there was growing division within it over tactics and over the extent to which leaders would go to defend rank-and-file interests. Persistent divisions occurred within the CT over whether strikes should be called over salary demands. While certain organizations within the CT, such as the CROM and the CROC, showed a willingness to acquiesce in the government's tough economic program, the CTM demonstrated growing resistance. As the CTM leadership came to recognize how its collaborationist position was eroding rank-and-file support, it adopted a harder line against government policy. The CTM's dilemma was an intractable one: if it lent support to a union struggle that was ultimately rejected by the government, it stood to lose credibility. If, on the other hand, it supported the government's position against the union, it would lose legitimacy in the eyes of more militant union leaders and rank-and-file members. The CTM appears to have tried to follow a middle ground, supporting the government in general while at the same time backing selected union demands. The regime's hard line meant that the CTM lost both legitimacy, for continuing to support the government, and credibility, for failing to win in those few cases in which it got behind worker demands.

While the CTM became more critical of the government after 1989, the CT remained generally quiescent throughout the entire post-1983 period. Despite the occasional threat to strike, the CT did not offer strong resistance to government-imposed labor settlements. Demanding salary increases often considered inadequate by its affiliates, the CT was repeatedly pressured by the government into the acceptance of wage settlements below even its original minimal demands, and it remained in support of the government's economic solidarity pacts, despite the erosion of salaries resulting from price increases.[26] While the CT's quiescence was not a problem for some of its labor organization affiliates (such as the CROC, the CROM, and the National Mining Metallurgical Union), others, especially those in public enterprise unions, such as the telephone and electrical (SME) workers, deeply resented the CT's failure to represent their interests.

One of the major factors in pushing the CTM to a more critical stance while severely undermining the CT was the growing militancy of the public enterprise unions, particularly in light of the CT's failure to defend their interests. An important turning point occurred in 1987, when Hector Hernández Juárez, head of the Telephone Workers' Union, was also leader of the CT. Pushed by unrest on the part of his own rank and file, Hernández Juárez declared the CT's intent to strike if a 23 percent wage increase was not granted to the workers of public enterprises. While Fidel Velázquez, as leader of the CTM, originally supported this initiative, he soon reversed his position, prevailing upon Hernández Juárez first to postpone the strike and then to cancel it. Nevertheless, two public enterprise unions, the SME (electricity) and the Telephone Workers' Union, went ahead with the strike. Neither the CT nor the CTM supported these strike actions, and both were ended with government intervention, leaving a residue of intense rank-and-file opposition against the official labor organizations.[27]

These events did much to undermine both the CTM and Velázquez's leadership. But probably more important in eroding Velázquez's credibility was the fact that virtually every economic proposal he presented to the economic cabinet and the president after 1983 was rejected. After 1985, the government unilaterally decided labor policy; it was not interested in even a facade of negotiations with official labor leaders. The corporatist arrangements whereby the official labor organizations had been allowed access to the policy process through their representation on various government bodies, such as the Minimum Salary Commission (La Comisión de Salarios Minimos), had effectively ceased to function.

Unlike the CT, which remained a firm supporter of the Economic Solidarity Pact, the CTM began to speak out against the pact's insufficient salary increases, threatening to break with the pact and to withdraw from the Minimum Salary Commission if the government continued to ignore its views.[28] By 1990, with strong backing from the telephone and electrical (SME) workers, the CTM was demanding a new agreement that would involve a 20 percent wage increase.[29] Sharp divisions within the official labor movement were now emerging. The CT failed to support the CTM in this latest demand, while the CROC and the CROM were actively opposed. Angered by the CT's acceptance of an 18 percent increase, the CTM then moved to distance itself from the CT, carrying out a threat to cease active participation in that organization.[30] Velázquez stressed the CTM's independence from the CT, necessary because the CT lacked "a truly revolutionary and syndicalist attitude without which it could not act in the true interests of workers." Changes, he declared, would have to be made in the CT so that it would be in a position "of sufficient force and authority to defend the interest of the workers."[31]

Despite this more critical stance, the CTM did not oppose the government's privatization policies in general. The failure of both the CT and the CTM to take strong stands against public enterprise restructuring and divestiture was instrumental in undermining support from the public enterprise unions. In fact, the CTM declared its support for the government's program of divestiture and public sector re-structuring, echoing the official line that the objective was to strengthen the state's economic leadership role. It declared further that despite the negative effect of such measures on employment, the program was necessary to eliminate inefficiencies.[32] Even when it be-came clear that divestiture and restructuring would signify massive layoffs in the public enterprise sector, the CTM defended divestiture as "necessary."[33] Although the CTM demanded an investigation of Cananea's declaration of bankruptcy, opposed the privatization of TELMEX, and questioned the restructuring of CONASUPO, it was notably silent on other major divestitures, including the privatization of the banks, which Velázquez had earlier gone on record as opposing.[34]

Given the failure of both the CT and the CTM to stand up for the interests of public enterprise workers, it is not surprising that a number of public enterprise unions (Sindical de Pilotos Aviadores, or APSA; Sindicato Mexicano de Electricistas, or SME, and the Tele-phone Workers' Union) began, as early as 1984, to discuss the for-mation of a new organization to confront the threats faced by their workers.

However, it was not until 1989 that the three public enterprise unions mentioned above proposed the creation of a new organization to represent the interests of public enterprise workers. The Federa-tion of Unions of Goods and Services Enterprises, (Federación de Sindicatos de Empresas de Bienes y Servicios, or FESEBES), estab-lished the following year, included among its objectives a halt to the privatization of public enterprises, the consolidation of state control of strategic areas of the economy, defense of collective contracts and the right to strike, and democratization of the labor movement.[35] It also declared as one of its major objectives the restructuring of the CT. The CT, according to FESEBES's first secretary general, Hector Hernández Juárez, "no longer represents nor satisfies worker aspi-rations." Moreover, he declared, the moment had come "for an end to the practices and structures that had caused the deterioration of the workers' movement."[36] The CT, according to Hernández Juárez, lacked the cohesion to support the struggles of the public enterprise unions. However, while FESEBES was strongly opposed by both the

CT and the CTM, it was willing to collaborate with the government. It supported both Salinas's objectives of transforming the state, and increasing productivity through economic modernization—what it wanted, it claimed, was participation in the process.[37]

As the struggle within the CT intensified, the deterioration of the CTM's predominance within the CT accelerated. The state opted for a divide-and-rule tactic. As the CTM seemed to be resisting state policy, the government favored the CROC; in 1986, the secretary of labor declared that the rival CROC was "destined to be the vanguard of the proletariat of Mexico, the great central of the workers," a thinly veiled threat to replace the CTM as the officially recognized labor confederation.[38] Salinista labor policy continued this reliance on the strategy of divide and rule, as reflected in a statement made by the secretary of labor in 1991 affirming that the CTM was no longer the major worker central.[39]

The deterioration of both salaries and employment after 1983 and the threats to labor rights presented official unionism with a formidable challenge: if it failed to defend the interests of labor, it risked rank-and-file unrest; if it resisted state policy, it faced possible dethronement from its privileged relationship with the state. Vacillating in its response, the CTM incurred the wrath of both union affiliates and workers when it did not go far enough to defend their interests[40] and of the state when it later took a more critical stance. It became increasingly clear that a corporatist structure based on a hegemonic labor organization was eroding rapidly. Indeed, CTM rival organizations were now demanding increased participation on the grounds that the CTM had lost its representative claim.[41]

But it was not just the fracturing of the official labor movement that was making the corporatist incorporation of workers increasingly problematic. In view of the restriction of resources available to the state and the firm commitment of the political elite to slash the public deficit, a corporatist system based on the selective distribution of material rewards had to be curtailed. With the ascent of Carlos Salinas to the presidency, the dismantling of many of the old *charro* clientelistic relationships became an explicit objective of policy. The growing conflict between the state and the leaders of the Petroleum Workers' Union, culminating in their arrest and imprisonment, reflected the resistance of official unionism to the demise of the old system of material bonds that tied the *charro* leaders to the party state apparatus. Most *charros,* however, had much less to defend than the Petroleum Workers' Union and therefore acquiesced in the state's demands, thereby undermining their hold on their rank and file.

The head of the Mining Metallurgical Union, Napoleon Gómez Sada, failed to support local resistance to restructuring in the steel industry. While he did question the closing of Fundidora Monterrey, his public opposition was by no means vigorous; he praised the privatizations of AHMSA and SICARTSA and acquiesced in the declaration of bankruptcy of Cananea, rejecting both workers' concerns that privatization would bring concentration in ownership and their aspirations for worker participation in ownership.[42] The consequence was local revolt against his *charro* leadership and, in some cases, against the PRI. Moreover, the political alienation often extended beyond the workers to include the local community devastated by plant closures and layoffs.

Such a situation occurred with the closure of Fundidora Monterrey, estimated to have affected some 100,000 in total—46,000 of them workers and employees in Fundidora, its affiliates, and various other activities related to the steel industry.[43] Powerful resistance emerged at the grassroots level: workers occupied the federal *palacio* in Monterrey, and at least five demonstrations involving 40,000–50,000 workers and their families occurred following the announcement of the closure. During the last of these, miners and their sympathizers are reported to have burned their PRI membership cards, with one of their leaders declaring that "the miners are free, we no longer have any political attachments."[44] The leader of the Mining Metallurgical Union, Juan García Argüelles, had fighting words for the PRI and the regime: "We are the backbone of the official party in power and look how they treat us. . . . We know that the number one enemy of the workers is the President of the Republic."[45] At the same time, a local PRI deputy, Arturo Quintanilla, threatened to resign from the party if Fundidora Monterrey was not reopened.

Although less dramatic, resistance from the rank and file against restructuring, along with the repudiation of *charro* leadership, occurred in other steel plants. As a consequence of restructuring measures, independent unionism made important inroads in the steel industry. The militant and independent labor organization, the Authentic Labor Front (Frente Auténtico del Trabajo, or FAT) helped to create an independent labor organization among the metal workers, and in July 1985 workers at the state-owned Aceros de Chihuahua steel plant voted to leave the official union headed by Gómez Sada and join the FAT. In this struggle the new independent union of steelworkers took over local offices of the Ministry of Labor, demanding the reopening of the steel mill.[46] In 1990, workers of SICARTSA also repudiated national leader Gómez Sada as a consequence of his dismissal of locally supported union leader Manuel Barreras and due to his agreement to renegotiate the forty-hour week, a hard-won gain they feared they would lose. These issues led to a two-month strike, which was declared illegal.[47] Similarly, workers of AHMSA (section 147) repudiated the national leadership and rejected the collective agreement signed by the company and the union's national committee. AHMSA workers rejected the national union's agreement to layoffs of 3,958 workers, denounced their union representatives, and demanded the enforcement of article 400 of the Labor Code, stipulating legal protection for workers against layoffs.[48]

The SME, a union with a long history of union independence, was divided over its leader's declaration of support for the presidential candidacy of Carlos Salinas. Opponents within the union saw this alliance as signaling the demise of the union's independence, while other recalcitrant groups accused the union leadership of corruption.[49] Indeed, rank-and-file opposition within both the SME and SUTERM (the union of the CFE) was increasing as a consequence of their leaders' acceptance of deteriorating working conditions, measures to increase productivity, and layoffs.[50] Changes in the collective agreement for railway workers also provoked opposition to traditional union *charro* leadership.[51] Hector Hernández Juárez, head of the Telephone Workers' Union, was opposed by a dissident group within his union, the Democratic Movement of Telephone Workers (Movimiento Democrático Telefonista), over the privatization of TELMEX, a measure Hernández Juarez had agreed to.[52] The repercussions of this intense alienation of the public sector union rank and file would soon surface with the 1988 federal election.

Worker Alienation, the Regrouping of Neopopulism, and the Challenge to the PRI

While the PRI, and in particular its ability to co-opt and control labor, had been in decline since the late 1960s, the 1982–1986 economic crisis accelerated the process. Prior to the Second World War, with no permanently organized opposition, Presidents Madero, Carranza, Obregón, and Cárdenas had each received an overwhelming 95–99 percent of the popular vote. By the 1950s, however, three opposition parties had been created, and in 1952, President Ruiz Cortines's share of the popular vote was reduced to 74 percent. In 1982, nine registered parties participated in the election, and the PRI candidate, Miguel de la Madrid, received the lowest proportion of the vote hitherto received by any PRI presidential candidate—71 percent.[53] The period 1976–1982 was an important one in the decline of the PRI: during those years, the PRI's proportion of the vote was reduced by approximately 20 percent. The biggest beneficiary of the PRI's decline was the rightist opposition PAN party: in 1982, it succeeded in obtaining 15.68 percent of the popular vote, while the left-wing Partido Socialista Unificado de México (Single Socialist Party of Mexico, or PSUM) candidate received only 3.48 percent of the vote.[54]

There is no question that reforms to the electoral laws facilitated oppositional activity. Proportional representation was first introduced in 1963 and further expanded in 1972. The electoral reform of 1977 eased registration requirements, allowing more political parties legal status, and guaranteed at least one-quarter of Chamber of Deputies seats for opposition parties.[55] These reforms are usually seen as attempts to restore the lagging legitimacy of the regime by making the electoral process more credible and by channeling opposition forces through institutionalized outlets.[56]

By 1982, therefore, opposition parties were in a position to provide vociferous criticism of government policy. All opposition parties, with the exception of the PAN, strongly opposed the economic restructuring programs of Presidents de la Madrid and Salinas. The most vigorous opponents of government policy during the early de la Madrid years were the Partido Mexicano de Trabajadores (Mexican Workers' Party, or PMT), the Partido Revolucionario de Trabajadores

170

(Revolutionary Workers' Party, or PRT), and the PSUM. These parties focused their attacks on Mexico's debt situation, condemning Mexico's subservience to the IMF and demanding suspension of payments on the debt.[57] They also declared their solidarity with workers' salary demands and their support for strikes.[58] By late 1985, a number of opposition parties, along with various independent trade unions, constituted a "national movement against indebtedness and in favour of moratorium."[59]

Most opposition parties (again, with the exception of the PAN) expressed fierce opposition to a diminished role for the state in the economy. Their vision of the appropriate role for the state was, in general terms, even broader than had been the case immediately following the 1982 bank nationalization. In 1984, for example, the PSUM was calling for greater controls on foreign investment and for the exclusive jurisdiction of the state over steel, food, transportation, and housing—that is, areas currently shared with the private sector.[60] The opposition left parties denounced the liquidation of Uranio Mexicano in 1984, the closing of Fundidora Monterrey in 1986, and each major privatization as it occurred thereafter, repeatedly reiterating their opposition to privatization in principle.[61] Privatization, they argued, must be stopped for two reasons: it significantly reduced the state's role in the economy, and was therefore "counterrevolutionary," and it constituted a direct assault on the rights of workers, insofar as it meant massive layoffs and fundamental alterations in collective agreements.[62]

At the same time, the government's economic restructuring program generated growing opposition within the official PRI party—an opposition that firmly resisted the abandonment of the party's nationalist and populist heritage. This growing opposition was articulated by a counterelite whose statist and nationalist views could no longer be accommodated within the party state apparatus. The catalyst for the emergence of this group was the allegation of electoral fraud during the 1985 elections.

Between 1982 and 1986, elections were a barometer of growing popular alienation from the PRI. The July 1982 federal election witnessed notable inroads by opposition parties into PRI sources of support, even in the face of substantial electoral fraud, with the opposition PAN making the greatest gains, winning 14.08 percent of the popular vote. In the face of growing unrest against electoral fraud, the de la Madrid administration was apparently persuaded to largely abandon the practice in the 1983 local elections.[63] The result: heavy defeats of the PRI by the PAN, which won seventeen municipalities in five states, including two state capitals. Hence, the 1985 state and local elections witnessed a return to large-scale electoral fraud and landslide PRI victories. The elections of 1986 also resulted in charges of electoral fraud. In Chihuahua, a PAN stronghold, so blatant were the electoral irregularities that the local church took the unprecedented action of accusing the PRI of massive electoral fraud.[64] The PRI's electoral manipulations produced rising demands, both from within the PRI and from opposition parties, for a greater respect for democratic processes.

Demands for democratization were expressed alongside demands for a revision of the government's current economic model. Indeed, the two types of demands were linked: it was argued that a more democratic political system was necessary to push political leaders to alter their economic policies. In the summer of 1986, the Democratic Movement (Movimiento de Renovación Democrática) emerged within the PRI. The movement represented the revolt of a counterelite: it was led by former PRI and government political bureaucrats who were now excluded from political power and who clung to the now circumscribed statist bent. The movement was led by Porfirio Muñoz Ledo, a then unemployed politician who had been chairman of the PRI, twice a cabinet minister, and ambassador to the United Nations. Among its ranks the movement counted one of the architects of the bank nationalization and a former head of the nationalized banking sector, Carlos Tello, also without a governmental or political position at the time. Probably the most well known of the movement's leaders was Cuauhtémoc Cárdenas, former governor of the state of Michoacán and son of Mexico's most popular president, Lázaro Cárdenas, who ruled Mexico between 1934 and 1940.[65]

The movement sought to return the PRI to its populist roots: it railed against the government's subservience to the IMF; the sellout to foreign interests, as demonstrated by membership in the GATT and the relaxation of restrictions on foreign investment; severe government budget cuts; and privatization. It demanded a tougher stance against Mexico's foreign creditors and called for a moratorium on the debt. It also attacked the secretive procedures by which the PRI presidential candidate is traditionally chosen, demanding a more open procedure.[66]

In general, the neoliberal political elite demonstrated very little tolerance of the movement's assorted demands. All of the movement's proposals involving greater intraparty democracy, along with the demand that the government adopt an alternative economic strategy, were overwhelmingly defeated at the May 1987 General Assembly of the PRI. The PRI leadership and key labor leaders such as Fidel Velázquez denounced the movement unequivocally and demanded its expulsion from the party.[67] The movement was denied facilities for meetings and was subjected to bomb threats and other forms of intimidation against its sympathizers.[68] Its march on PRI headquarters to demand Cárdenas's registration as a contestant for the PRI presidential candidacy was turned away by armed railway workers.[69] Finally, in October 1987, shortly after announcing his presidential candidacy for the Partido Auténtico de la Revolución Mexicana (Authentic Party of the Mexican Revolution, or PARM), Cárdenas and other members of the Democratic Movement were expelled from the PRI.

At this point, negotiations began for the establishment of an electoral coalition, bringing together various left-wing opposition parties, a number of smaller left-wing organizations, and the recently expelled Democratic Movement.[70] Constituted as the Frente Democrático Nacional (National Democratic Front, or FDN), it fielded Cuauhtémoc Cárdenas as its presidential candidate in the 1988 federal election. As the FDN presidential candidate, Cárdenas called for a return to nationalism and to the state interventionism of earlier years. The FDN's program also called for a suspension of debt-service payments and debt negotiation, a commitment to a mixed economy, and "the assumption by the state of its full responsibilities towards public and social enterprises . . . in transport, communications, hydrocarbons, large scale mining, petrochemicals and pharmaceutical products, radioactive, steel, banking, insurance, foreign trade, power generation and distribution, and military industries"; that is, in a variety of sectors in which privatization was already under way.[71]

Opposition to the government's privatization program was a major issue raised by the FDN during the 1988 election campaign. Defending a strong role for the state, Cárdenas denounced the government's divestiture of state enterprises as dismantling the ability of the government to provide economic leadership, favoring multinationals, and representing an attack on the workers' movement.[72] The sale of Cananea, according to Cárdenas, represented "the handing over of [national] sovereignty," while government policy in the petroleum industry, particularly the opening up of basic petrochemicals to private investment, was "anti-national."[73]

The FDN worked hard to cultivate support from public enterprise trade unionists. In 1987, the leftist parties overwhelmingly supported the SME's strike for a 23 percent salary increase.[74] But perhaps the most well-known case is their support for the Petroleum Workers' Union. As a consequence of the government's restructuring program, the relationship between the PRI party and the Petroleum Workers' Union, particularly its leader, La Quina, had been deteriorating. While relations were tense during the early de la Madrid years, with hints from the Petroleum Workers' Union that it was contemplating leaving the PRI,[75] they declined even further once Carlos Salinas was designated PRI presidential candidate. It was well known that Salinas had been the force behind the removal of the Petroleum Workers' Union's privileges. It has even been suggested that La Quina campaigned heavily to stop Salinas's nomination as PRI presidential candidate.[76]

Under these circumstances, La Quina became an outspoken critic of government policy, charging that the impact of the government's policy "errors" was being born by the ever more impoverished majority.[77] The Petroleum Workers' Union openly opposed the economic solidarity pact and the government's anti-inflation program, which involved wage and price controls.[78] Strong statements of opposition from the Petroleum Workers' Union leadership caused leaders of the FDN to admit that on certain issues, particularly issues of economic policy and privatization, they shared a convergence of views with the *charro* petroleum union leadership, which could serve as the basis for "discussion."[79]

Hence, while Cárdenas obtained the support of a group of professionals and technicians affiliated with the Petroleum Workers' Union, Heberto Castillo of the Mexican Socialist Party (Partido Mexicano Socialista, PMS), one of the organizations belonging to the FDN, had obtained the support of the Democratic Petroleum Movement (Movimiento Democrático Petrolero) of the Petroleum Workers' Union.[80] And although the Petroleum Workers' Union remained formally and officially in support of the PRI, it retained ties to the FDN, and many of the union's rank and file deserted the PRI. La Quina's supporters are believed to have been active in Cárdenas's electoral campaign; La Quina himself is reported to have supported Cárdenas's campaign through the provision of supplies and office equipment. The 1988 election was the first time the Petroleum Workers' Union failed to send its usual memorandum to the union membership directing the rank and file to vote for, and to show militancy for, the PRI.[81] The electoral results in the petroleum zones are revealing: the presidential vote went overwhelmingly in favor of Cárdenas, and while the PRI petroleum deputies in the Chamber of Deputies were reelected, all had links with dissident groups within and outside the PRI.[82] Other angry public enterprise workers appear to have backed the FDN and Cárdenas as well. Telephone and airline workers organized committees in support of Cárdenas, while dissident workers of the SME held a rally and a march in his support.[83]

The July 1988 federal election resulted in a considerably reduced majority for the ruling party and a strengthening of the opposition parties, particularly the leftist parties. Official results, heavily contested in the face of overwelming evidence of large-scale fraud, gave Carlos Salinas 50.36 percent of the popular vote, Cuauhtémoc Cárdenas 31.29 percent, and Manuel Clouthier, the PAN candidate, 17.07 percent.[84] Absenteeism was also high.

As mentioned earlier in this chapter, some of the literature has focused on the surge of support from new social movements in accounting for the 1988 electoral success of the Cardenista coalition. This view is not incompatible with the interpretation that draws political implications from the erosion of corporatist control stemming from privatization. Rank-and-file workers experiencing a dramatic decline in wages and benefits, workers cast into the ranks of the unemployed as a consequence of restructuring, who then turned against their *charro* union leadership or the PRI (or both), would be prime candidates for both new social movements and oppositional organization. In the big cities, the PRI lost with a clear margin.[85] Cárdenas, on the other hand, received a high percentage of the vote in all voting districts of the Federal District, which were principally working class.

The same occurred in the state of Mexico and in numerous other cities.[86] Proportionately, labor suffered more legislative losses than any other sector.[87] One interpretation suggests that voters went out of their way to repudiate union bosses who were congressional candidates: eighteen of sixty-six official labor candidates were defeated.[88] Indeed, a CTM document presented to the president blamed government economic policy for worker absenteeism from the polls and for their abandonment of the PRI in support of opposition parties, declaring that "everything in the economy which goes against workers is paid back by the worker at election time."[89] Fidel Velázquez was more blunt, explaining that while credibility had been lost by the CTM, the unions, and the party, the workers had "settled the account by voting against the PRI and the worker candidates."[90]

The privatization issue and associated policies, such as wage restrictions and alterations in collective agreements, were instrumental in dividing and weakening the official labor movement. The growing alienation of the rank and file of the public enterprise trade unions was abundantly apparent by the 1988 federal election: neither the leadership nor the rank and file of these unions were dependable sources of PRI support.

The Salinas Years:
Neocorporatism and Efficient Clientelism

The federal election of 1988 was a turning point in Mexican politics. The results of that election—the failure of the corporatist core of organized labor to deliver the vote—produced an explicit decision on the part of Mexico's political bureaucratic rulers to alter existing political arrangements so as to reestablish a "popular" support base, but one no longer so dependent on organized labor.

The most important development involved the attempt to reduce the importance of the labor sector within the PRI. In 1990, collective membership in the PRI by virtue of membership in a sector was eliminated, with membership henceforth being individual and free. In addition, the number of deputy and senate candidates allocated to labor was reduced.[91] In 1992, despite the fierce opposition of Fidel Velázquez, incoming party president Gerardo Borrego Estrada announced a reorganization of the PRI involving a more dramatic reduction in the importance of organized labor. The stated purpose of the changes was to broaden the base of the support for the party, in particular, to make the party attractive to the middle classes. The PRI would be, Borrego declared, "a party of citizens as well as of organizations and sectors."[92] The sectoral groups of the PRI (the worker, peasant, and popular sectors) would be replaced by three "great movements": (1) the Movimiento Popular Territorial (Popular Territorial Movement), (2) the Frente Nacional de Ciudadano (the National Citizens' Front), and (3) the Pacto Obrero-Campesino (the Worker-Peasant Pact). Not only would the worker sector no longer be one of the main organizations of the party, but it was to be merged with the peasant sector.

These proposals, however, met with stiff labor opposition. By 1993, the CTM succeeded in securing the restitution of traditional sectoral representation within the party by obtaining agreement that three secretaries (one for each of the old sectors) would sit on the PRI executive.[93] Although the neoliberal elite's modernization of the party had been stalled, the outcome of the change desired by Mexico's technocratic elite was clearly a reduction in the influence of the traditional corporate sectors.

But while the political bureaucrats were abandoning organized labor and sought to cultivate the middle classes, they also saw the importance of building clientelistic ties with the popular classes. Indeed, the political purpose of the National Solidarity Program (PRONASOL) was overwhelmingly acknowledged by government officials interviewed in the course of this research. Announced by President Salinas in 1989, PRONASOL drew a significant proportion of its funding from resources obtained by the sale of privatized companies,[94] with further infusions of capital coming from the World Bank. It represented, according to government officials, a more efficient allocation of resources for political purposes. Set up to alleviate extreme poverty by providing matching funds for locally generated projects, the program substituted for privatized state firms in direct ways. It has, for example, provided funds for such projects as electrification and for schools in fishing communities that had previously been provided these services by the state-owned fishing company, Productos Pesqueros Mexicanos (PROPEMEX), now privatized.[95] Workers laid off from SICARTSA, one of the privatized steel companies, were provided with business credits from PRONASOL, and credits previously distributed by BANRURAL (the state rural development bank, now liquidated) were until 1993 distributed to farmers through PRONASOL.[96] In 1993, due to difficulties in the rural sector created by recent neoliberal reforms, especially the privatization of ejidal lands, the government announced its Program for Direct Support of the Countryside (Programa de Apoyos Directas al Campo, PROCAMPO). This program gave direct subsidies to peasant producers of corn, beans, wheat, rice, soya, sorghum, and cotton for a transition period during which guaranteed prices would be removed. In addition, a PRONASOL fund was set up to offer loans to small companies, providing such support for 3,000 of them in 1993 alone.[97]

There seems to be little dispute that PRONASOL funds have gone to regions of opposition party strength in order to win back PRI support.[98] Indeed, more than 80 percent of the people of the state of Michoacán—a Cárdenas stronghold—became incorporated into solidarity committees, and Michoacán has been one of the regions most favored by the solidarity program.[99] In those cases where the opposition holds office locally, PRONASOL funds bypassed the municipal government (through which they are normally distributed) and gone directly to local committees.[100] Through over 150,000 solidarity committees (the establishment of such committees being necessary for the receipt of funds), the president of the republic was able, through the ministry set up to administrate the program (SEDESO), to establish direct clientelist ties with the citizenry. Despite the fact that World Bank funding for PRONASOL was contributed for the purpose of encouraging decentralization and regional development, some observers argue that the program strengthened the presidency.[101] Indeed, PRONASOL was presented as the president's program; from its inception, President Salinas spent at least one day a week visiting local communities to dispense funds for various local projects.[102]

At the same time, however, PRONASOL was also linked to the PRI and to the old sectoral labor organizations. In Oaxaca, the CNC is reported to have received 60 percent of the PRONASOL budget going to that state.[103] Government officials pledged that PRONASOL would provide financial support for joint projects of the CTM and the CNC.[104] And PRONASOL funds were earmarked to help create more malleable sectoral leaders: a Solidarity Institute (Instituto de Solidaridad) was proposed to "prepare better worker and farmer leaders."[105]

Its support bolstered by PRONASOL programs, the PRI made an apparent comeback in the August 1991 mid-term elections. The PRI won all but one seat in the senate and 320 of the 500 seats in the Chamber of Deputies, giving it control (more than 60 percent of the vote) in each of the two chambers.[106] PRONASOL was held largely responsible for the improvement in the PRI's electoral fortunes, particularly in opposition strongholds such as Michoacán where, in 1991, twenty-five municipalities with strong FDN support in the 1988 election supported the PRI with 60 percent of the popular vote.[107] However, serious doubts have been raised about the reliability of these electoral results, since, according to official figures, 5 million more people voted than in the 1988 election, highly unusual for mid-term elections. While the absolute number of opposition votes increased in many states, the number of PRI votes increased even more.[108] Steep electoral campaign spending is believed to have been important, both in these elections and in the PRI's performance in the 1992 elections, particularly in highly contentious contests.[109]

The clearest proof of the electoral worthiness of PRONASOL and PROCAMPO was the 1994 federal election, which returned the PRI presidential candidate to office with 48.8 percent of the popular vote. A combination of both old and new clientelistic arrangments account for the PRI's political resiliency.[110] Electoral observers reported the practice of making a vote for the PRI a condition for receiving PROCAMPO credit.[111] PRONASOL money was poured into areas of potential electoral difficulty, such as the Valley of Chalco, and was withheld from regions known to be bastions of opposition support.[112]

Traditional corporatist structures were less important than in the past. Some important labor organizations, such as the Telephone Workers Union, the Teachers Union (Sindicato Nacional de Trabajadores de la Educación, SNTE) and the Federation of Unions of Public Service Workers (Federación de Sindicatos de Trabajadores al Servicio del Estado, FSTE) repudiated the idea of collective labor support for the PRI, leaving the rank and file free to vote as they chose.[113] Similarly, the leader of the CNC declared himself against a peasant corporatist bloc vote for the PRI, and the press reported that local CNC leaderships were overturned when they attempted to secure rank-and-file votes for the PRI.[114] However, the CTM exhorted all members to vote for the PRI. And the Petroleum Union, facing problems of rank-and-file resistance, used methods of intimidation such as threats of job dismissal, contract termination, and violence to convince members to vote for the PRI.[115]

Concessions to the opposition (albeit the opposition right) have given the regime a veneer of democratic legitimacy. In 1989, the government conceded the governorship of Baja California (Norte) to the opposition PAN, thereby allowing the first opposition governor in modern Mexican history to take power. Hailed by President Salinas as yet another step forward in the process of democratization, this action was repeated in 1992 and two times in 1995, giving the PAN a total of four governorships. Charges of electoral fraud by the opposition have been rampant throughout the Salinas years, however, particularly in the municipal elections of Michoacán (1989) and the state of México (1990). Since President Zedillo assumed power, the gubernatorial contests in Chiapas and Tabasco have been marred by charges of electoral fraud.

At the same time, violent political repression has not been absent. The opposition PRD party claims that 230 of its party militants were assassinated between 1988 and May 1993,[116] and both Americas Watch and Amnesty International have condemned the rising number of human rights violations, including those with political motivations. In the 1980s, more that thirty journalists were murdered, while the increasing use of violence in rural areas has continued unabated.[117] One of the regime's opponents, Jorge Castañeda, a university professor who writes articles critical of government policy in the foreign press, received death threats from a source believed to have connections with the administration.[118]

Opposition leftist parties, particularly the PRD, articulated a nationalist, populist position throughout the second half of the 1980s: they condemned subservience to the IMF, economic policies that failed to develop the domestic consumer market, deregulation, the opening to foreign capital, and privatization, particularly the bank privatization.[119] The PRD, in particular, cultivated disaffected trade unionists in the former public enterprise sector. It emphasized the impact of privatization on employment. In a speech to the miners of Cananea in 1989, Cárdenas urged workers to resist its privatization, characterized the government's declaration of bankruptcy as fraudulent, and condemned the violations of collective agreements and the use of the army in labor conflicts.[120]

But the struggle against neoliberalism has created unexpected alliances. The PRD and other leftist parties sided with the powerful and undemocratic Petroleum Workers' Union and its corrupt leader, La Quina (now in prison), over a variety of issues: opposition to the reclassification of basic petrochemicals, demands that the conduct of PEMEX's director general, Ramón Beteta, over the tanker issue be investigated, and opposition to the 1989 arrest of La Quina and other petroleum union leaders and the use of the army in the maneuver.[121] Leading members of the PRD also denounced the government's dismantling of the Petroleum Workers' Union's collective agreement.[122] During the 1989 electoral campaign in Tamaulipas, the PRD was reported to have successfully cultivated the support of workers who had close ties with La Quina, with the result that the PRD became the second most important party in the southern part of the state (Madero and Tampico).[123] As a consequence of the bitter labor strife in SICARTSA, the population openly supported the PRD, resulting in the election of a local PRD deputy and later a municipal president.[124]

Perhaps the clearest evidence of the regime's failure to contain resistance to its neoliberal reforms is the Chiapas rebellion initiated on 1 January 1994. In that state, the drop in international coffee prices, the termination of the commercial networks and technical assistance provided by state enterprises such as the Mexican Coffee Institute (INMECAFE, Instituto Mexicano de Café), in charge of directing the production and marketing of coffee, combined with the psychological impact of privatizing ejidal lands, which effectively put an end to land reform, have all been factors behind this recent uprising.[125] Peasant demands have met with little government sympathy. The Salinas administration's initial response was to attempt full-scale military represssion of the rebels, with widespread human rights violations.[126] While the administration later dropped its hard line, it was unable to arrive at a settlement with the rebels. With the support of the opposition PAN party and the country's major business associations, the Zedillo administration launched a major offensive across north and central Chiapas in early 1995 before making overtures toward a negotiated solution.[127] The Chiapas rebellion initiated a wave of political and social protest across the country, involving opposition leftist parties and the organized working class alongside peasant organizations.[128] The opposition PRD has supported the rebels, calling for a reversal of the Constitution's revised article 27, which made possible the sale of ejidal landholdings.

Populist resistance to the government's economic restructuring program continued to emerge within the PRI into the 1990s—the expulsion of the Democratic Movement did not succeed in uniting the party around Salinas's neoliberal economic strategy, although the party leadership has been fairly successful at keeping intraparty opposition under wraps. In November of 1988, the National Direction of the PRI formally accepted the Corriente Critica (Critical Current), headed by former ambassador Rodolfo González Guevera, who had been a participant in the old Democratic Movement. Its concerns echoed those of the Democratic Movement: it denounced the lack of democracy in the PRI and protested privatization, the bank privatization in particular.[129] In addition, two other groups demanding democratization also emerged: the Movement for Democratic Change (Movimiento para el Cambio Democrático, or MPCD) and the Progressive Democratic Current (Corriente Democratica Progresista, or CDP).[130] However, by 1994, opposition to the regime's neoliberal economic model had moderated considerably. Although condemning the corruption of the privatization drive and the inroads made by private capital into the petroleum industry, Cárdenas, the PRD's 1994 presidential candidate, rejected the notion of the renationalization of privatized firms and promised an important role for both foreign and domestic private capital.[131]

Mexico's rulers have not contained popular resistance easily nor entirely successfully. While relatively successful until the 1994 election in stemming the flow of popular alienation from the regime, neocorporatism and the new clientelism have had to be supplemented with various forms of violent repression. The use and threat of force to dismantle collective contracts and bring about privatization and the use of intimidation to rout out opponents of the government's economic model within the PRI have paralleled the use of violent repression against extragovernmental opposition parties and individuals. Despite predominant neoliberalism in current policy, there remains an underlying current of populist-statist opposition in the leftist parties and within society itself.

Business and the State
in the Era of Neoliberal Reform

While the reduction of the state's role in the economy, particularly the sale of state enterprises in strategic sectors, contributed heavily to the deterioration of the state's alliance with labor, these same policies have produced growing business confidence—a consequence the government had anticipated and one of the reasons for the acceleration of the program—and have solidified the government's alliance with the most powerful business interests. This process was set in motion during the de la Madrid years. As we saw in the previous chapter, the country's most important privatized companies passed into the hands of the most important industrial and commercial conglomerates.[132]

A variety of other economic policies over the past ten years have also favored the interests of big business. The de la Madrid government had bailed out the highly indebted industrial-commercial Monterrey group, channeling substantial state credits there.[133] These businesses had been the major beneficiaries of the Trust for Foreign Exchange Protection (Fideicomiso para la Cobertura de Riesgos Cambiarios, or FICORCA), a program introduced in 1983 to provide coverage of the private sector's exchange risks originating from the external debt.[134] Moreover, once economic restructuring was under way, the biggest firms benefited most from the government's export promotion program. The 1986 Program for Exporting Companies (Programa de Empresas Altamente Exportadora, or ALTEX) provided preferential treatment in the areas of credit and tax relief for those enterprises already exporting an important proportion of production—that is, the country's largest firms, many of which are transnational corporations.[135]

Hence, Mexico's largest industrial conglomerates and transnational corporations are rapidly preempting the state's leadership role in the economy. This is due to the fact that only transnationals and national firms with large amounts of available capital have had the resources to institute industrial reconversion and become export competitive. Industrial reconversion, initiated halfway through the last decade, had already been accomplished in most transnational companies (in such industries as electronics, automobiles, chemicals, and *maquiladoras* (assembly plants). A minority of big national enterprises were able to undergo reconversion: synthetic fibers, for example, was able to modernize and enter the international market from 1982, as were the cement, glass, and beer industries.

But in order to compete internationally—to acquire the necessary technology—many big Mexican businesses have found it necessary to make strategic alliances with transnational capital: the sale to the U.S. brewery Anheuser-Busch of a 17.7 percent stake in Mexico's top beer company, Cervecería Modelo, the merger of General Tire's manufacturing operation in Mexico with that of Grupo Carso S.A., and the sale to Coca-Cola of a 30 percent stake in the soft drink operation of FOMEX (Fomento Económico Mexicano S.A.) are a few examples.[136] Meanwhile, small and medium enterprises were not able to modernize due to the absence of an adequate government financing program, while public firms were faced with insufficient resources and corrupt and clientelistic labor relations. Indeed, according to data available from SECOFI, by 1992 barely 5 percent of industrial establishments had modern technology.[137]

Most of the enterprises that export are large firms, manufacturing motors and autoparts. The top three exporting companies, after PEMEX, are transnational auto manufacturers: Chrysler, Ford, and GM of Mexico.[138] By 1992, 267 companies accounted for 70 percent of the value of all exports; 100 of these companies are transnational corporations, and 60 percent of the value of total export sales is concentrated in only ten product lines.[139] Indeed, the president of the Business Coordinating Council (CCE) was forced to admit that the increase in manufactured exports had benefited the country's biggest businesses while small and medium firms accounted for only 6.3 percent of the value of export sales.[140]

The profound economic changes that have occurred since 1985 have resulted in a degree of economic concentration at least equal to that in existence prior to 1982. With the bank privatization, the government has authorized the establishment of financial groups that include a variety of financial institutions, usually combinations involving a major privatized bank and brokerage and investment houses, whose directors also have ties to important industrial firms through directorships. An exception is the Grupo Financiero Inbursa, whose major shareholder is Carlos Slim Helú. Instead of acquiring one of the existing banks, Carlos Slim announced plans to establish his own bank to concentrate business in commerce, telecommunications, and construction. By early 1994, fourteen such groups had been authorized. Table 7.1 shows the financial holding companies, their affiliated banks, investment houses, and other companies registered in the Mexican stock exchange in 1992. The appendix lists the individual shareholders of the most important of these financial groups illustrating their links to holding companies other than their own through directorships on the boards of banks and investment houses. The appendix also illustrates considerable overlap between the boards of financial institutions and major industrial companies. All those listed are members of the CMHN, the Mexican Council of Businessmen, an organization comprising the top thirty-seven business leaders in the country.

Not much has changed since Roderic Camp's analysis of the concentration of industrial-financial ownership prior to the bank nationalization. (See Appendix.) As Camp found, there are not only horizontal ties, linking financial holding companies, banks, and industrial

TABLE 7.1

Major Financial Holding Companies and Affiliates

Holding Company	Bank	Investment Houses	Other[a]
Grupo Financiero Monterrey	BANCOMER	Acciones Bursátiles	6
Grupo Financiero BANAMEX/Accival	BANAMEX	Acciones y Valores de México, Fundo Integral BANAMEX	5
Grupo Financiero SERFIN	SERFIN	Operadora de Bolsa	7
Grupo Financiero Inbursa	Inbursa	Inbursa Bursátil Fondo Inbursa	2
Grupo Financiero Inverlat	COMERMEX	Casa de Bolsa Inverlat	3
Grupo Financiero Mexival/ BANPAIS	BANPAIS	Mexival	2
Grupo Financiero Probursa	Mercantil	Casa de Bolsa Probursa	7
Grupo Financiero Abaco	Banca Confía	Abaco Casa de Bolsa	4
Grupo Financiero Invermexico	SOMEX	—	3

Source: Bolsa Mexicana de Valores and Asociación Mexicana de Casas de Bolsas, *Mexican Company Handbook, 1992.*

a. Includes insurance companies, foreign exchange houses, real estate, tourism, and leasing establishments.

firms, but there are also numerous vertical ties, linking the most powerful financial industrial groups to each other.[141] The Bailleres family is represented in three groups (Grupo Financial Monterrey, BANAMEX/Accival, and Inverlat), the Garza Sada family (Garza Lagüera, Bernardo Garza Sada, and Adrían Sada Treviño) in four groups (Grupo Financial Monterrey, BANAMEX/Accival, Grupo Financiero SERFIN, and Inverlat), the Helú family (Carlos Slim Helú and Alfredo Harp Helú, cousins) are in two groups (BANAMEX/Accival and Inbursa), the Zambrano family (Lorenzo and Marcelo, nephew and uncle) in two groups (BANAMEX/Accival and Grupo Financiero SERVIN), and Claudio X. González is a major shareholder in two financial groups (BANAMEX/Accival and Grupo Financiero SERVIN). The distinctions between these financial groups is further blurred by the fact that their most important shareholders come together on the boards of directors of the country's most important industrial firms.

There are, however, some new faces. Roberto Hernández and the

Helú family, controlling BANAMEX/Accival and Inbursa, did not appear in Camp's analysis. As noted in the previous chapter, they arose during the 1960s and 1970s with profitable stock brokerage businesses. With regard to old money, Mexico's industrial and financial magnates have played a game of musical chairs with the bank privatization: Alberto Bailleres has moved from Banca CREMI and COMERMEX to BANCOMER and BANAMEX; E. Garza Lagüera from COMERMEX to BANCOMER; and B. Garza Sada, whose family had interests in SERFIN and COMERMEX, now has interests in BANAMEX and COMERMEX. The younger generation of Mexico's industrial and financial elite has moved into a more prominent position than it occupied prior to 1982: A. F. Legorreta Chauvet has expanded his family's interests beyond a variety of industrial concerns into banking; similarly, J. Larrea Ortega has expanded his family's interests beyond mining into banking and other activities.

One study suggests that the Grupo Financial Monterrey, BANAMEX/Accival, Grupo Financiero SERFIN, and Grupo Financiero Inbursa control the most important financial, industrial, commercial, and service activities of the country.[142] According to a similar study, the Grupo Financial Monterrey and BANAMEX/Accival account for 67 percent of the shares of all financial groups registered in the stock market and 71 percent of the profits for the first quarter of 1992.[143]

The industrial enterprises held by the major shareholders of these powerful financial-industrial groups are the most important national firms involved in exporting: CEMEX (cement), VITRO (glass), Peñoles (mining), TELMEX (telecommunications), and Celanese (petrochemicals). Four mining companies linked to these financial groups control 80 percent of mining production in Mexico: Frisco, Corporación Industrial San Luis, Peñoles, and Grupo Industrial Minera México.[144] As the case of mining illustrates, there is now greater economic concentration in certain sectors by virtue of the fact that the state has sold its holdings to already powerful private sector firms.

Economic concentration appears to be integral to the new export model. As suggested, public policy has been instrumental in bringing about the reconcentration of economic power, particularly with privatization. Moreover, the growth of financial concentration is seen by the business community as necessary to become internationally competitive.[145] Despite business opposition to trade liberalization, particularly during the early years, the Salinas administration has succeeded in restoring much of the business confidence (at least on the part of Mexico's most powerful business interests) that had been lost as a consequence of the 1982 bank nationalization. Virtually all the enterpreneurs interviewed in the course of research for this book praised the Salinas administration.

President Salinas has established close links to big business. Their representatives were found on the PRI's Committee for the Financing and Consolidation of Resources, responsible for raising funds for Salinas's election campaign.[146] In 1992, entrepreneurs were incorporated into the PRI through so-called committees for campaign financing (Comités de Financiamiento de Campañas) in charge of securing financial donations to the party. These groups have become instruments through which businessmen are able to express their political preferences, organize meetings with candidates, and gain media exposure.[147] The Mexican Council of Businessmen (CMHN), grouping together Mexico's most powerful business interests, continues to have the closest and most readily available access to public authorities.[148] The 1994 federal electoral campaign involved even closer ties to the big business community. Business leader Miguel Alemán Velasco served as the PRI's finance secretary. In early 1993, Mexico's top business leaders, the beneficiaries of privatization, were invited to a dinner party where each was asked to pledge $25 million to the PRI's 1994 campaign.[149] At the same time, a number of the country's top businessmen such as Claudio X. González (president of Kimberly Clark and former leader of the peak business association, the CCE) are believed to be close advisors of Salinas,[150] while critics have charged that Carlos Slim Helú and Carlos Salinas have been secret business partners, enabling Salinas to personally benefit from the privatization drive.

Close personal contacts between SECOFI (the Ministry of Commerce and Industrial Development), the presidency, and powerful individuals in the private sector continue to be more important than formal channels for big business.[151] One owner of an ALTEX (export-oriented) company had this to say about his relationship with the Salinas administration:

> Consultation between the public and private sector is largely on an informal basis between cabinet secretaries and individual companies. My company has very good relations with the current administration. A cabinet secretary will call me to arrange a meeting, and I speak with Carlos Salinas every two or three weeks or so. . . . Formal business organizations exist just to give a show of democracy.

Along similar lines, Matilde Luna suggests that with particular reference to exporting companies, personal contacts between businessmen and the state play a much more important role than enterpreneurial associations.[152]

At the same time, the country's most powerful conglomerates continue to dominate the most powerful business associations. The most important of these at the present time is the Coordinating Committee for Commercial Export Business Organizations (Coordinadora de Organizaciones Empresariales de Comercio Exterior, or COECE), established in June 1990 to represent the private sector in the NAFTA negotiations. The CCE (Business Coordinating Council), controlled by the big financial and industrial conglomerates, plays a central role in this organization, as do a variety of other organizations representing the big exporters.[153]

Small and medium businessmen, on the other hand, believe themselves to be excluded almost completely from the new economic strategy. Their questioning of the privatization program has already been noted. Organizations representing small and medium firms, CANACINTRA and the National Association of Transformation Industries (Associación Nacional de Industriales de la Transformación, or ANIT), were much more critical of trade liberalization than were other business organizations, claiming that it was particularly harmful to small and medium firms. This group has also demanded that increased credit support be made available to small and medium firms generally and not just to export firms. They have called on the government to pursue a strategy less concerned with export markets and more concerned with domestic markets. These businessmen have criticized government policy as benefiting the largest firms, which had already broken into such markets. And they see free trade negotiations as a process that encourages input from only the country's most powerful economic interests, ignoring the interests of smaller firms. CANACINTRA has made public demands for antimonopoly measures and for measures to guarantee the use of domestic inputs by industry.[154]

During the late 1980s and early 1990s, small and medium business became increasingly critical of what it viewed as the unrepresenative nature of such organizations as the CCE. Indeed, intense conflict occurred within that organization over the election of an interim president during 1989–1990, featuring small and medium business on one side and big business on the other.[155] Similarly, CANACINTRA and other associations representing small and medium business have repeatedly questioned the representativeness of COECE. ANIT alleges that information on the NAFTA negotiations was circulated only among the top echelons of COECE (the big groups) and not made available to small and medium firms.[156] In sum, economic restructuring and its logicial extension, NAFTA, have entailed an increasing polarization within the private sector, as the big financial-industrial conglomerates draw closer to the state and small and medium firms are increasingly excluded.

There have been distinct political ramifications to this exclusion, as a study of the political activities of enterpreneurs in the state of Chihuahua shows. While the most prominent enterpreneurs gave overt support to the PRI in the 1992 elections, many small and medium enterpreneurs reasserted their support for the PAN. Yemile Mizrahi links this political scenario to the fact that big entrepreneurs usually have economic and personal links with the government while small and medium firms do not. Moreover, since small and medium firms believe that they are not well represented in Mexico's political institutions, they seek a redefinition of the rules that govern the political game.[157]

The 1994 financial crisis may not alter the current situation in any fundamental way. While Mexican banks and big firms such as TELMEX and CEMEX have been hit hard by the devaluation, once again the state seems prepared to bail them out.[158] Funds have been provided to help commercial banks rebuild capital drained by the peso crisis. And the government has said that it is prepared to provide additional funds to Fabraproa, the bank bailout fund.[159] Meanwhile, the situation has provided an opportunity for one of the country's wealthiest businessmen, Carlos Slim Helú, to buy up shares, at bargain prices, in a number of the country's most important companies such as ALFA, Celanese Mexicana, and Kimberly Clark of Mexico.[160]

Conclusion

Economic restructuring, particularly that involving the dismantling of the state, has precipitated two related simultaneous transformations: (1) a change in the basis of state support, as it has shed labor and the small and medium business sector as allies and moved closer to big business, and (2) a change in the mechanisms (corporatism and clientelism) by which authoritarian control is excercised. As a consequence of the new economic policies put into effect after 1982, the rank and file of the country's most powerful trade unions—especially those in the public enterprise sector—began to turn against their *charro* leadership and against the PRI. The severe reduction in opportunities for patronage also undermined *charro* leadership support for the PRI.

The 1988 electoral results triggered a rapid unraveling of the old corporatist system. Following the PRI's poor showing, President Salinas pursued an explicit strategy designed to reduce the importance of organized labor within the party state apparatus. But he did not abandon the use of cooperative *charro* leadership, as the discussion in chapter 5 of his handling of the Petroleum Workers' Union showed. There was an explicit attempt to reorganize the PRI, to downgrade the importance of the labor (and peasant) sector, while providing a revised structure designed to attract the middle class.

At the same time, a new form of clientelism was put in place in an attempt to tie the marginalized masses to the political bureaucratic elite, in particular to the presidency. Instead of a centralized corporatist-clientelist system in which organized labor had a central role through a hegemonic worker central (with the trade unions of the public firms occupying a core position), the system became more segmented. Corporatist structures still operate, but they are weaker and more fragmented. Moreover, clientelism, while it continues to operate through some of the old corporatist structures, operates outside those structures as well and became linked directly to the presidency through a powerful new ministry. These developments do not suggest a trend toward increased democratization, as much of the current literature on Mexico argues. We are not witnessing the emergence of pluralism, which would entail the eradication or reduction of corporatism and clientelism, in order to give freer rein to societal organizations and to open the possibility of their influence on public policy. Rather, we are witnessing a system that combines corporatism and clientelism in new ways and entails an extreme degree of policy centralization in the hands of the president and his closest advisors.

The tough treatment of labor unrest that has been integral to public enterprise reform and privatization generated stiff political opposition. But the government has not gracefully accepted the loss of political support stemming from this and other neoliberal policies. Electoral irregularities and violent intimidation of opposition have remained features of the regime, a clear sign that the "new" methods of political control have been less than adequate. This fact has been recently demonstrated in the sector most economically marginalized both from the earlier import-substitution economic model and from the current neoliberal one. As the Chiapas rebellion shows, neither PRONASOL nor harsh repression has been able to stem the tide of rising unrest engendered by a commitment to market forces and export competitiveness that exclude traditional Indian communities. The danger presented to the regime by this recent event and its aftermath lies in its demonstration of the depth and breadth of popular alienation and the specter of the emergence of a broad-based popular alliance opposed to the extremes of the current neoliberal model, particularly as it pertains to such issues as petroleum and ejidal peasant landholdings. Without the old system of co-opted *charros*, who in the past have had the resources to keep their rank and file in line, a great many workers and former workers of the old public enterprise sector can be expected to join an opposition alliance.

There is no evidence that economic restructuring in general or privatization in particular have produced a dispersal of economic or political power. The policy-making process is highly concentrated in the hands of the president and his closest advisers, whose ties with powerful business groups are closer now than they have ever been.

192

Economic power is at least as concentrated as before 1982, and in some sectors, more so. Increased business influence on policy has not occurred within a context of more open decision making: if anything, decision making has become more closed in light of the homogeneity of bureaucrats involved (the by now complete exclusion of statist bureaucrats) and the personal nature of big business links with the cabinet and the president.

8

—

From Statism to Neoliberalism

Transition in an Authoritarian Regime

Privatization and Political Transition

The process of privatization has been linked to important changes in the coalitional base of the state and in the mechanisms of authoritarian political control that have been at the core of Mexican political stability. While these transformations were set in motion in earlier years, the economic crisis that began in 1982 and continued through 1986, and the economic restructuring measures that resulted from that crisis, dramatically accelerated the process. The manner in which pre-1982 political arrangements account for Mexico's relatively high degree of political stability has been one of the most important areas of scholarly concern. Much of the literature has stressed the reinforcing principles of corporatism and patron clientelism as mechanisms mitigating dissent and potential dissent from the most militant and organized among the popular classes. Although the role of the party has been central to most of these analyses, this work has emphasized the importance of state enterprises in the co-optative process. As the state extended its role, it became the locus of class and group struggle. State agencies and institutions, and particularly state enterprises, provided important benefits to state bureaucrats and to their labor and business clienteles. While this process may well have been counterproductive in terms of economic efficiency, it has been extremely functional in terms of its enhancement of the incorporative capacities of the state, particularly with regard to the militant workers of public companies.

Originating as a group of foreign enclaves, the state enterprise sector spawned a work force with a history of strong organization and militancy. Because of the strategic nature of the activities carried out by public firms—petroleum and electrical energy, for example, were crucial to the state's industrialization drive—labor quiescence in these sectors came to be of overriding importance. Hence, the mechanisms of corrupt union clientelist control, known as *charrismo,* achieved their fullest expression in the unions of state enterprises. Under this system, public firms contributed to the wealth of both unions and union leaders, affording them the instruments by which to control the rank and file. Further, these co-optative arrangements resulted in the emergence of a powerful labor bourgeoisie able to exercise a certain degree of political influence. The power of the Petroleum Workers' Union during the petroleum boom years is the most well-known case. Until the economic crisis of the 1980s, the incorporative political arrangements were fairly successful not only in containing unrest but also in securing support for the PRI, although difficulties arose when economic recession obstructed the delivery of economic benefits.

The political role of state enterprises has gone beyond that of the distribution of patronage, however. Public enterprises in Mexico became nationalist symbols, intimately linking the regime responsible for their creation to the popular goals of the Mexican Revolution. The central role they played in Mexico's postwar economic expansion established them as essential instruments of the state's developmentalist role, while their social welfare responsibilities strengthened the regime's image as a government concerned with popular living standards.

The heterogeneity of Mexico's political bureaucratic elite has also enhanced the co-optative capacities of the system. A variety of views and bureaucratic types could be accommodated within the expanding state apparatus and were by convention represented in the highest reaches of political power. This was the case even after 1970, when Mexico's top political leaders were less often recruited from the ranks of the PRI and came increasingly from within the state bureaucracy. The expansion of the public enterprise sector facilitated the entrenchment of public servants and political bureaucrats fully committed to an interventionist vocation for the state. In the past, the incorporative nature of the system assumed a certain degree of tension between the state and the private sector, particularly big business, despite the fact that this group was undeniably the greatest beneficiary of state policy. This tension between the state and big business increased as the state enterprise sector expanded, and the country's biggest business interests hardened their opposition toward this form of state intervention. Small and medium firms, on the other hand, with a predisposition toward statism, felt their interests accommodated by an expansionary state.

Hence, while policy rested in the hands of a heterogeneous political bureaucratic elite (particularly with regard to statist and antistatist policy tendencies), Mexico's policy makers were constrained by an increasingly powerful and hostile private sector. At the same time, a variety of subelite groups were also incorporated through a system of material rewards and came to feel that they could exercise some influence on particular issues.

By the late 1960s, economic difficulties were beginning to seriously impinge upon the smooth functioning of the political process as I have described it. Balance of payments difficulties stemming from policy neglect of agriculture were compounded by the world petroleum crisis of the early 1970s. The state began to experience a growing fiscal crisis. Although a brief respite was afforded during the petroleum export boom (1976–1982), the petroleum export strategy in fact aggravated Mexico's economic difficulties. By 1982, the country was saddled with an enormous foreign debt, an uncompetitive manufacturing sector, and serious problems in agricultural production. Public enterprises were particularly hard hit: most had severe deficits and had acquired substantial foreign debts.

After 1982, debt negotiations began to take on overriding importance. From here on, external pressures patterned the distribution of power within the state. The debt negotiations reinforced the power and the objectives of the finance sector within the state, largely because its neoliberal vision of reality became the only possible choice under the circumstances. The debt negotiations patterned the outcome of the political bureaucratic struggle within the state and encouraged the predominance of a political bureaucratic faction demanding an alleviation of strict austerity but at the same time fully committed to both public deficit reduction and economic liberalization—goals that assumed an acceleration in privatization.

There is no question that Mexico's post-1983 policy drive has been mightily influenced by the growing predominance of neoliberal economic ideas, ideas that have taken root not simply as a consequence of pressures exercised by multilateral institutions but also as a consequence of more subtle processes. Since the mid to late 1970s, neoclassical economic thought has become so pervasive that it has influenced the choices of most policy makers in developed and developing countries, overriding original ideological predispositions and independent of direct pressures from creditors. Historically, certain sectors within the Mexican public bureaucracy have been more open than others to neoliberal ideas. The institutional responsibilities of the Ministry of Finance, which is in charge of revenue collection, have predisposed it to oppose the expansion of the state. This opposition intensified over the years as the Finance Ministry witnessed the erosion of its powers and their transfer to a competitor ministry responsible for administering the bulk of the industrial public enterprise sector. At the same time, both the Finance Ministry and the Central Bank have historically recruited from academic institutions with neoliberal tendencies while further reinforcing this predisposition by socializing new recruits along antistatist lines. Moreover, their close contacts with the country's most powerful financial interests have further facilitated a similarity of views.

Hence, events occurring after 1983 reinforced these policy predispositions and institutional interests. Ongoing and protracted negotiations with the IMF fortified the preoccupations of these political bureaucrats with the public deficit and the size of the state. The further decline in petroleum prices in 1986 and the increase in interest rates strengthened the pressure to reach agreement with the country's creditors and to implement their policy prescriptions. In the absence of this external pressure, the statist bureaucratic opposition would no doubt have been stronger, and Mexico's economic liberalization drive would have been weaker.

The economic crisis and the process of debt negotiations has rendered the state highly permeable to outside influences on the policy process. While it is true that the finance sector supported neoliberal ideas in 1983, most highly placed government officials did not envision the deep restructuring that would ultimately occur. Indeed, the state's ruthlessness in implementing economic restructuring is linked to the debt negotiation process; that process implanted the conviction that no policy option other than economic liberalization was possible.

The successful implementation of economic liberalization in general and privatization in particular entailed increasingly exclusionary and concentrated decision making. Only when decision-making power rested in the hands of a homogeneous superpolitical bureaucratic elite could intrastate resistance to economic restructuring be overcome. In the realm of economic policy, decision-making authority is now monopolized by a homogeneous superelite. The economic policy-making process is now more closed than ever: under President Carlos Salinas, statist political bureaucrats were totally excluded from economic decision-making authority.

A closed decision-making process, that is, one that denied all but the most powerful members of the economic cabinet an opportunity to influence decisions, was particularly important in the success of the privatization program, as resistance from political bureaucrats, from bureaucrats within state firms, and from the trade unions of public companies was enormous. In addition, during the de la Madrid administration, the strength of the presidency and the pervasiveness of neoliberal ideas and their "correctness" discouraged the bureaucratic opponents of privatization from opposing privatization in principle. Opposition was never to the principle of privatization but only to its pace, as bureaucrats did not want to endanger their career interests by being perceived as opposing a policy fully accepted by the president. As privatization got under way, statist political bureaucrats either changed their views or were permanently removed from the picture, allowing the privatization drive to gain rapid momentum.

The traditional mechanisms of corporatist-clientelist control reduced but by no means eliminated labor resistance to public enterprise restructuring and divestiture. Resistance from rank-and-file dissidents and even from *charro* leadership concerned about eroding rank-and-file support made state strong-arm tactics unavoidable. Strikes were intervened and declared illegal, and the military was used to occupy public company premises. *Charro* tactics were used to rout out uncooperative *charro* leaders and implant more cooperative ones. Such tactics were dictated both by the logic of the new economic model, which required a reduction in the cost of labor, and by the requirements of privatization, where generous collective agreements were making public firms unmarketable.

Privatization signaled the definitive hegemony of the finance sector within the state. Divestiture meant the permanent removal of statist bureaucrats and the elimination of the institutions responsible for their socialization into the statist mold. It also permanently weakened SEMIP, the ministry responsible for the greatest number of, and the most important, public firms. Wage restrictions, divestiture, and public enterprise reform also severely undermined the alliance between the leaders of the country's most powerful trade unions, those of the public enterprise sector, and the state and undermined rank-and-file support for union leaders.

The potential negative impact of these policies on state-labor relations was not an important consideration for policy makers. Indeed, the 1988 electoral results came as a shock to the administration. After 1988, however, since it was by then apparent that labor had left the fold, the Salinas administration pursued an explicit hard-line policy against labor in general and against the unions of public firms in particular. There appears to have been a mix of motives behind this policy. Finance sector bureaucrats saw their conflict with these official labor leaders as a power struggle, resented their undue influence over policy, and wanted to ensure that they would be permanently removed from any future influence. Second, Finance Ministry officials' overriding concern with the public deficit predisposed them to view labor privileges as an unnecessary and expendable drain on public resources. Labor union involvement in administrative decisions, such as promotions, state contributions to union companies and various other union projects, and the absence of competitive tendering, were seen as contributing to the inefficiency and high costs of public firms. Moreover, particularly with the Salinas administration, the political bureaucratic elite in charge of economic policy espoused a strong doctrinal commitment to neoliberal ideas and hence to privatization.

Changes in the collective contracts of public enterprises, which have considerably reduced the resources made available to unions, have eroded the power of official labor leaders. The mechanisms by which they can manipulate the rank and file have been diminished by recent contract changes. With the elimination of exclusive access to lucrative government contracts, the loss of their right to distribute benefits to rank-and-file workers, and the loss of the state's financial contribution to various facilities (health clinics, sports facilities), union leaders' capacity to distribute patronage has been seriously eroded. This fact, combined with the inability of unions to defend workers against the erosion of wages, resulted in the emergence of a variety of dissident groups within unions and, in a number of instances, in the rejection of *charro* leaderships.

Public enterprise unions have been instrumental in weakening the worker centrals (the CT and the CTM), the central mechanisms of worker incorporation under traditional corporatist arrangements. They have pushed the CTM toward a position more critical of the government and in so doing have opened the way for state cultivation of opposing centrals, in particular, the CROC. Public enterprise trade unions have formed their own organization, which, although collaborationist, has called for a complete revamping of the CT in view of its failure to protect the interests of public enterprise workers. These developments have signaled the breakdown of the old corporatist-clientelistic arrangements that depended on trade union incorporation into worker centrals and their incorporation, in turn, into the party.

While privatization has removed statist bureaucrats from the policy process and substantially reduced, if not eliminated, the influence of official labor leaders, the new economic model requires that state managers win the confidence of the private sector, particularly big domestic business and transnational corporations. Circumstances and doctrine have reinforced each other in causing political bureaucrats to court the private sector. The state's fiscal crisis and the pressure to reduce the deficit significantly diminished the state's capacity to lead economic growth. In view of the state's fiscal difficulties, Mexico's rulers now felt compelled to rely on the private sector to restore economic growth through investment and to expand export markets. It was therefore necessary to pursue policies that would maintain the confidence of the private sector. This was a formidable challenge, particularly during the early de la Madrid years.

A number of aspects of government policy, such as trade liberalization and a tight money policy, were intensely disliked by the private sector. Acceleration of the privatization program was not only favored by the finance sector and multilateral lending institutions; it was also a policy strongly advocated by the private sector. Indeed, with trade liberalization, the pressure from the private sector for privatization deepened. Trade liberalization, according to the private sector, must be accompanied by privatization, since privatization would lower the private sectors' costs and make it more export competitive. Despite state subsidies, the private sector's disapproval of state intervention, and especially state companies, was sincerely and strongly felt. No doubt, doctrine has heavily supplemented some real disadvantages presented by certain statizing measures, such as the bank nationalization, to account for the intensity of private sector hostility toward state enterprises.

Privatization in combination with other policies geared to stimulate manufacturing export activities has strengthened the country's most powerful financial and industrial conglomerates and their transnational allies. These conglomerates have been the purchasers of the most important public firms, and they have benefited the most from many other aspects of government policy over the last decade. Greater reliance on them as leaders of economic growth means that the government will have to remain sensitive to their policy preferences. Although initiative in policy matters appears at the moment to remain in the hands of the president and his closest advisors, this may well alter in time. At the same time, the potential for disagreement between state managers and the most powerful private sector interests is now considerably less than in the past, given the high degree of doctrinal convergence and the expulsion of statist political bureaucrats from the highest reaches of political power.

Changes in the state's coalitional basis have paralleled alterations in the institutional arrangements of political control. Although there is a continuity with past practices, it is possible to speak of a transition in progress. The transition has been toward a more exclusionary and probably less stable form of authoritarianism. Some of the regime characteristics remain unchanged.

The use of *charrismo* and the threat of charrification as a mechanism to ensure the political docility of trade unions remains an essential trait of the system. The most obvious case is that of the Salinas administration's treatment of the Petroleum Workers' Union, where the *charrazo* was employed to remove an uncooperative *charro* leader and impose a cooperative leadership. And while considerably diminished by fiscal restraint, *charro* leaders are still allowed to enrich themselves and thereby gain a foothold in the system. The cultivation of trade union leaders in economic sectors essential to the government's present economic model is another lingering feature: President Salinas fostered support from the Telephone Workers Union and one of the electrical workers' unions, the SME. Although important reforms of the PRI were attempted, sectoral representation (of workers and peasants) continues to operate. The distribution of patronage, the glue that has kept the traditional authoritarian arrangements together, remains the central feature of the system. In part, it continues to be channeled through traditional party mechanisms. But it was also channeled through the PRONASOL and PROCAMPO programs, which, although much more important than any previous similar program, were not themselves entirely new.[1] Some of PRONASOL's funding came from the privatization of public firms, and it took on a variety of the distributive functions previously carried out by public firms. Finally, electoral fraud, the use of the army, various forms of intimidation, and political assassinations have continued.

But while these continuities are important, the weakening of some of the features of the pre-1982 arrangements has meant the introduction of a number of new elements into the old authoritarian order. These new elements, emerging with the presidency of Carlos Salinas, appeared to have been fairly successful in shoring up regime support following the electoral debacle of 1988.

One of the most politically dangerous aspects of privatization was the potential erosion of legitimacy stemming from the nationalist significance of Mexico's most important public firms. Opposition criticism of government policy as antinational and as a betrayal of the Mexican Revolution was a powerful and effective political weapon of the opposition during the de la Madrid administration. The regime was forced to find ways to defend itself against the loss of legitimacy accruing from charges that privatization had meant the handing over of national patrimony to private, including foreign, interests. The Salinas administration demonstrated considerable political savvy in coming to terms with this dilemma. President Salinas was able to incorporate his neoliberal policy agenda into a discourse that continued the major lines of the PRI's nationalist revolutionary mythology—one of the most important mainstays of PRI rule. Privatization was justified to the public on the grounds of social necessity. By divesting itself of functions that can more effectively be carried out by the private sector, the state would be able to focus on its revolutionary mission: improving living standards for the majority. The evidence of this commitment is the fact that funds from privatization are handed over to PRONASOL.

Even more important, however, was the nature of PRONASOL's clientelist ties. Whereas the clientelism of Mexico's traditional authoritarian arrangements was pyramidal, with patronage distributed at various levels of the state-party and trade union structures, PRONASOL tied local communities directly to the presidency, unmediated by corporatist structures. It is therefore a more segmented arrangement: PRONASOL communities do not come together in a regional or nationwide organization. They are involved in administration, not in influencing the policy process. The heavy concentration of policy-making power in a superpolitical elite, the reduction in the importance of the traditional corporatist structures (particularly in light of the decline in the role of organized labor), and the dispersed and clientelist ties developed by PRONASOL suggest the evolution of a segmented system of authoritarian control. The dismantling of the state has not, therefore, signified greater pluralism, because the weakening of the old corporatist-clientelist instruments of popular control (the trade union, confederation, and party arrangements) has not been accompanied by a diminishment in control by the political bureaucratic elite.

On balance, there is no clear trend toward political liberalization, much less democratization, despite the fact that there have indeed been some changes suggesting a greater tolerance for oppositional activity. Subject to strong criticism both from the opposition and from within its own party, opposition (PAN) victories for a number of governorships have been tolerated for the first time in Mexican history. In fact, what appears to be occurring is a movement toward a form of authoritarian rule that may tolerate a certain degree of popular mobilization at the local level for the purpose of distributing patronage, but is highly exclusionary in formulating and implementing economic policy.

The question of political transition must also address the issue of the stability of these new arrangements. The great strength of the Mexican political system has been its incorporative capacity. Both the party and the state apparatus have had important roles here. State enterprises have provided jobs and lucrative contracts. They have been a source of enrichment both to the private sector and to labor leaders; they have provided clear rewards to subelites willing and able to keep the rank and file in line. They have also provided unions with the patronage mechanism to successfully manipulate the rank and file.

The inadequacy of the PRONASOL model lies in the greater potential for autonomous political action on the part of local communities in the absence of malleable subelites whose job it is to ensure that such a political threat does not materialize. Changes that facilitate grassroots organization, even if the intention is to ultimately limit that organization, may inspire demands for more autonomous forms of political participation. The political difficulties arising from the absence of sufficient mechanisms to co-opt alienated subelites is suggested by the impact of the Democratic Movement—a frustrated counterelite that did not hesitate to challenge the ruling elite. Commitment to fiscal austerity and the dismantling of the state signifies a permanent loss of one of the most important instruments by which subelites were co-opted. At the same time, ideological homogeneity and the intense exclusivity of the current political elite means that political mobilization by excluded groups is practically the only way the system will be forced to open up. By excluding all but the established political currents from the state, Mexico's rulers are leaving alienated subelites no alternative but opposition from outside the state-party system.

Moreover, political liberalization and democratization is contingent on the sustained success of Mexico's new economic model. Mexico's rulers will make a sustained commitment in this direction only when they become convinced that they can maintain political power under the new rules. The success of the current economic model is therefore of paramount importance. Sustained economic growth will demonstrate the correctness of the economic choices made and shore up regime legitimacy. A downturn into economic stagnation, on the other hand, will demonstrate the folly of the leadership and strengthen opposition critics. As Mexico slipped into recession in the second half of 1993, then into economic crisis in 1994, the rebellion in Chiapas and two political assassinations—that of PRI presidential candidate Luis Donaldo Colosio and PRI secretary general José Francisco Ruiz Massieu—have combined to produce a full-scale political crisis.

The economic model itself places important constraints on just how far political liberalization can be allowed to go. That model depends on a compliant and cheap labor force to maintain investor confidence and to achieve export competitiveness. Abandoning the use of force against union activity and instituting union democracy are therefore incompatible with the current economic model. The danger of unleashing pressures that would demand modification or reversal of the current economic model means that popular demands cannot be allowed to drive the PRI agenda. Business confidence, now more critical than ever to economic growth, is contingent on maintaining the neoliberal reforms carried out since the mid-1980s.

Privatization has signified the abandonment of some of the instruments of co-optation and control that were essential to the operation of traditional Mexican authoritarianism. It has also meant a decline in the state's ability to influence the direction of economic change. A homogeneous superpolitical bureaucratic elite, now heavily dependent on an economically powerful business elite, presides over an authoritarian state apparatus that, although it may allow more leeway in the pursuit of the neoliberal policy agenda, is probably inherently less stable than under previous arrangements.

The folly of orchestrating deep structural adjustment by means of a closed and politically isolated policy process is amply demonstrated by the consequence of Mexico's privatization drive. The imposition of privatization has been instrumental in breaking down traditional co-optative arrangements. These old sources of legitimacy have not been replaced by a legitimacy rooted in a popular political consensus that favors the various privatization measures carried out. For the most part, neoliberal measures, particularly privatization, have been imposed in an authoritarian fashion, leaving a legacy of public resentment, now manifest in political unrest and growing political violence. Indeed, the very characteristics of the Mexican political system that made neoliberal economic reforms possible—the ability to concentrate economic decision making while controlling political discontent—may threaten the continued viability of the new economic model as the interests and demands of ignored social groups erode political stability.

Privatization is a global phenomenon: as such, the process in Mexico shares certain commonalities with parallel processes in other countries, especially other Latin American countries. Furthermore, the features of the Mexican case that facilitated the decisive move toward privatization may help to illuminate cases where privatization is seemingly stalled or is taking longer to bring about.

Mexico in Comparative Perspective

Privatization has been a worldwide policy drive with a number of features common to both developed and developing countries. According to one recently published comparative study, privatization programs are linked to the onset of economic crisis, making it necessary to remove what is believed to be structural impediments to efficiency; the exposure of policy leaders to a common policy culture of privatization; and the presence of strong political motives among political leaders, in particular, the desire to reduce the power of labor.[2] All these characteristics were certainly present in the Mexican case.

There are, however, important differences in the privatization experiences of developed and developing countries, and the Mexican case clearly demonstrates those differences. One of the most important of these distinctions is that privatization in developing countries has been formulated and implemented within the broader policy context of heavy foreign indebtedness and structural adjustment, a package that includes a severe cutback in public expenditures, the removal of subsidies, trade liberalization, and wage restraints. Hence, public deficit reduction emerges as a much more important motivating factor for privatization in developing countries. Furthermore, the social repercussions are believed to have been far more severe in developing countries than in developed ones, where (with the exception of Great Britain) the state's social responsibilities remained largely intact.

The expansion of popular capitalism in developed countries through the spread of shareholding by workers in their own and in other privatized firms has blocked the concentration of ownership in a few hands.[3] In developing countries, on the other hand, monopolies and oligopolies are the more likely consequence of privatization. Although systematic studies of economic concentration in Mexico since privatization are not yet available, the evidence suggests that privatization has resulted in a high degree of concentration in some sectors. Economic concentration is likely to occur is developing countries like Mexico because of thin capital markets and because of the relative weakness of the middle strata, which makes the distribution of shares among smallholders difficult.[4] Even in developed countries, incentives have been necessary to encourage the dispersal of shared ownership. But a variety of obstacles block the implementation of such incentives in developing countries. In Chile, for example, despite an official policy of promoting popular capitalism, financial restrictions prevented the expansion of loans to popular capitalists, loans that could have brought about a dispersal of ownership. Moreover, the government may well have feared that the real expansion of popular capitalism would have cut into the revenues from the sale of public enterprises.[5] In Mexico, the notion of popular capitalism never entered the policy discourse, either privately or publicly.

Mexico's privatization drive shares a number of other common features with the phenomenon as it has evolved in other developing countries. It has been, as in other such countries, a response to an economic crisis bred of high indebtedness and the failure of alternatives.[6] Just as the failure of López Portillo's petroleum-led growth model gave credibility to those within the state who had been critical of that model, so the failure of heterodox experiments in Argentina and Brazil gave additional weight to those advocating orthodoxy.

Presidential support for the new policy and the predominance of a cohesive, politically insulated, and dedicated technocratic elite with a narrow coalitional base committed to privatization occurred in Mexico, as in other successful cases of privatization in developing countries.[7] The nature of Mexico's liberalizing technocratic elite was not atypical. The international training of developing-country economists in the graduate departments of universities in the United States and Europe has contributed to the creation of a cadre of technocrats within these countries committed to economic orthodoxy. And, as in Mexico, their views have been strengthened by ongoing links with multilateral lending institutions.[8] The ongoing conflict that occurred in Mexico between neoliberal finance technocrats, involved most directly in negotiations with international financial institutions, and more expansionist-statist bureaucrats, located in ministries such as industry, is not unusual. Such struggles emerge as a common feature of structural adjustment and have occurred also in Jamaica, Sri Lanka, Brazil, and Peru.[9]

The shedding of labor as a coalitional partner and the emergence of a new alliance involving big business has been a common feature of structural adjustment programs in general and privatization in particular. Ezra Suleiman and John Waterbury argue that in most developing countries a new coalition emerged combining the military with big agricultural, industrial, and export interests. This new coalition supports measures to bring about economic efficiency and export competitiveness.[10] This has been the situation in Mexico—without the military. Even the less successful privatization drive in Brazil has been associated with a new state alliance with oligopolistic domestic groups allied with multinational corporations (MNCs).[11] In Argentina, the movement of the Afonsín administration away from heterodoxy toward greater orthodoxy has been associated with the movement of that administration toward a closer alliance with big business, the country's most powerful agribusiness enterprises, and the elite of the most modern manufacturing firms, including some MNCs.[12]

More recently, in Argentina, Carlos Menem's privatization drive has involved intense resistance from elements within the state bureaucracy, especially within state enterprises and from the trade unions of the state firms.[13] The successful implementation of that program has, as in the Mexican case, involved a heavy hand against labor resistance: the right to strike by the public sector was severely restricted, and collective agreements were annulled.[14] In Argentina, as in Mexico, the country's biggest conglomerates have been the purchasers of the most important privatized public companies.[15]

Mexico's prizatization stands out in the Latin American context for its rapidity and depth, particularly given the historically important role of the Mexican state in that country's economy. Privatization, on the other hand, has gone forth haltingly in Brazil, where it has been stalled by fierce political opposition.[16] At the same time, although the Argentine privatization drive did not get under way until after 1990, it has gone forward at least as rapidly as Mexico's— a development that could not have been predicted, given the historical strength and independence of trade unions in that country.

Differences in the international pressures faced by each of these countries help explain these divergencies. The severity of Mexico's 1982 and 1985–1986 economic crises undoubtedly increased the leverage of orthodox hard-liners within the state and drove many who were wavering into orthodoxy. On the other hand, Brazil's greater resistance to economic orthodoxy may be related to its greater degree of maneuverability in relation to the IMF and the World Bank.[17] More important, however, has been the interaction of this international context with domestic economic and political circumstances. Certain domestic factors have been viewed as important in explaining the differences in the stabilization and structural adjustment policies pursued by Mexico, Brazil, and Argentina. These factors also account for the differences in their experiences with privatization.

The Nature of the Political System

As suggested in chapter 1, "new" democratic regimes, such as Argentina under Raúl Alfonsín and Brazil under José Sarney, are highly subject to popular pressures due to the sudden appearance of previously repressed demands. Pressure from trade unions and the fear of their newly elected governments of exacerbating social tensions and thereby possibly raising the specter of renewed military intervention may be important in accounting for the reluctance of such regimes to move decisively forward with such politically unpopular policies as privatization. This situation, in combination with the technical capacities of their bureaucracies and their substantial international reserves at the time, is the explanation usually given for the Argentine and Brazilian attempts at heterodox adjustment in 1985–1986.[18] But this does not explain why Argentina was able to privatize more rapidly than Brazil in subsequent years.

Stephan Haggard and Robert Kaufman, writing on the ability of developing countries to implement stabilization programs, link success to the insulation of the policy elite from social pressures, particularly from trade union pressure.[19] Since public enterprises are closely tied with redistributive mechanisms for the working class, their observations may be useful here. Haggard and Kaufman argue that countries with fragmented party systems are those least likely to successfully implement stabilization, while institutionalized two-party systems are more likely, and monist (single-party) systems most likely, to be successful, because they provide the least political space for organized groups such as trade unions while giving technocratic elites the greatest degree of autonomy in policy. Mexico's corporatist-clientelist system allowed technocratic elites to ride roughshod over labor resistance to privatization. Only in those rare occasions in which constitutional amendments were required were such matters presented to the congress—bureaucratic manipulation was used to get around restrictions on privatizations in such areas as basic petrochemicals.

By mid-1991, Argentina was consolidating as a two-party political system, the mid-term elections having given Menem's Justicialist Party control of the Chamber of Deputies—a fact that may be helpful in understanding the recent success of the Argentine privatization drive. While opposition within the congress presented some difficulties for Menem's privatization program, he was able to secure legislation allowing him to privatize through presidential decree; and with a majority in the congress, he was able to force through the necessary constitutional amendments. Brazil, on the other hand, during the same period, continued to have a fragmented party system, with the president dependent on a coalition of political parties within the congress. The Brazilian president was extremely vulnerable politically. He could not allow counterelites the opportunity to mobilize alienated groups; he was forced to compromise on policy goals, and in such a tenuous political situation, he was reluctant to dispense with essential patronage tools such as public enterprises. Furthermore, in 1993 the congress amended recent economic policy legislation, allowing itself the right to veto any sale of state enterprise for up to sixty days after the divestment resolution is published.[20]

The Technocratic Elite

The greater relative strength of Mexico's technocratic elite compared with its counterparts in Brazil and in Argentina until recently may help explain its earlier privatization drive. As argued earlier, Mexico's neoliberal technocrats have been a historically powerful and cohesive group. Their neoliberal predisposition has been reinforced by ongoing contacts with the country's most powerful bankers and with historically close and ongoing relations with international financial institutions. Presidential support is believed to be essential to a successful privatization program.[21] In Mexico, the president arose from this group and led the privatization drive himself. In Argentina and Brazil, on the other hand, such technocratic groups have been weaker. A similar neoliberal group was purged from the Argentine Central Bank (Banco Central de la República Argentina) during the Peronist era, while Brazil has not had an integrated central bank mechanism.[22] The Brazilian technocrats supporting privatization are found in that country's industrial development bank, BNDES, not at the senior levels of any ministry. With only lukewarm support from Brazil's post-military-era presidents, they have not, until recently, been able to enforce their policy preferences. In stark contrast to the Mexican case, ideological opponents of privatization in Brazil continued to exist in the upper reaches of the state bureaucracy, including the cabinet.[23] On the other hand, privatization got rapidly under way once President Carlos Menem became committed to it and once he assembled a neoorthodox policy team in the Economic Ministry.[24]

Relations with the Labor Movement

Available evidence suggests that regimes whose coalitions include labor and that have established ties with the labor movement are more likely to successfully institute structural adjustment than regimes lacking such ties.[25] According to Jennifer McCoy, a party-dominated labor movement "facilitates the capacity of the state to impose austerity without risking severe social disruption"; such an arrangement provides for symbolic participation in the decision-making process.[26] In the Mexican case, state leverage over the major worker centrals and the corrupt *charro*-led public enterprise trade unions were instrumental in the imposition of public enterprise reform and privatization. Similarly, Justicialist Party leaders were in a better position to persuade trade union leaders than the previous Alfonsín administration, which experienced extremely disruptive labor unrest. Brazilian presidents, on the other hand, lacked this sort of leverage, facing strong and successful resistance to privatization from the labor movement. Major court challenges and successful demonstrations by the labor movement, combined with the government's lack of commitment to privatization, resulted in its backing down on a number of planned privatizations.

Support from Veto Groups

Strong support from the private sector was important in propelling the Mexican privatization drive forward. In the Brazilian case, on the other hand, the private sector may well be less enthusiastic about this policy option, while opposition may also be present from another veto group not present in the Mexican case, the military. The private sector in Brazil, for example, has not been supportive of stabilization, and it opposed President General Figueiredo's attempt to move toward greater economic orthodoxy.[27] There are also indications that military opposition to privatization has been cultivated by the government's opponents.[28] While elements within the Argentine military have also resisted privatization,[29] the statist strain has been relatively weaker, and the influence of the Argentine military has been diminished by the Falkland Islands fiasco.

The case study of Mexico presented here and the cursory comparative discussion in the preceding paragraphs point to disturbing features of the privatization decision-making process, which may not augur well for democratization. The process of privatization has involved a closed and exclusionary decision making by an ideologically homogeneous technocratic elite. Even in political systems that are procedurally democratic, the decision-making process is a closed technocratic one, involving strong-arm tactics against organized labor. Popular capitalism has not been an important feature of this process, as it has been in the developed nations, raising the likelihood of a heavy concentration of assets in the hands of a few conglomerates and their transnational allies. These private sector elites acquire access to the highest reaches of political power. While the process by which privatization has been achieved must be distinguished from its long-term consequences, an examination of that process suggests that the path toward political liberalization and democratization is now more arduous.

Appendix

—

Notes

—

References

—

Index

Appendix

Mexico's Economic Elite

Major Shareholders in Financial Holding Companies, Interlocking Directorships in Banks, Investment Houses, and Major Companies

Alemán Velasco, E.
Investment House: Casa de Bolsa Inverlat
Other Major Companies: AEROMEXICO, Corporación Industrial San Luis, Seguros América, Grupo Industrial Minera México

Aranguren Castiello, I.
Financial Holding Company: Grupo Financiero SERFIN
Banks: BANCOMER, SERFIN
Investment House: Acciones Bursátiles, Operadora de Bolsa
Other Major Companies: Unión Carbide, Seguros América, and others

Bailleres, A.
Financial Holding Company: Grupo Financiero Monterrey
Banks: BANCOMER, COMERMEX
Investment House: Casa de Bolsa Cremi
Other Major Companies: DESC, Peñoles, Palacio de Hierro, and others

Ballesteros, C.
Financial Holding Company: Grupo Financiero SERFIN
Bank: COMERMEX
Investment Houses: Casa de Bolsa Inverlat, Operadora de Bolsa
Other Major Companies: DESC, Corporación Industrial San Luis, Kimberly Clark, Hoteles Hyatt, and others

Garza Lagüera, E.
Financial Holding Company: Grupo Financiero Monterrey
Bank: BANCOMER
Investment Houses: Acciones Bursátiles, Casa de Bolsa Probursa

Other Major Companies: ALFA, CYDSA, VIRTO, VISA, VAMSA, FOMEX, and others

Garza Sada, B.

Financial Holding Company: Grupo Financiero SERFIN
Banks: BANAMEX, SERFIN, COMERMEX
Investment Houses: Casa de Bolsa Inverlat, Operadora de Bolsa
Other Major Companies: ALFA, CYDSA, VIRTO, Seguros América, DESC, and others

Sada Treviño, A.

Financial Holding Company: Grupo Financiero SERFIN
Investment House: Operadora de Bolsa
Other Major Companies: CYDSA, VISA, VITRO

González, C. X.

Financial Holding Company: Grupo Financiero SERFIN
Bank: BANAMEX
Investment House: Operadora de Bolsa
Other Major Companies: Corporación Industrial San Luis, Grupo Industrial Minera México, Sanbornes, Hoteles Hyatt, and others

Harp Helú, A.

Financial Holding Company: Grupo Financiero BANAMEX/Mexival
Bank: BANAMEX

Hernández, R.

Financial Holding Company: Grupo Financiero BANAMEX/Accival

Hernández Pons, E.

Financial Holding Company: Grupo Financiero Monterrey
Bank: BANCOMER
Other Major Companies: Peñoles, Refactorios Mexicanos, and others

Legoretta Chauvet, A. F.

Financial Holding Company: Grupo Financiero Inverlat
Bank: COMERMEX
Investment House: Casa de Bolsa Inverlat
Other Major Companies: ALFA, Corporación Industrial San Luis, DESC, Seguros América, Celanese Mexicana, TELMEX, Hoteles Hyatt, and others

Ortega Larrea, J.

Banks: COMERMEX, SERFIN
Investment House: Casa de Bolsa Inverlat
Other Major Companies: DESC, Seguros América, Grupo Industrial Minera
México, Mexicana de Cananea, Mexicana Cobre, and others

Sada Zambrano, A. M.

Financial Holding Company: Grupo Financiero SERFIN
Investment Houses: Operadora de Bolsa, Casa de Bolsa Abaco
Other Major Companies: ALFA, CYDSA, VITRO, DESC, and others

Slim Helú, C.

Financial Holding Company: Grupo Financiero Inbursa
Banks: SERFIN, COMERMEX, BANAMEX, BANCOMER, SOMEX
Investment House: Inbursa Bursátil
Other Major Companies: TELMEX, Celanese Mexicana, Grupo Frisco, San-
bornes, Grupo Carso, and others

Zambrano, L.

Bank: BANAMEX
Other Major Company: CEMEX

Sources: "Perfil de la Jornada," *La Jornada*, 1–2 April 1991; 5 July 1992, 32;
3 July 1992, 11; *Proceso*, no. 819, 13 July 1992, 6–7, 10; *Mexico and NAFTA
Report*, 23 September 1993, 7.

Notes

Chapter 1. Economic Liberalization and Political Change

1. Cook and Kirkpatrick, "Privatization," 3.

2. While little was accomplished in the area of privatization during the presidency of Raúl Alfonsín, a dramatic shift occurred during the administration of Peronist Carlos Menem. By the end of 1993, the Argentine state had divested itself of most state companies, including those in strategic sectors, such as petroleum, gas, electricity, railways, and steel. Venezuela's program has also involved the divestiture of core state enterprises (Ramamurti, *Privatization*). For a discussion of divestitures and planned divestitures under Argentina's President Menem since 1989, also see Angel Abdala, "Regulation of Newly Privatized Firms."

3. *La Jornada,* 6 April 1992, 3.

4. *El Financiero,* 25 May 1992, 2.

5. Pirages, "Technology, Ecology, and Transformations," 2; Ballance, *International Industry,* 9, table 1.1; 40.

6. Ballance, *International Industry,* 248.

7. Armstrong, Glyn, and Harrison, *Capitalism,* 357.

8. On this, see, Wilkinson, "Trade Liberalization."

9. Discussed in chapter 6.

10. Peet, introduction to *International Capitalism,* 27. Capital flight was also an important factor in debt expansion for Latin American debtors (see Rodríquez F., "Consequences of Capital Flight," 129–44).

11. *Economic liberalization* has been defined as "any policy action which reduces the restrictiveness of [government] controls" (Krueger, "Problems of Liberalization," 15). In practice, this has come to mean the virtual elimination of restrictions on international trade, deregulation, internationalization of the financial sector, privatization, and the elimination of a variety of state regulatory arrangements.

12. Armstrong, Glyn, and Harrison, *Capitalism,* 402.

13. These include Bela Balassa, Jagdish Bhagwati, Anne Krueger, Ronald McKinnon, and Jeffery Sachs.

14. In fact, however, most of the Asian NICs were characterized by highly interventionist state policies. Fajnzylber, "Sobre la impostergable

transformación," 103. Moreover, the distinction drawn between Latin American import-substitution industrialization policies and Southeast Asian export-oriented strategies is unfounded: each region has followed both strategies. Gereffi, "Los nuevos desafíos," 221. For a comparison of the East Asian and Latin American experiences, also see Ellison and Gereffi, "Explaining Strategies."

15. Cook and Kirkpatrick, "Privatization," 14.

16. Barbara Stallings argues that structural adjustment became a major focus of creditor policy with the announcement of the Baker Plan in 1985. Stallings, "International Influence on Economic Policy," 76.

17. Ibid., 265; Mosely, "Privatization," 127, 129.

18. Babai, "World Bank and the IMF," 254, 265–69.

19. Ibid., 265. The IMF does, however, acknowledge that divestiture may increase the public deficit in the future due to measures required to make public enterprises marketable. The IMF, therefore, prefers liquidation to divestiture. Ibid., 267.

20. Ramamurti, *Privatization,* 164–65.

21. Kahler, "External Influence," 95–109.

22. Ibid, 118.

23. Ikenberry, "International Spread of Privatization Policies," 103; Kahler, "Orthodoxy and Its Alternatives," 39.

24. Ikenberry, "International Spread of Privatization Policies," 103.

25. Kahler, "External Influence," 124.

26. Ibid., 126–27.

27. On the pressures exerted by multilateral lending agencies for privatization, see Biersteker, "Logic and Unfulfilled Promise of Privatization."

28. Nelson, introduction to *Economic Crisis and Political Choice,* 7.

29. Chile's first privatization program occurred between 1974 and 1981, its second (reprivatization) program between 1985 and 1989.

30. Friedman, *Capitalism and Freedom,* 7–10. For a full discussion of the political assumptions of neoliberal political economists, see Toye, "Is There a New Political Economy of Development?"; and Grindle, "A New Political Economy," 41–68.

31. For a discussion of the political advantages of privatization, see Biersteker, "Logic and Unfulfilled Promise of Privatization," 204–05; Savas, *Privatization,* 3–4; and Van de Walle, "Privatization in Developing Countries," 606–16.

32. Schneider, "Partly for Sale," 95.

33. Butler, "Changing the Political Dynamics."

34. Indeed, the large transfer payments made to public sector firms to compensate for operational losses has been mainly due to the underpricing policies of such firms, instituted to make cheap industrial inputs available. Anglade and Fortin, "Accumulation, Adjustment, and Autonomy," 261.

35. Commander and Killick, "Privatization in Developing Countries," 100. For a discussion as to why privatization tends to increase income inequality in developing countries, see Biersteker, "Logic and Unfulfilled Promise of Privatization," 209–10.

36. For industrial countries, the share of public enterprises in capital formation actually declined during the period. Figures for Latin America were calculated from Short, "Role of Public Enterprises," 116–22.

37. Anglade and Fortin, "Accumulation, Adjustment, and Autonomy," 257.

38. An example of the former is Hamilton, *Limits of State Autonomy,* and of the latter, Fitzgerald, *State and Economic Development*. For more extensive bibliographical references, see Teichman, *Policymaking in Mexico,* 3–8.

39. Although in its original formulation the term *bureaucratic authoritarian* (O'Donnell, *Modernization and Bureaucratic Authoritarianism*) referred to a statist policy orientation carried out by a technocratic coalition (the two case studies are Brazil, 1964, and Argentina, 1966), the term also came to be used (incorrectly) to describe military regimes with a neoliberal bent, such as the Chilean military regime of Augusto Pinochet. The term has also been used to describe the Mexican case (post-1940) where a "blander" form of bureaucratic authoritarianism is said to be attributable to the prior institution of corporatist controls. Kaufman, "Mexican and Latin American Authoritarianism."

40. Petras, "State Capitalism and the Third World," 5.

41. As observed, for example, by Chalmers, "Politicized State in Latin America," 31.

42. Trebat, *Brazil's State-Owned Enterprises,* 36.

43. Glade, "Privatization in Rent-Seeking Societies," 680; Stallings, "Politics and Economic Crises," 165.

44. Haggard, "Politics of Adjustment," 183. See also Haggard and Kaufman, "State in the Initiation of Market-Orientated Reform," 226.

45. Grindle and Thomas, *Public Choices and Policy Change,* 155.

46. Waterbury, "Management of Long-Haul Economic Reform," 40.

47. Remmer, "Politics of Economic Stabilization"; Haggard, "Politics of Adjustment." Barbara Stallings argues that the harshness of the Chilean program was only possible under a highly repressive military government. Stallings, "Politics and Economic Crises," 165.

48. Haggard and Kaufman, "Economic Adjustment in New Democracies."

49. McCoy, "Venezuela," 205–07.

50. Nelson, introduction to *Economic Crisis and Policy Choice,* 3, 25.

51. Ibid., 24.m

52. Conaghan, Malloy, and Abugattas, "Business and the Boys," 26. On the implementation of the structural adjustment policy in Peru between

1980 and 1985 by means of presidential decree, see Pastor and Wise, "Peruvian Economic Policy," 91.

53. Haggard and Kaufman, "Economic Adjustment in New Democracies," 70–71.

54. Smith, "Heterodox Shocks," 152–53.

55. Kaufman, "Stabilization and Adjustment," 78.

56. On the progress of various privatization programs in Latin America, see Angel Abdala, "Regulation of Newly Privatized Firms"; Saulniers, *Public Enterprise in Peru;* Wernick, "Uneasy Steps"; and Kelly de Escobar, "Venezuela."

57. Wernick, "Uneasy Steps," 70; González Fraga, "Argentine Privatization," 75, 84, 85.

58. The analysis here assumes a distinction between political liberalization, which guarantees certain individual and group freedoms, and democratization, which assumes the presence of a minimum set of procedures allowing for the orderly transfer of power and, theoretically, public participation in the choice of policy. The former generally precedes the latter. See O'Donnell and Schmitter, *Transitions from Authoritarian Rule,* 9. Procedural changes, may, however, obscure the perpetuation of highly centralized policy-making processes.

59. The globalization of production presents an interesting challenge to the issue of the relative autonomy of the state. Not only are Latin American countries faced with the restricted options imposed by indebtedness, but they are also subject to vastly increased bargaining power of MNCs because of their mobility and increased choice of investment sites. See Ross, "Relative Decline of Relative Autonomy," 218; Anglade and Fortin, "State and Capital Accumulation," 14, 25.

60. Hansen, *Politics of Mexican Development,* 83.

61. Purcell, "Decision Making in an Authoritarian Regime."

62. A classic work dealing with the operation of patronage in the Mexican political system is Brandenburg, *Making of Modern Mexico.* See also Handelman, "Unionization, Ideology, and Political Participation." Brandenburg also deals with the evolution of Mexican corporatism, as do most standard works on Mexican political history. Good discussions of the particular nature of Mexican corporatism are found in Reyna and Weinert, *Authoritarianism in Mexico.*

63. Powell, "Peasant Society and Clientelistic Politics," 412–13.

64. On this, see Coleman and Davis, "Preemptive Reform and the Mexican Working Class"; Hellman, *Mexico in Crisis,* 162–68 and Stevens, *Protest and Response in Mexico,* 188–217.

65. Discussed further in chapter 5.

66. See Purcell, "Business-Government Relations in Mexico"; Camp, *Entrepreneurs and Politics,* 172; Story, *Industry, the State, and Public Policy,* 105.

67. Camp, *Making of a Government*, 93–125; "Camarillas in Mexican Politics," 96; Ronfeldt, "Prospects for Elite Cohesion," 435; Maxfield, *Governing Capital*, 12, 118. On achieving a balance of ideological tendencies in the cabinet, see Bailey, *Governing Mexico*, 45; Newell and Rubio F., *Mexico's Dilemma*, 207–08.

68. Purcell and Purcell, "State and Society in Mexico," 194.

69. Numerous studies demonstrate this point. A few examples: Purcell, *Mexican Profit-Sharing Decision;* Grindle, *Bureaucrats, Politicians, and Peasants;* Spalding, "Welfare Policymaking"; Story, *Industry, the State, and Public Policy;* Maxfield, *Governing Capital.*

70. The classic formulation of the notion of "revolutionary family" is found in Brandenburg, *Making of Modern Mexico*, 5–7.

71. Story, *Industry, the State, and Public Policy*, 139.

72. For further elaboration, see Teichman, "The Mexican State and Political Implications."

73. Baer, "Mexico's Second Revolution," 51–53; Rubio, "Economic Reform and Political Change in Mexico," 37–40; Roett, "At the Crossroads," 12; Aguayo Quezada, "Inevitability of Democracy," 123–26; Weintraub and Baer, "Interplay Between Economic and Political Opening," 200.

74. Middlebrook, "Political Liberalization"; Story, *Mexican Ruling Party*, 44–45; Cornelius, Gentleman, and Smith, "Overview of Political Change in Mexico," 15; Smith, "1988 Presidential Succession," 411. For a review of some of the more recent literature, see Morris, "Political Reformism in Mexico."

75. Foweraker, "Popular Movements and the Transformation of the Political System," 111; Meyer, "Democratization of the PRI," 330; Coppedge, "Mexican Democracy," 130. Roderic Camp sees political liberalization as linked to the question of whether the chosen growth model generates greater economic equality. Camp, "Political Liberalization," 38.

76. While the peasant sector has clearly been the most disadvantaged by the statist 1940–1982 economic model, it has been even further alienated by the more recent neoliberal thrust.

Chapter 2. The Evolution of Public Enterprise in Mexico

1. Witker and Eslava, "Aspectos generales," 336.

2. Ayala Espino, *Estado y desarrollo*, 77.

3. Besserar, Novelo, and Sariego, *El sindicalismo minero*, 16, 19. One of the largest investors was Guggenheim-Asarco, which set up a mining enterprise involving mines, foundries, and railways, accounting for 40 percent of the total capital invested in mining in 1910. Ibid., 14.

4. Shabot, *Los orígenes de sindicalismo ferrocarrilero*, 35.

5. Powell, *Mexican Petroleum Industry*, 23. Royal Dutch Shell acquired control of El Aguila in 1919.

6. Manke, *Mexican Oil and Natural Gas,* 17.

7. Pineda Gómez, "Movimiento sindical," 38.

8. Haber, *Industry and Underdevelopment,* 172.

9. Ruiz Dueñas, *Empresa pública,* 117.

10. Seventeen American and European corporations were expropriated, the most important of which were the Royal Dutch Shell Group and Standard Oil of New Jersey, which controlled more than 70 percent of total Mexican oil production.

11. Powell, *Mexican Petroleum Industry,* 26–28.

12. Mining concessions were limited to 100 hectares, and all new plants were required to dedicate 25 percent of their capacity to the production of minerals for small producers. The legislation also provided for the constitution of a national system of mineral reserves (for co-ops and small mineral producers and the state) and for the establishment of the Commission for Mining Development (Comisión de Fomento Minero, or CFM). Its function was to directly exploit mining reserves, to set up metallurgical plants, and to provide technical advice and credit to Mexican mining companies and co-ops. Sariego et al., *El estado y la minería Mexicana,* 151.

13. From a rate of growth of 1.1 percent during 1925–1934 to 7.6 percent between 1934 and 1940. Ayala, Aroche, and Galindo, "El papel del sector público," 159.

14. Blair, "Nacional Financiera," 210; Maxfield, *Governing Capital,* 62.

15. Ayala Espino, *Estado y desarrollo,* 188.

16. Ibid., 194.

17. Ibid., 228, 302–03, 397.

18. Ibid., 193.

19. Maxfield, *Governing Capital,* 10–13, 35, 59.

20. Martínez Nava, *Conflicto estado empresarios,* 88.

21. According to Roger Hansen, "no other Latin American political system has provided more rewards for its industrial, commercial, and agricultural elites." Hansen, *Politics of Mexican Development,* 87.

22. Insofar as the public sector invested in branches that provided key inputs to the private sector and went into areas with less return and greater risk, the state, it has been argued, sustained economic growth. Ayala Espino, *Estado y desarrollo,* 371.

23. Newell and Rubio F., *Mexico's Dilemma,* 83.

24. Amparo Casar and Peres, *El estado empresario en México,* 69.

25. Tamayo, "Las entidades parastatales en México," 266.

26. Blair, "Nacional Financiera," 212.

27. Ayala Espino, *Estado y desarrollo,* 319. Of nearly 1.5 billion dollars in long-term loans obtained with NAFINSA's help between 1942 and 1960, more than four-fifths went to the public sector. Blair, "Nacional Financiera," 229.

28. Blair, "Nacional Financiera," 196.

29. Sariego et al., *El estado y la minería Mexicana,* 159.

30. The new law stipulated that foreign capital could not control more than 49 percent of the shares in the mining industry, with certain strategic minerals, such as uranium, reserved exclusively to the state, while in other sectors national capital could not be less than 60 percent. Ibid., 250.

31. Ayala Espino, *Estado y desarrollo,* 373.

32. At the same time, the government amended article 27 of the constitution, giving the state the exclusive right over the production and administration of electrical energy and thereby empowering it to proceed to full nationalization. Ruiz Dueñas, *Empresa pública,* 117.

33. Ayala Espino, *Estado y desarrollo,* 375–76.

34. On Mexico's social welfare institutions, see Ward, *Welfare Politics in Mexico.*

35. Green, "Mexico's Economic Dependence," 106.

36. Ayala, Aroche, and Galindo, "El papel del sector público," 159.

37. Looney, *Mexico's Economy,* 17.

38. Ayala Espino, *Estado y desarrollo,* 251.

39. Amparo Casar and Peres, *El estado empresario en México,* 47.

40. Tello, *La politica economica en México,* 76.

41. Gribomont and Rimez, "La politica ecónomica," 784.

42. It increased from 7.5 percent of GDP in 1975–1979 to 16.1 percent in 1982–1983. Villarreal, "Las empresas públicas," 12.

43. See Teichman, *Policymaking in Mexico,* 136.

44. *Mexico and Central America Report,* 17 February 1984,

45. Private investment as a percentage of total investment dropped from 56.8 percent in 1975 to 23.6 percent in 1982, while public enterprise investment as a percentage of total investment increased from 36.7 percent to 44.3 percent in the same period. Ayala Espino, *Estado y desarrollo,* 467.

46. Amparo Casar and Peres, *El estado empresario en México,* 45.

47. Carrillo Castro and García Ramírez, *Las empresas públicas en México,* 150.

48. Teichman, *Policymaking in Mexico,* 88.

49. Villarreal, "Las empresas públicas," 39.

50. Indeed, according to a study carried out by Jorge Tamayo, the heavy subsidies provided by PEMEX, CFE, FERTIMEX, and FERRONALES due to their low prices account for their total deficits. Tamayo, "Las entidades parastatales en México," 278. See also Philip, "Public Enterprise in Mexico," 33; and Dávila Mendoza, "La empresa pública," 15.

51. Ayala Espino, *Estado y desarrollo,* 433.

52. Ibid., 427.

53. Tamayo, "Las entidades parastatales en México," 260.

54. Carrillo Castro and García Ramírez, *Las empresas públicas en México,* 156.

55. Ibid., 157.

56. Ibid.

57. Amparo Casar and Peres, *El estado empresario en México,* 52. State enterprise industrial production remained concentrated in eight industrial branches, comprised largely of intermediate goods and petroleum production. Ibid., 47. See also Tamayo, "Las entidades parastatales en México," 264–65.

58. Ayala Espino, *Estado y desarrollo,* 60–61.

59. Salinas de Gortari, *Segundo Informe de Gobierno,* 170.

60. Ibid., 165.

61. Maxfield, *Governing Capital,* 13.

62. PEMEX's board of directors, for example, had six representatives from the federal government appointed by the president and five from the union. Two of the presidential appointees had to be from the Ministry of Finance and two from the then Ministry of National Economy. Powell, *Mexican Petroleum Industry,* 36.

63. Witker, "Relaciones y controles exterior de la empresa pública," 355.

64. Bailey, "Presidency, Bureaucracy, and Administrative Reform in Mexico," 36.

65. Ibid., 41.

66. Carrillo Castro and García Ramírez, *Las empresas públicas en México,* 85.

67. In 1976, the Ministry of Natural Resources became the Ministry of Natural Resources and Industrial Development.

68. On the creation of the SPP, see Bailey, "Presidency, Bureaucracy, and Administrative Reform in Mexico."

69. This split in the revenue collection and expenditure functions is believed to have generated considerable conflict between the Ministry of Finance and the SPP. Bailey, "Presidency, Bureaucracy, and Administrative Reform in Mexico," 50.

70. For an explanation of how and why this occurred, see Teichman, *Policymaking in Mexico.*

71. On the autonomy of PEMEX during the petroleum boom years and the power of its director general to contravene the directives of the secretary of natural resources, see Teichman, *Policymaking in Mexico,* 65–69. Díaz Serrano's power, however, lasted only as long as the viability of his expansionary petroleum-led growth strategy. When petroleum prices began to slide on the international market, Díaz Serrano was forced out of his position as director general. He was later convicted and imprisoned for the misappropriation of government funds while director general of PEMEX.

72. Schafer, *Mexico: Mutual Adjustment Planning,* 69; Benveniste, *Bureaucracy and National Planning,* 60; Bailey, *Governing Mexico,* 76–77.

73. Schmidt, *Deterioration of the Mexican Presidency,* 54. On the clienteles of public enterprises, also see Poitras, "Welfare Bureaucracy and Clientele Politics in Mexico," 23.

74. Greenberg, *Bureaucracy and Development,* 51. Although referring to the Ministry of Agriculture and Hydraulic Resources, Greenberg's comments are equally applicable to public enterprises.

75. Witker, "Relaciones y controles exterior de la empresa pública," 401.

76. This process with regard to the unions is dealt with in the following chapter.

77. Purcell, for example, argues that one of the obstacles to reform during the administration of Luis Echeverría was the fact that "too many *camarillas* include members of the private sector." Purcell and Purcell, "State and Society in Mexico," 220–22. According to Merilee Grindle, the head of CONASUPO's *camarilla* included not only officials of other government agencies but also party officials in the peasant and popular sectors of the PRI (the CNC and the CNOP) and university students without formal ties to either government or party. Grindle, *Bureaucrats, Politicians, and Peasants,* 65.

78. Purcell and Purcell, "State and Society in Mexico."

79. Bailey, *Governing Mexico,* 76–77; Ronfeldt, "Prospects for Elite Cohesion," 439. The findings of this study confirm this point, as discussed further in later chapters.

80. On this, see Camp, "Camarillas in Mexican Politics"; Ronfelt, "Prospects for Elite Cohesion," 444.

81. The issue of institutional loyalties and conflicts is explored further in chapter 4.

Chapter 3. Labor Relations in the Public Enterprises

1. Gómez Tagle, *Insurgencia y democracia,* 24.

2. Ibid., 23.

3. Bizberg, "La crisis del corporativismo Mexicana," 714.

4. Gómez Tagle, *Insurgencia y democracia,* 22.

5. That relationship has not been, however, either as direct or as manipulative as has been the relationship between the state and its non-public-enterprise federal employees, represented by the Federation of Unions of State Workers (Federación de Sindicatos de Trabajadores al Servicio del Estado, or FSTSE), a group whose labor history has lacked the militancy of the public enterprise unions. The FSTSE also provided the state with crucial support and loyalty. The way in which restrictions on public spending has impacted the workers of these unions and the implications for Mexico's political transition is a major study in itself.

6. Basurto, *El proletariado industrial,* 103.

7. Shabot, *Los orígines de sindicalismo ferrocarrilero,* 173.

8. López Aparicio, *El movimiento obrera,* 141.

9. Indeed, it has been suggested that without labor's support it is unlikely that Obregón and Calles would have triumphed. Clark, *Organized Labor in Mexico,* 101.

10. Ibid., 71.

11. By 1946, this ministry had been split into the Ministry of the Economy and the Ministry of Labor and Social Welfare. In 1976, the Economy Ministry lost its responsibility for industry, becoming the Ministry of Commerce.

12. The CROM's influence declined precipitously with the assassination of Obregón in 1928, since it was believed that the CROM was involved in the murder.

13. Either coercion was used to bring unions into the CROM or parallel acquiescent unions were set up. Strikes carried out by non-CROM unions were declared illegal and were often violently repressed.

14. Besserar, Novelo, and Sariego, *El sindicalismo minero,* 26.

15. In 1940, the electrical industry was added; in 1942, electronics; and in 1964, steel, the lamination of iron and steel, petrochemicals, and cement. Bizberg, *Estado y sindicalismo en México,* 105.

16. Basurto, *Cárdenas y el poder sindical,* 13.

17. Ibid., 19.

18. Clark, *Organized Labor in Mexico,* 128.

19. Strikes occurred in the petroleum industry in 1937 and 1939, in the railway industry in 1936, in electricity (Veracruz) in 1935, and in mining, against American Smelting and Refining Company, in 1937. The most important labor conflicts during the period were in railways and petroleum, along with a strike carried out by peasants in the Laguna region. Ashby, *Organized Labor,* 176.

20. Shortly after the railway strike was declared nonexistent, Cárdenas announced his intention to expropriate the interests of the minority shareholders of the railway company. In mining and electricity, on the other hand, the negative U.S. reaction to the petroleum expropriation caused the Cárdenas administration to pledge that the government would not take over activities in these sectors, despite intense worker agitation that it do so. Besserar, Novelo, and Sariego, *El sindicalismo minero,* 37; Gómez Tagle, *Insurgencia y democracia,* 30.

21. Alonso, *El movimiento ferrocarrilero,* 36.

22. Ashby, *Organized Labor,* 73.

23. Middlebrook, "State-Labor Relations in Mexico," 6.

24. The consensus appears to be that Cárdenas courted the support of the popular classes (workers and peasants) in order to consolidate his power but at the same time sought to limit the power and autonomy of their or-

ganizations. The fact that Cárdenas opposed the establishment of a single national organization representing both workers and peasants is seen as evidence of what a threat to the state such combined strength would have posed. In fact, some have seen his as a strategy to limit the autonomy of the workers' movement from the start. See, Camacho, *La clase obrera,* 39.

25. A new national miners' union, El Sindicato Nacional Minero Metalúrgico y Similares de la República Mexicana (National Mining Metallurgical and Similar Activities Union, SNMMSRM) was established in 1934, following the dissolution of the Unión Minera Mexicana.

26. Pineda Gómez, "Movimiento sindical," 72; Besserar, Novelo, and Sariego, *El sindicalismo minero,* 38.

27. Barbosa Cano, "El movimiento petrolero," 68.

28. Bermúdez, *Mexican National Petroleum Industry,* 133; Alonso and López, *El sindicato de trabajadores petroleros,* 74.

29. Barbosa Cano, "El movimiento petrolero," 79.

30. Basurto, *La clase obrera,* vol. 11, 294.

31. La Botz, *Crisis of Mexican Labor,* 85.

32. Ibid., 118–19.

33. Mining at that time was still basically in the hands of American Smelting and Refining Company (ASARCO), American Metal Company, and Anaconda, although, as discussed in the previous chapter, the government had begun to intervene in the mining sector. Unlike the petroleum and railway unions, the National Mining Metallurgical Union grouped together union sections, which neither achieved a single collective agreement nor worked for a single enterprise. This union represented workers in mining, metallurgy, and (increasingly) in steel. The implantation of *charrismo* in the unions of mining and metallurgy in both the public and private sectors established the pattern by which later unions, such as those in the steel sector, would be incorporated into the national union structure.

34. At least three of these unions had connections with an opposition party: the National Railway Workers Union, the SME (electricity), and the National Mining Metallurgical Union have been linked to the Partido Popular. One source suggests that the brutal repression of the miners stemmed from their support for the Partido Popular. Gaítan Riveros, "El movemiento minero," 159.

35. Rivera Flores, "Union General de Obreros y Campesinos de Mexico," 39. While considered progressive during this period, Gómez Zepeda would later become very corrupt. Basurto, *La clase obrera,* vol. 11, 121.

36. Cortés A., "Golpe al movimiento ferrocarrilero," 77.

37. Salazar Segura, "El movimiento sindical petrolera," 208.

38. Cortés A., "Golpe al movimiento ferrocarrilero," 95.

39. For details, see, Basurto, *La clase obrera,* vol. 11, 218.

40. Cortés A., "Golpe al movimiento ferrocarrilero," 93.

41. This occurred as a consequence of the election of a more combative secretary general, following state imposition of a leadership that had resulted in the losses of union gains. Rivera Castro, "Periodizatión del sindicalismo petrolero," 30; Basurto, *La clase obrera,* vol. 11, 187.

42. Basurto, *La clase obrera,* vol. 11, 246. It has, however, been argued that since the opposition delegates were in the minority, they did not have sufficient weight to challenge these illegalities. Besserar, Novelo, and Sariego, *El sindicalismo minero,* 52.

43. Upon their arrival in Mexico City, workers were herded by police into a park near the Zólcalo, where they were attacked with clubs. Gaítan Riveros, "El movimiento minero," 153.

44. Cortés A., "Golpe al movimiento ferrocarrilero," 93.

45. Additional clauses, added between 1958 and 1961, stipulated that when unions form their own companies, PEMEX must give them preference. Pérez Linares, "El Charrismo sindical," 127.

46. Teichman, *Policymaking in Mexico,* 72.

47. Camacho, *La clase obrera,* 61.

48. Members of opposition parties (the Partido Popular, the Communist Party, and the Partido Obrero Campesino de México, or POCM) sat on the railway union's executive.

49. Alonso, *El movimiento ferrocarrilero,* 153.

50. Vallejo was not released until 1971. The workers who were able to return to work had their salaries reduced and lost their seniority. Overall, about ten thousand railway workers lost their jobs in three enterprises. Trejo Delarbre, "Los trabajadores y el gobierno de Adolfo López Mateos," 123.

51. Alonso, *El movimiento ferrocarrilero,* 153.

52. Union insurgency also emerged within the unions of UNAM (Universidad Nacional Autónoma de México), the teachers' union, and some sections within the Petroleum Workers' Union, including temporary workers who sought to establish their own union. Independent worker coalitions established during the period included the Unidad Obrera Independiente and the Frente Aútentico de Trabajo. Camacho, *La clase obrera.*

53. Rodríquez and Mauro Saldána, "El movimiento sindical," 97.

54. The Railway Workers' Movement (Movimiento Sindical Ferrocarrilero, or MSF), constituted within the Railway Workers' Union in 1971, supported veteran dissident leader Demetrio Vallejo in union elections, calling for union democracy.

55. Rodríquez and Mauro Saldána, "El movimiento sindical," 96.

56. Its effectiveness in containing workers' demands is demonstrated by the fact that salaries and benefits were much lower than in private industry. Gómez Tagle, *Insurgencia y democracia,* 211.

57. The FNTICE became the Sindicato de Trabajadores Electristas de la República Mexicana (STERM) in 1959, with the fusion of fifty-two small unions.

58. Particularly the FNTICE is characterized as having had a strong democratic tradition. Sylvia Gómez Tagle takes issue with the commonly accepted view that the SME had a strong democratic tradition, arguing that although the leadership rotates in power, leaders have responded more to group interests than to rank-and-file interests. The clearest exponent of the democratic current, she argues, was found within the FNTICE, later the STERM. Gómez Tagle, *Insurgencia y democracia*, 90, 146. The greater degree of democracy in the private sector unions stemmed from the private sector's unlimited ability to raise electricity rates. Management, therefore, had no reason to promote the corruption of union leaders or promote their adherence to the progovernment union umbrella organizations. Ibid., 96.

59. This struggle affected largely the FNTICE/STERM, since the Mexican Light and Power Company (whose workers were represented by the SME) was not fully nationalized until 1975. Having observed the fate of STERM, the SME steadfastly refused all attempts at amalgamation.

60. Gómez Tagle, *Insurgencia y Democracia*, 204–05.

61. On this see, Minello, *Siderúrgica Lázaro Cárdenas*, 230.

62. Ibid., 233.

63. The CT, in which the CTM was dominant, was created in 1966 to keep rebellious unions depoliticized and under control. Created at the instigation of the government, it marked the successful establishment of a national organization that incorporated the recalcitrant public sector unions.

64. Basurto, *La clase obrera*, vol. 14, 179.

65. For a detailed explanation of the way in which patron clientelism operates to preserve the political status quo and for a review of the classic literature on the topic, see, Gamer, *Developing Nations*, 100–74.

66. There has, as a consequence, been a considerable amount written on the operation of *charrismo* in the Petroleum Workers' Union. See, for example, Alonso and López, *El sindicato de trabajadores petroleros;* Colmenares, "Pemex: Crisis y restructuración."

67. Bizberg, *Estado y sindicalismo en México*, 123.

68. Alonso and López, *El sindicato de trabajadores petroleros*, 52.

69. Sariego et al., *El estado y la minería Mexicana*, 341.

70. Basurto, "El nacionalismo revolucionario," 12.

71. Alonso and López, *El sindicato de trabajadores petroleros*, 247.

72. Bizberg, *Estado y sindicalismo en México*, 141; Sariego et al., *El estado y la minería Mexicana*, 340.

73. La Botz, *Crisis of Mexican Labor*, 149.

74. A partial exception is the National Mining Metallurgical Union, which does not have a single collective agreement.

75. Bizberg, *Estado y sindicalismo en México*, 128.

76. Garza,"La democratización en la sección 147 (Monclova)," 206.

77. Basurto, "El nacionalismo revolucionario," 29.

78. Ibid, 28.

79. In 1977, PEMEX conceded to the union the right to subcontract 40 percent of all drilling contracts. In 1980, this right was extended to the transportation of hydrocarbons, and in 1983, this figure was raised to 50 percent. In 1980, the union and PEMEX signed an extracontractual agreement whereby PEMEX would tolerate the granting of contracts without tender.

80. Pérez Linares, "El Charrismo sindical," 132.

81. Ibid., 176–77.

82. Garza, "La democratización en la sección 147 (Monclova)," 13.

83. Pérez Linares, "Vigencia y formas del charrismo," 135.

84. Grayson, *Mexican Labor Machine,* 51.

85. Ibid.

86. Middlebrook, "State-Labor Relations in Mexico," 8.

Chapter 4. Debt Negotiations and the Triumph of Economic Liberalism

1. The term *political bureaucrat,* first used by Raymond Vernon *(Dilemma of Mexico's Development),* distinguishes cabinet appointees recruited through the public bureaucracy from those recruited through the party (PRI) (politicos). The terms *bureaucracy* and *bureaucrats* are used to refer to public servants in general. Finance sector bureaucrats are those working in the most important ministries dealing with macroeconomic matters: the Ministry of Finance, the Central Bank and the Ministry of Budget and Planning (SPP).

2. Maxfield, *Governing Capital,* 93.

3. Purcell and Purcell, "State and Society in Mexico," 212–13.

4. Story, *Mexican Ruling Party,* 141. See also Purcell, "Business Government Relations in Mexico," 220.

5. Newell and Rubio F., *Mexico's Dilemma,* 208, 223; Teichman, *Policymaking in Mexico,* 87–110; Bailey, *Governing Mexico,* 45, 130–31; Maxfield, *Governing Capital,* 137. This is contrary to Angel Centeno's analysis, which sees power as concentrated in the presidency during the years López Portillo was in power. Angel Centeno, *Democracy Within Reason,* 84–85.

6. Angel Centeno, *Democracy Within Reason,* 45, 56. Angel Centeno refers to this group as Mexico's "new technocratic elite." He argues that its homogenization began with the Alemán years and contends that this process, along with certain institutional changes between 1970 and 1980, in particular the concentration of power in the presidency, accounts for the neoliberal policy thrust of the Salinas years. See especially 55–75.

7. Bennett and Sharpe, "State As Banker and Entrepreneur," 175.

8. Camp, "Camarillas in Mexican Politics," 98–99.

9. Kaufman, *Politics of Debt,* 64.

10. Both Miguel de la Madrid and his successor, Carlos Salinas de Gortari, had served in the Ministry of Budget and Planning during the expan-

sionary López Portillo years, and both had won the confidence of the president through the pursuit of expansionary policies.

11. Of fourteen cabinet secretaries, all but Manuel Bartlett Díaz (secretary of state), Jesús Reyes Heroles (secretary of education), and Sergio García Ramírez (attorney general) came from either the Ministry of Finance or the Central Bank. From the Ministry of Finance: Carlos Salinas de Gortari (SPP), Francisco Rojas (comptroller general), Bernardo Sepúlveda (foreign affairs), Labastida Ochoa (mines and public industries), Ramón Aguirre Velázquez (federal district); from the Central Bank: Silva Herzog (finance), Hector Hernández Cervantes (trade and industrial development), Antonio Enrique Sivignac (tourism), Horacio García Aquilar (agriculture and hyraulic resources), Luis Martínez Villicaña (agrarian reform), and Marcelo Javelly Girard (urban development and ecology). *Proceso,* no. 507 (21 July 1986): 6.

12. The director general level is two steps below ministerial rank. Angel Centeno, *Democracy Within Reason,* 138.

13. The changeover in state personnel at the beginning of each *sexenio* has been a persistent feature of the Mexican public bureaucracy. What changed with de la Madrid, according to a number of key informants, was the clearing out of well-known statists and the appointment of those known to share the president's views.

14. Before, cabinet secretaries and directors of public enterprises could bypass the SPP and seek government approval for expenditures beyond the original budget allocation. This was one of the most important sources of government overspending and was especially prevalent within public companies.

15. All senior-level officials willing to discuss this point in interviews stressed the policy predominance of these two ministries.

16. Most of those government officials interviewed felt that the predominance of the Ministry of Finance was largely a function of the personalities occupying these secretaries, the secretary of finance being the stronger personality with more support from the president.

17. Interviews. *Mexico and NAFTA Report,* 12 May 1994, 4. It is generally believed that this position was created especially for Córdoba, since the Mexican constitution barred him from the post of secretary of state because he had not been born in Mexico.

18. This was the characterization of the process given by virtually all middle- and senior-level officials interviewed, although middle-level bureaucrats said that they had no direct knowledge of how the process worked—this was just their impression.

19. He was replaced by the former secretary of the SPP and secretary of education, Ernesto Zedillo.

20. The Salinas cabinet is also notable for the almost total disappearance of politicos, people linked to mass mobilization in one of the three PRI sectors. See Angel Centeno and Maxfield, "Marriage of Finance and Order," 71.

21. Miguel Mancera (central bank), Jaime Serra Puche (trade and industry), and Ernesto Zedillo (SPP) all have graduate degrees from Yale. Pedro Aspe (finance) has a doctorate from MIT, while Salinas has a Ph.D. from Harvard.

22. Salinas, for example, appointed Fernando Gutiérrez Barrios, a member of the PRI old guard, as secretary of state (governación). He also kept on Manuel Bartlett Díaz as secretary of education, Jorge de la Vega Domínquez as agriculture secretary, and Hank González as secretary of tourism. The secretary of labor's role is discussed further in chapter 6.

23. David Ibarra Muñoz, secretary of finance during the administration of López Portillo (1977–1982), was critical of the government's ambitious spending program and was eventually forced to resign, due to his desire for greater restraint.

24. See Teichman, *Policymaking in Mexico*, 98.

25. Interview, senior-level finance official.

26. Aspe and Cordoba, "Stabilization Policies."

27. The threat of dismissal is believed to have been extremely effective in winning over many public servants to the new economic policy direction. According to one middle-level informant, most either came to terms with the new reality or were replaced.

28. Carvaunis, *Foriegn Debt/National Development Conflict*, 31; "Carta de intención del gobierno al FMI," 29. These latter reforms were at the insistence of the IMF. See *Quarterly Economic Review of Mexico*, no. 1 (1983): 8.

29. "Carta de intención al Fondo Monetario Internacional," *El Trimestre Económico* (1983), 1128.

30. Mexico, *Plan Nacional de Desarrollo*, 133, 145. Strategic areas included mail, telegraph, radio-telegraph, communications via satellite, issuance of money from a single bank, petroleum and other hydrocarbons, basic petrochemicals, radioactive minerals, generation of nuclear energy, electricity, railways, and "activities specifically designated by laws passed by the Congress of the Union." "Reformas constitucionales," 164–65.

31. This was possible because of the usual absence of pressure to increase government spending typical of all administrations during their first two years. Teichman, *Policymaking in Mexico*, 91.

32. In 1984, for example, CONASUPO's responsibilities were expanded with a new food program providing discounts of 25 to 50 percent on basic food items in its stores, while 100 new stores were opened in the federal district. *Quarterly Economic Review of Mexico*, no. 3 (1984): 35; *Mexico Update*, 15 August 1984, 11 (21): 10.

33. BANAMEX, *Examen de la situación económica*, August 1987, 290, 339.

34. *Globe and Mail*, 1 October 1983, sec. 1B, 5.

35. Purcell and Purcell, "State and Society in Mexico," 26; Bailey, *Governing Mexico*, 130–31. More will be said about the reaction of the private sector in the following chapter.

36. "Informe anual de labores de la Secofi," 1033–35.

37. *Proceso*, no. 474 (2 December 1985): 20.

38. Story, *Industry, the State, and Public Policy*, 144.

39. Compare Angel Centeno, *Democracy Within Reason*, 26.

40. According to senior government officials interviewed, there was no alternative but to, in the words of one official, "take the required medicine."

41. *Quarterly Economic Review of Mexico*, no. 3 (1983): 9; no. 1 (1986): 9; BANAMEX, *Examen de la situación económica*, March 1986, 116.

42. Green, *La deuda externa de México*, 151–52.

43. *Quarterly Economic Review of Mexico*, no. 4 (1985): 16. The postponement, later agreed to by the banks, was for six months and was later extended.

44. "Carta de intención del Gobierno de México," *Mercado de Valores* (1985).

45. Brailovsky, Clarke, and Warman, *La política económica*, 25; Cypher, *State and Capital Accumulation in Mexico*, 181.

46. The initial cutback involved the elimination of fifteen undersecretaries of state and fifty auditors general. *Latin American Weekly Report*, 2 April 1985, 10; 2 August 1985, 10.

47. *Quarterly Economic Review of Mexico*, no. 2 (1985): 17; no. 2 (1986): 10; no. 3 (1986): 11; *Financial Times*, 25 April 1986, 5.

48. *New York Times*, 18 June 1986, 29.

49. *Quarterly Economic Review of Mexico*, no. 3 (1986): 6; *Latin American Weekly Report*, 13 June 1986, 4.

50. *Economist*, 21 June 1986, 79; *Latin American Weekly Report*, 26 June 1986, 4. *Globe and Mail*, 9 June 1986, B15. *Latin American Weekly Report*, 26 June 1986, 4.

51. *Economist*, 14 June 1986, 74; *Proceso*, no. 503 (23 June 1986): 10.

52. *Globe and Mail*, 9 June 1986, B15; *Economist*, 14 June 1986, 11.

53. *Quarterly Economic Review of Mexico*, no. 2 (1986): 15.

54. *Quarterly Economic Review of Mexico*, no. 3 (1986): 7; *Wall Street Journal*, 6 October 1986, 32; 23 June 1986, 32.

55. For the terms of this agreement, see, *Quarterly Economic Review of Mexico*, no. 3 (1986): 7; "Carta de intención del gobierno de México al FMI," *Mercado de Valores* (1986), 751; *Mexico and Central America Report*, 17 July 1986, 1; *Wall Street Journal*, 15 July 1986, 26.

56. *Economist*, 26 July 1986, 73; *Mexico and Central America Report*, 30 October 1986, 1.

57. Solís advised that Mexico break with the IMF if it would not alter its negotiating stance. *Proceso*, no. 500 (2 June 1986): 8.

58. *Economist,* 21 June 1986, 79; *Proceso,* no. 487 (3 March 1986): 9; "La deuda externa," 38.

59. Two senior-level officials interviewed suggested that Silva Herzog was less supportive of economic liberalization than Salinas.

60. *Latin American Weekly Report,* 15 October 1987, 4.

61. Petroleum prices fell from about $16.00 per barrel in 1987 to less than $10.00 per barrel by late 1988. Difficulty in obtaining agreement from the private banking sector meant that Mexico went for two years without any new loans from international banks. U.S. Embassy, *Economic Trends Report,* May 1989, 4; *Latin American Weekly Report,* 20 August 1987, 3.

62. *Latin American Weekly Report,* 28 May 1987, 8.

63. Ibid.

64. Loans were made available to exporters for the importation of inputs, the modernization of productive plant, commercial missions, and the acquisition of training and technical advice. These loans were provided by BANCOMEXT (Banco Nacional de Comercio Exterior). "El Financiamiento," 244. By 1988, BANCOMEXT was providing 80 percent of the credits to stimulate exports through its various programs. Ibid., 727.

65. *Comercio Exterior* 38 (9): 781–82.

66. This "strategy" is inferred from the results of the negotiation process. Those political bureaucrats involved in negotiations with the IMF were very closed about the process and sensitive to any suggestion that their economic policies were not entirely their own. They claimed that they only agreed to policies they wanted to implement anyway. On the other hand, senior- and middle-level bureaucrats in SEMIP and SECOFI, marginalized from the debt negotiation process, were convinced of the IMF's enormous influence in the drive toward economic liberalization.

67. Interviews, senior-level finance officials.

68. Indeed, even if some officials were opposed to the policy itself, they would not have felt free to say so. To be heard by the president it was necessary to present any opposition as opposition to the pace of economic restructuring.

69. Carsten Etenroth and Gándara, "El plan Brady," 302.

70. Ramamurti, *Privatization,* 165.

71. The political fallout of the government's economic program is discussed at length in chapter 7.

72. Carlos Salinas de Gortari, "Discurso de toma de posesión," 1140; *Latin American Weekly Report,* 19 July 1989, 10.

73. *Proceso,* no. 644 (6 March 1989): 6.

74. "Convenio del gobierno de México con el Fundo Monetario Internacional" (documento), 255–59, 359.

75. *Mexico and Central America Report,* 8 June 1989, 5; *El Mercado de Valores* 49, no. 3 (1 July 1989): 35.

76. Further reduction of tariffs, reduction in the regulation of the financial sector, and the reduction or elimination of food subsidies continued to be major concerns. *Latin America Weekly Report,* 30 March 1989, 7. *Proceso,* no. 730 (29 October 1990): 6.

77. The results were the following: 49 percent of the external debt would benefit from a reduction in interest rates, 41 percent would have the principal reduced, and a small group of banks chose to lend new money, affecting 10 percent of the debt. *Latin American Weekly Report,* 25 January 1990, 4. This account of the negotiations is taken from, *Latin American Weekly Report,* 16 February 1990, 12; 15 March 1990, 12; 8 June 1990, 7; 22 June 1989, 6–7.

78. Salinas's Pact for Stability and Economic Growth (Pacto para la Estabilidad y el Crecimiento Económico, or PECE) replaced de la Madrid's pact (Pacto de Solidaridad Económica) and, like his predecessor's, was renewed every three to eight months. Salinas so much as admitted the importance of convincing creditors of Mexico's commitment to restructuring when he said that the renewal of the pact, signed by the state, business, peasants, and labor in June of 1989, would give Mexico a "strengthened negotiating position" in debt negotiations. *Proceso,* no. 660 (26 June 1989): 36.

79. At this point, foreign investment continued to be limited to minority ownership in mining (34–40 percent, except for oil, gas, and uranium, which continued to be reserved exclusively to the state), petrochemicals, autoparts, and telecommunications (except telegraph). Foreign investment could reach 100 percent if the project investment was less than US$100 million, the project was financed from foreign sources, and the project would generate permanent employment, be established outside of Mexico's major industrial centers, use adequate technology, and observe environmental regulations. "Política Actual en Materia de Inversión Extranjera," 22–24.

80. Mexico, *Legal Framework,* 46. With the 1993 Foreign Investment Law, the 40 percent foreign ownership limitation on secondary petrochemicals was removed, as was the 49 percent restriction on mining, while foreign investment on auto parts was allowed to reach 49 percent, instead of being limited to 40 percent.

81. Aspe Armella, "Nuevos créditos," 389.

82. Mexico received numerous warnings regarding the negative impact of its current account deficit, from the OECD, from the Clinton administration and from the IMF. *Mexico and NAFTA Report,* 21 July 1994, 6; *New York Times,* 2 January 1995, 10, and 24 January 1995, 3.

83. *Latin American Weekly Report,* 22 December 1994, 578.

84. *Mexico NAFTA Report,* 19 January 1995, 7.

85. *New York Times,* 2 January 1995, 14; *Latin American Weekly Report,* 22 December 1994, 591; *Mexico NAFTA Report,* 20 October 1994, 4.

86. Another reason frequently cited for Mexico's failure to devaluate

earlier was Salinas's attempt to head up the new World Trade Organization—devaluation would have signaled to the world that there were serious problems in Mexico's economic management. *New York Times*, 24 January 1994, 12.

87. *Mexico NAFTA Report*, 23 February 1995, 1; *Washington Post*, 1 January 1995, 12.

88. In 1994, two banks in financial difficulties had already been taken over by the state.

89. *Latin American Weekly Report*, 9 February 1995, 51.

90. *Latin American Weekly Report*, 26 January 1995, 26; *Miami Herald*, 11 January 1995, 17.

91. *Latin American Weekly Report*, 19 January 1995, 19.

92. *Mexico NAFTA Report*, 23 February 1995, 2.

93. *Mexico NAFTA Report*, 30 March 1995, 2.

94. *Mexico and NAFTA Report*, 23 February 1995, 2.

95. *Latin American Weekly Report*, 23 March 1995, 122.

96. Ibid.; *Latin American Weekly Report*, 30 March 1995, 134.

97. Compare Angel Centeno, *Democracy Within Reason,* 39–41, 152–71.

Chapter 5. Power and Public Enterprise Reform

1. The classic discussion is found in Poulantzas, ''Problem of the Capitalist State.''

2. Examples include Hamilton, *Limits of State Autonomy,* 25, 63; and Aquilar Mora, *El Bonapartismo Mexicano,* 35. While the structuralist argument concerning the constraints on policy by the capitalist context is convincing, I have argued that presumptions about the long-term implications of state actions are questionable. See Teichman, ''Mexican State and Political Implications of Economic Resructuting,'' for a discussion of this issue for the de la Madrid years.

3. Brandenburg, *Making of Modern Mexico;* Reyes Esparza et al., *La burguesía Mexicana;* Cockcroft, *Mexico: Class Formation, Capital Accumulation, and the State.*

4. A few examples are Purcell, *Mexican Profit-Sharing Decision;* Grindle, *Bureaucrats, Politicians, and Peasants;* Story, *Industry, the State, and Public Policy;* Maxfield, *Governing Capital;* Whiting, *Political Economy of Foreign Investment.*

5. See, for example, Vernon, *Dilemma of Mexico's Development*; and Purcell, ''Business-Government Relations in Mexico.''

6. Purcell and Purcell, ''Mexican Business and Public Policy,'' 221.

7. Camp, *Entrepreneurs and Politics;* Story, *Industry, the State, and Public Policy,* 146.

8. The existence of this group was first observed by Mosk, *Industrial Revolution in Mexico,* 22. A split within CANACINTRA produced the Asociación Nacional de la Industrial de Transformación (ANIT).

9. Haber, *Industry and Underdevelopment,* 84–102.

10. Saragoza, *Monterrey Elite,* 116, 143, 151.

11. Ibid, 11.

12. Carrillo Arronte, "Role of the State," 53.

13. Camp, *Entrepreneurs and Politics,* 171.

14. Saldívar, *Ideología y política,* 175; Basáñez, *La lucha por la hegemonia en México,* 114.

15. Hernández Guttierrez, "La burguesía comercial nativa," 190–91.

16. The National Confederation of Industrial Chambers (Confederación Nacional de Cámaras Industriales) and the Confederation of Chambers of Commerce (Confederación Nacional de Cámaras de Comercio). Cockcroft, *Mexico: Class Formation, Capital Accumulation, and the State,* 208; Puga E., "Los empresarios y la política en México," 192. Although CANACINTRA, CONCAMIN, and CONCANACO were established under official auspices, they gradually became independent.

17. Perhaps as a consequence of the influx of foreign firms into CANACINTRA. See Story, "Industrial Elites in Mexico," 362; and Cockcroft, *Mexico: Class Formation, Capital Accumulation, and the State,* 210.

18. Story, "Industrial Elites in Mexico," 362.

19. William Glade notes the growing hostility of the private sector toward the state in many developing countries by the 1970s. Glade, "Privatization and Denationalization," 89–90.

20. Cypher, *State and Capital Accumulation in Mexico,* 142.

21. The government argued that the plant would produce for a market not provided for by the private sector: the biscuits were for popular consumption. *Unomásuno,* 22 March 1985, 12.

22. Escobar Toledo, "Rifts in the Mexican Power Elite," 73.

23. Maxfield, "Introduction," *Government and Private Sector,* 2.

24. Escobar Toledo, "Rifts in the Mexican Power Elite," 75.

25. Luna, Tirado, and Valdés, "Businessmen and Politics in Mexico," 18.

26. *Proceso,* no. 322 (3 January 1983): 29.

27. *Proceso,* no. 397 (11 June 1984): 31.

28. *Proceso,* no. 385 (14 March 1984): 41; no. 397 (11 June 1984).

29. Garavito, Montes de Oca, and Rodríquez, "Pronafice, más que programa, un pacto," 13, 14.

30. Bravo Mena, "Coparmex and Mexican Politics," 102.

31. Ibid., 6; Story, "The PAN, the Private Sector, and the Future of Mexican Opposition," 261.

32. Maxfield, "Introduction," *Government and Private Sector,* 11. *Proceso,* no. 430 (28 January 1985): 28.

33. *Proceso,* no. 430 (28 January 1985): 28; no. 472 (18 November 1985): 16; *Mexico and Central America Report,* 29 December, 1985, 2. As a consequence, the board of directors of the conglomerate VITRO passed a regulation prohibiting officials in the top three levels of management from par-

ticipation in politics. The ruling produced at least one resignation—that of Rogelio Sada Zambrano, a director of VITRO and PAN activist, who said that the regulation infringed upon his freedom of expression and protested the growing authoritarianism of the government. In 1991, he ran as the PAN candidate for the governorship of Nuevo León. *Proceso*, no. 474 (2 December 1985): 6.

34. *Proceso*, no. 401 (2 July 1984): 26; "Lo que se dijo en Excelsior," 10.

35. Mizrahi, "Rebels Without a Cause?" 5.

36. Ibid. The political activities of the private sector will be explored further in chapter 7.

37. *Proceso*, no. 482 (27 January 1986): 14.

38. Due to the fact that the extensiveness of such state intervention caused a great deal of uncertainty. Vargas Velázquez, Martínez Oregón, and de la Torre Punzo, "La agonia Mexicana," 19.

39. *Mexico and Central America Report*, 14 February 1986, 2; *Proceso*, no. 482 (27 January 1986): 14.

40. Camp, *Entrepreneurs and Politics*, 243.

41. *Quarterly Economic Review of Mexico*, no. 3 (1984): 11.

42. *Quarterly Economic Review of Mexico*, no. 1 (1986): 16; *Proceso*, no. 481 (20 January 1986): 11.

43. *El Financiero*, 10 March 1987, 31. A report produced by CANACINTRA said that approximately two hundred enterprises producing capital goods (about half the enterprises in the metallurgical sector) had gone bankrupt due to a combination of the contraction of the domestic market and the commercial opening. Textile firms in Nuevo León were reportedly hard hit by the commercial opening. *Proceso*, no. 602 (6 May 1988): 22.

44. *El Sol de México*, 23 February 1988, 1B.

45. *Heraldo*, 24 June 1989, 1; see also Luna, "La derecha empresarial," 73.

46. Fundamental alteration in the 1970 Ley de Trabajo (Labor Code) has been one of the major demands of business. Business demanded a fifteen-day limit on strikes followed by obligatory arbitration, a reduction in vacation time, greater flexibility in instituting layoffs, and the abolition of the forty-hour work week. *Proceso*, no. 602 (6 May 1988): 26. Business wanted labor legislation "deregulated" and "rigidities" in collective agreements removed. *La Jornada*, 15 January 1990, 1. These public pronouncements were echoed in interviews.

47. See *Proceso*, no. 580 (14 December 1987): 9.

48. *Proceso*, no. 592 (7 March 1988): 33.

49. *Mexico and Central America Report*, 20 September 1985, 5.

50. *Proceso*, no. 580 (14 December 1987): 9.

51. *Unomásuno*, 27 January 1989, 17; *La Jornada*, 27 October 1991, 21; *Unomásuno*, 13 January 1989, 16.

52. *Excelsior*, 27 September 1989, 1E.

53. These, in turn, assemble their own loyal subordinates. See Grindle, *Bureaucrats, Politicians, and Peasants,* 55–70.

54. This was the case even when it was headed by fiscal conservative Miguel de la Madrid. Teichman, *Policymaking in Mexico,* 97. The apparent reversal from spenders to fiscal conservatives of both de la Madrid and Salinas, who also served in the SPP, was explained by one senior-level finance official in terms of what he described as the "chameleon nature" of Mexican policymakers: "Mexican political leaders change their positions quickly and frequently in accordance with circumstances . . . that is, in accordance with their understanding of presidential objectives." Each did what was necessary to curry presidential favor (under López Portillo, this entailed the pursuit of an expansionary policy); the results in terms of the advancement of their careers speak for themselves.

55. Both middle- and senior-level finance sector bureaucrats interviewed suggested that Salinas had been particularly ruthless in routing out bureaucrats not entirely dedicated to the objectives of neoliberalism. All of the SPP officials interviewed for this book were recent finance ministry recruits.

56. The sympathy of finance officials for Mexico's financial conglomerates was apparent with the 1982 bank nationalization, a decision from which they were completely marginalized and to which they were strongly opposed. Teichman, *Policymaking in Mexico,* 137.

57. The Mexican Bankers' Association is the private sector group with the largest proportion of enterpreneurs who have held public office. Camp, *Entrepreneurs and Politics,* 83.

58. According to most officials interviewed.

59. "Nuevas disposiciones," 538.

60. Excluded from this legislation were public firms forming part of the financial system and firms governed by their own specific legislation, such as the Mexican Institute of Social Security (Instituto Mexicana de Seguridad Social, or IMSS), indicative of the fact that this reorganizational thrust reflected the financial sector's primary objective of exercising control over other ministries of state, particularly SEMIP.

61. "Ley federal de las entidades parastatales."

62. Secretaría de Controlaría General de la Federación, *Restructuración del sector parastatal,* 62–63, 98.

63. Ibid., 107.

64. SEMIP, *Informes de labores* (1985–1986), 32.

65. Grayson, *Mexican Labor Machine,* 57.

66. *Proceso,* no. 571 (12 October 1987): 8; *Latin American Weekly Report,* 23 April 1987, 11; *Proceso,* no. 551 (25 May 1987): 6–8.

67. Cited in Bensusan, "Instituciones en crisis," 50.

68. In 1986, layoffs as a consequence of reorganization and plant closures were estimated at seventeen thousand. "La deuda externa," 47.

69. The cases recorded in table 5.5 are those corroborated in the print media. Officials interviewed suggested that this threat had been used in virtually all cases.

70. With the objective of eventually unifying the administration of all nationalized electrical companies, the CFE had taken over important administrative, financial, and technical functions from the CLFC in that year.

71. By 1988, employment reduction was being imposed. Vásquez Rubio, "Telmex por los caminos," 12; "Los telefonistas," 64.

72. Two senior-level finance officials made this point in interviews.

73. *Novedades,* 12 February 1984, discussed in Colmenares, "Pemex: Crisis y restructuración," 202.

74. *Proceso,* no. 380 (13 February 1984): 26.

75. The Ley de Obras, therefore, effectively overturned the advantages given the union in clause 36 of the collective agreement. Clause 36, included in the 1947 collective agreement, gave union consent for the company to contract out work. The clause was revised in 1977 to give the union 40 percent of PEMEX maintenance and service work contracts, which the union would then subcontract. The PEMEX union was, however, able to continue to receive contracts for the construction of houses for petroleum workers.

76. *Proceso,* no. 484 (10 February 1986): 16.

77. In 1939, President Cárdenas passed a decree that took technical and administrative personnel out of the union, forming a group known as confidence personnel, who were recruited or appointed by either the president or, in the case of a public company, the director general. A changeover in confidence employees, especially at more senior levels, is a common occurrence with new administrations. López, "Crisis en la industria petrolera," 17.

78. Colmenares, "Pemex: Crisis y restructuración," 211. See also Angel Cruz B., "La modernización de Pemex," 13.

79. Angel Cruz B., "La modernización de Pemex," 12.

80. Colmenares, "Pemex: Crisis y restructuración," 137, 142. The decline in productivity was the result of the greater growth in numbers of personnel employed with respect to product.

81. López, "Tres problemas obrero-patronales," 15.

82. The contract went to a Flota Petrolera Mexicana, a new petroleum tanker company established at the instigation of PEMEX. Its most prominent and principal shareholders were Isidoro Rodríquez, president of the Mexican Chamber of Transport, two members of the Chamber of Deputies, and a number of highly placed PEMEX officials. López, "Crisis en la industria petrolera," 26; *Proceso,* no. 534 (26 January 1987): 7.

83. *La Jornada,* 18 December 1988, 11; *Proceso,* no. 574 (2 November 1987): 27.

84. *Proceso,* no. 567 (14 September 1987): 32, 67; López, "Tres problemas obrero-patronales," 63.

85. This is dealt with in more detail in chapter 6. *Proceso,* no. 637 (16 January 1989): 22. La Quina's supporters claimed that he had been jailed because he had proof that PEMEX was going to be privatized. *Unomásuno,* 25 January 1988, 8.

86. *Latin American Weekly Report,* 2 February 1988, 8. Cabrera had been ousted as leader of local 10 of the Petroleum Workers Union on corruption charges by his rival, La Quina, in 1988, when it appeared that Cabrera might take over the secretary generalship of the union.

87. Armed thugs operating as goon squads against groups seeking reform.

88. *Proceso,* no. 639 (3 January 1989): 14; *Unomásuno,* 26 January 1989, 8; *Proceso,* no. 727 (8 October 1990): 22; no. 729 (22 October 1990): 16; no. 739 (31 December 1990): 8.

89. *Proceso,* no. 694 (19 February 1990): 23–24. Indeed, his company was set up just one month before the union accepted changes in the collective agreement, which expanded PEMEX's ability to contract out. *La Jornada,* 25 March 1991, 10.

90. *La Jornada,* 3 August 1989, 1; *Proceso,* no. 666 (7 August 1989): 31; no. 658 (12 June 1989): 23, 31.

91. *Proceso,* no. 652 (1 May 1989): 31.

92. Barbosa Cano, "La restructuración de Pemex," 24.

93. *Proceso,* no. 806 (13 April 1992): 16.

94. *Los Angeles Times,* 22 June 1993, 12.

95. *El Día,* 6 July 1992, 21; *La Jornada,* 5 June 1992, 41. Indeed, according to a middle-level finance official interviewed, dividing up PEMEX and thereby fracturing labor negotiations was an explicit strategy to weaken the Petroleum Workers' Union.

Chapter 6. *Dismantling the State*

1. Poder Ejecutivo Federal (SPP), *Plan nacional de desarrollo,* 133.

2. Villarreal, "Las empresas públicas," 236; Ruiz Dueñas, "El redimensionamiento del sector parastatal," 425.

3. "Primer informe," 14.

4. Ruiz Dueñas, "El redimensionamiento del sector parastatal," 425.

5. Ibid.

6. *Financial Times,* 13 May 1986, 4.

7. Some of this reduction was to be accounted for by fusions. Grupo SIDERMEX, *Informes de Labores* (1986–1987), 129; (1988–1989), 20.

8. *Financial Times,* 28 December 1986, 6.

9. *La Jornada,* 23 May 1988, 6.

10. Ibid.; *La Jornada,* 20 April 1988, 28.

11. *Comercio Exterior* 38 (4): 294.

12. *La Jornada,* 11 May 1987, 3; 14 April 1988, 25; 27 May 1988, 27; *Latin American Weekly Report,* 3 December 1988, 10; *La Jornada,* 12 March 1988, 6.

13. *La Jornada,* 8 June 1988, 27.

14. *La Jornada,* 6 December 1988, 17; 3 December 1988, 23; 8 December 1988, 23.

15. Secretaría de la Contraloría General de la Federación, *Restructuración del sector parastatal,* 90.

16. Amparo Casar and Peres, *El estado empresario en México,* 162.

17. Ibid., 91.

18. Ibid., 167.

19. Ruiz Dueñas, "El redimensionamiento del sector parastatal," 803.

20. All senior-level government officials involved in the Salinas administration referred to this decision. The country's nuclear company had already been closed in 1983.

21. *Mexico and NAFTA Report,* 6 May 1993, 2.

22. *Latin American Weekly Report,* 12 May 1994, 185.

23. *Latin American Weekly Report,* 26 July 1990, 4.

24. *El Financiero,* 19 August 1992, 14.

25. Ibid., 14.

26. Interview, owner of petrochemical company.

27. Molina, "Pemex, la reprivaticación de facto," 27.

28. It is also involved in the construction of petrochemical plants in Venezuela and a new refinery in Columbia. *El Sol de México,* 29 December 1989, 1.

29. *Mexico and Central America Report,* 16 July 1992, 2.

30. Two of these companies are involved in the distribution of gas. *El Financiero,* 21 July 1992, 3A.

31. *La Jornada,* 8 April 1993, 1.

32. The government has gotten around the constitutional stipulation that all mineral resources "belong to the nation" by explaining that this in no way inhibits the state from giving out mining concessions to the private sector.

33. *La Jornada,* 18 February 1991, 34. Through a revision in regulations, coal mining had been opened up to foreign capital several months earlier (*News,* 22 April 1992, 2).

34. *La Jornada,* 20 February 1991, 30.

35. Several plants have already been constructed under such arrangements. *El Financiero,* 18 May 1992, 36.

36. Private initiative may participate in the construction and ownership of railway yards and loading docks, the maintenance of railway tracks, telecommunications, and the purchase of rolling stock. *El Financiero,* 16 July

1991, 2; *Mexico and Central America Report,* 20 August 1992, 3; *Proceso,* no. 824 (17 August 1992): 10.

37. *Proceso,* no. 652 (1 May 1989): 8; no. 752 (1 April 1991): 24.

38. *El Financiero,* 31 August 1989, 12; *Proceso,* no. 679 (6 December 1989): 18.

39. Banco de Mexico, *Mexican Economy, 1992,* 251; Salinas de Gortari, *Quinto Informe de Gobierno,* Anexo, 239, 252.

40. *El Día,* 18 April 1992, 9.

41. *Latin American Weekly Report,* 19 January 1995, 14.

42. Mexico (SEMIP), *Informes de labores* (1987–1988), 46–57, 90–93, 123.

43. Grupo SIDERMEX, *Informes de labores* (1985–1986), 8; 1986–1987, 33; FERTIMEX, *Informes institutional de labores* (1985–1986), 63.

44. *Latin American Weekly Report,* 13 May 1983, 6; 20 January 1984, 2.

45. According to one account, Carlos Salinas (then secretary of budget and planning) took advantage of Labastida's absence from the country in February of 1986 to formulate a list of forty SEMIP enterprises to be sold or liquidated. Labastida opposed the proposal as soon as he returned and succeeded in paring down the list to sixteen. Fundidora Monterrey was one of the firms about which there was considerable dispute. Labastida did not believe "it was the moment" for the state to divest itself of Fundidora. Hence, it was only after his departure that Fundidora and other firms whose divestiture he had opposed were let go. *Proceso,* no. 500 (2 June 1986): 10.

46. SEMIP, *Informes de labores* (1984–1985), 25.

47. Grupo SIDERMEX, *Informes de labores* (1985–1986), 8; FERTIMEX, *Informes institutional de labores* (1985–1986), 23.

48. "Comparencia del Alfredo del Mazo," 110l.

49. Interview, senior-level SECOFI official.

50. All officials interviewed agreed on this point. According to finance officials, this had been one of the factors slowing down the divestiture process.

51. Interview, senior-level official.

52. *El Día,* 1 July 1987, 11.

53. FERTIMEX, *Informes institutional de labores* (l985–1986), 30; *La Jornada,* 20 September 1988, xi.

54. *La Jornada,* 18 June 1988, 1.

55. Interview, middle-rank finance official.

56. *Unomásuno,* 21 February 1991, 20; *Journal of Commerce,* 26 February 1993.

57. This was attempted in the case of PEMEX, with disastrous results, as discussed in chapter 5.

58. *La Jornada,* 23 January 1991, 29.

59. John Waterbury, in his comparative study of divestiture in Egypt,

Mexico, India, and Turkey, also found that it was driven by the desire for public deficit reduction. Waterbury, *Exposed to Innumerable Delusions,* 36.

60. *Latin American Weekly Report,* 5 December 1991, 10.

61. *El Día,* 15 April 1992, 13.

62. *News,* 3 June 1992, 1, 15; *La Jornada,* 2 June 1992, 40.

63. Originally established in 1979, the commission consisted of the secretaries of finance and of budget and planning and the comptroller's office, two subsecretaries each from finance and budget and planning, and one subsecretary from the comptroller's office. It gained importance during the de la Madrid years after being given responsibility for the coordination of the three financial ministries and the provision of advice to the economic cabinet.

64. Interview, senior-level finance official.

65. Ibid.

66. Ibid.

67. According to John Waterbury, Pedro Aspe was the driving force behind Mexico's privatization program. Waterbury, *Exposed to Innumerable Delusions,* 155.

68. In each of these cases, the declaration of bankruptcy followed labor strife in which management attempted to alter collective contracts.

69. *El Día,* 10 May 1988, 1F.

70. *Latin American Weekly Report,* 16 August 1990, 6.

71. For CMHN membership list, see *La Jornada,* 1 April 1991, "perfile de *La Jornada*" (suplemento), 3.

72. *Latin American Weekly Report,* 4 July 1991, 10.

73. *La Jornada,* 16 July 1992, 10.

74. *La Jornada,* 10 October 1990, 20.

75. *Mexico and NAFTA Report,* 20 October 1994, 5.

76. *La Jornada,* 16 July 1992, 6.

77. *Proceso,* no. 819 (13 July 1992): 7.

78. *Mexico and NAFTA Report,* 29 September 1994, 5.

79. *Financial Times,* 14 May 1986, 6.

80. *Proceso,* no. 598 (8 April 1988): 30.

81. Rodríguez Reyna, "La privatización de la petroquímica basica," 16–22.

82. *El Financiero,* 23 August 1989, 23.

83. *Latin American Weekly Report,* 20 May 1993, 219; *Mexico and NAFTA Report,* 18 February 1993, 1.

84. *Mexico and NAFTA Report,* 21 July 1994, 7.

85. One petrochemical entrepreneur recounted the case of the privatization of a state petrochemical company where the sale to the highest bidder would have created a monopoly in that particular sector. Although the government wished to avoid this, it eventually allowed the sale to go for-

ward because of the belief that to maintain two companies in the sector would inhibit the sector from becoming internationally competitive.

86. *Proceso,* no. 478 (30 December 1985): 31.

87. *El Día,* 21 May 1992, 15; *Unomásuno,* 20 January 1989, 1; *La Jornada,* 25 August 1992, 6.

88. *El Financiero,* 8 July 1992, 20.

89. An exception is the bank privatization. In order to gain the PAN's support for the constitutional amendment necessary to privatize the banks, legislation stipulated that no individual could hold more than 5 percent of the shares of any bank. The establishment of holding companies, however, allow Mexican business to skirt this regulation.

Chapter 7. The Politics of Privatization

1. Bailey, "Can the PRI be Reformed?" 79; Baer, "Mexico's Second Revolution," 37–38; Weintraub and Baer, *Interplay Between Economic and Political Opening,"* 200; Cornelius, Gentleman, and Smith, "Overview of Political Change in Mexico," 12; Aguayo Quezado, "The Inevitability of Democracy," 119; Gómez and Bailey, "La transición política," 66; Pacheco Méndez, "Los sectores del PRI," 259.

2. Gómez and Bailey, "La transición política," 87.

3. Alvarez Bejár, "Economic Crisis," 44. Similar views are expressed in Baer, "Mexico's Second Revolution," 52–53; and Cornelius, Gentleman, and Smith, "Overview of Political Change in Mexico," 13.

4. Baer, "Mexico's Second Revolution," 54.

5. Carr, "The PSUM," 286; "Mexican Left, the Popular Movements, and the Politics of Austerity"; "Labor and the Political Left," 10; Prieto, "Mexico's National Coordinadoras"; Ramírez Laiz, "Urban Struggles," 235.

6. Foweraker, introduction to *Popular Movements and Political Change,* 12; Monsiváis, "From '68 to Cardenismo," 390.

7. Ramírez Laiz, "Urban Struggles," 235.

8. Haber, "Political Change in Durango," 278; Molinar Horcasitas and Weldon, "Electoral Determinants," 140; Fox, "Targeting the Poorest," 180.

9. Baer, "Mexico's Second Revolution," 55.

10. Smith, "1988 Presidential Succession," 35.

11. Cornelius, Gentleman, and Smith, "Overview of Political Change in Mexico," 15.

12. Meyer, "El corporativismo Mexicano," 28; Middlebrook, "The CTM and the Future of State-Labor Relations," 303.

13. Rubin, "Popular Mobilization," 262.

14. Coppedge, "Mexican Democracy," 128; Dresser, "Bringing the Poor Back In," 148.

15. Foweraker, "Introduction," *Popular Movements and Political Change,* 10.

16. Cornelius, Gentleman, and Smith, "Overview of Political Change in Mexico," 36.

17. Foweraker, "Introduction," *Popular Movements and Political Change,* 114.

18. Camp, "Political Liberalization," 27.

19. Bailey, "Centralism and Policy Change in Mexico," 101.

20. Bizberg, "La crisis del corporativismo," 726; Meyer, "El corporativismo Mexicano," 22.

21. Bensusan and García, introduction to *Estado y sindicatos,* 15; Micheli, "Sindicatos y futuro," 96.

22. The CTM, an affiliate of the CT, has been the core of the PRI in terms of numbers, organization, and militancy. It is composed of thirty-six national unions, the most important of which is the Petroleum Workers' Union. Bailey, *Governing Mexico,* 94.

23. *Proceso,* no. 398 (18 June 1984): 23; no. 503 (23 July 1986): 61. *Latin American Weekly Report,* 9 August 1985, 11; 7 March 1986, 10; 13 June 1986, 4; *Unomásuno,* 5 May 1989, 13.

24. *Proceso,* no. 434 (25 February 1985): 31.

25. *Proceso,* no. 487 (3 March 1986): 18.

26. First signed in December 1987 and renewed every three months, the objective of these pacts was to control inflation.

27. *Proceso,* no. 542 (23 March 1987): 31; no. 551 (25 May 1987): 11.

28. *El Día,* 23 December 1989, 6.

29. *La Jornada,* 27 March 1990, 35; 29 March 1991, 5.

30. *La Jornada,* 9 February 1991, 23.

31. *La Jornada,* 5 March 1991, 25. See also *La Jornada,* 19 February 1991, 18.

32. *El Día,* 9 June 1986, 3; Vargas, "Recortes al gasto público," 20.

33. *La Jornada,* 18 January 1986, 13.

34. *Unomásuno,* 22 August 1989, 1; 19 September 1989, 1; *La Jornada,* 25 October 1991, 1; *Proceso,* no. 322 (3 January 1983): 13.

35. In addition to the three unions already mentioned, also included were the Flight Attendants Union (Asociación Sindical de Sobrecargos de Aviación, ASSA), Alliance of Transit Workers of Mexico (Alianza de Tranviarios de Mexico, ATM), and Technicians and Workers in the Motion Picture Industry (Tecnicos y Manueles de Producción Cinematografía). *La Jornada,* 27 March 1990, 16; 3 January 1990, 3.

36. *La Jornada,* 28 April 1990, 9; 26 April 1990, 10.

37. "Conflictos obreros-patronales," 53–54.

38. *Proceso,* no. 529 (22 December 1986): 24. The tactic of divide and rule is not a new one. President Ruiz Cortines had helped in the creation of the CROC to rival the CTM, and various presidents have wooed both the CROC and a renewed version of the CROM whenever they felt the CTM was becoming too strong. Story, *Mexican Ruling Party,* 86.

39. *Proceso,* no. 752 (1 April 1991): 28.

40. As a consequence, the CTM began to experience a hemorrhage of defections, and more were threatened—it was reported that more than a thousand workers had abandoned it and had joined the CROC. *Proceso,* no. 734 (26 December 1990): 31.

41. *La Jornada,* 25 August 1990, 5.

42. *La Jornada,* 9 March 1990, 11.; *Proceso,* no. 715 (16 July 1990): 28.

43. *Proceso,* no. 502 (16 June 1986): 28; Quintano López, "La bancarrota de Fundidora," 27.

44. Quintano López, "La bancarrota de Fundidora," 44; *Proceso,* no. 501 (9 June 1986): 22.

45. *Proceso,* no. 501 (9 June 1986): 22.

46. La Botz, *Crisis of Mexican Labor,* 177.

47. *La Jornada,* 6 March 1990, 1.

48. Méndez, "Espisodos de lucha obrera," 66.

49. *Proceso,* no. 496 (4 April 1988): 26; no. 658 (12 June 1989): 12–13.

50. *Proceso,* no. 679 (6 November 1989): 8.

51. Leyva and Campos, "Ferrocarriles, luz verde a la modernidad," 52.

52. *Proceso,* no. 596 (4 April 1988): 18–19.

53. Story, *Mexican Ruling Party,* 28.

54. Ibid., 50, 56.

55. Ibid., 47–49.

56. Cockcroft, *Mexico: Class Formation, Capital Accumulation, and the State,* 273; Hellman, *Mexico in Crisis,* 129.

57. *Proceso,* no. 406 (13 August 1984): 31; no. 451 (24 June 1985): 13; no. 466 (7 October 1985): 29; *Latin American Weekly Report,* 2 August 1985, 10; 2 May 1986, 10.

58. *Proceso,* no. 345 (13 June 1983): 10.

59. *Proceso,* no. 468 (21 October 1985): 7.

60. *Proceso,* no. 386 (26 May 1984): 22.

61. Ibid.; *Proceso,* no. 425 (24 December 1984): 228.

62. *Unomásuno,* 29 December 1987, 7; *La Jornada,* 3 December 1988, 7; 4 December 1989, 13. The PAN opposed the government's privatization program, arguing that it did not go far enough fast enough.

63. Wayne Cornelius suggests that the virtual absence of electoral fraud in the 1983 elections was the consequence of the adoption by the government of a strategy to allow political frustrations a political outlet, in view of the severe restrictions that austerity imposed on the distribution of patronage. Cornelius, "Political Liberalization," 22.

64. *Latin American Weekly Report,* 7 August 1986, 4.

65. The common denominator of this counterelite appears to have been their close ties to former president Luis Echeverría (1970–1976), whose administration had overseen a massive expansion of the state and state intervention. *Proceso,* no. 520 (27 October 1986): 6.

66. *Latin American Weekly Report,* 30 October 1986, 6. The sincerity of this criticism may, however, be disputed. Muñoz Ledo himself had benefited from traditional nondemocratic procedures within the PRI. He had obtained his appointment as PRI chairman through presidential appointment, not through democratic election. *Proceso,* no. 520 (27 October 1986): 6. Most officials interviewed characterized the democratic movement as a group of former government officials who were deeply dissatisfied, largely because they no longer were in positions of power. Muñoz Ledo was allegedly unhappy because of his frustrated presidential aspirations—he apparently saw himself in the running during his tenure as secretary of education in the administration of López Portillo.

67. *Proceso,* no. 556 (29 June 1987): 14.

68. *Proceso,* no. 557 (6 July 1987): 14; *Latin American Weekly Report,* 17 September 1987, 2.

69. *Proceso,* no. 569 (28 September 1987): 17; *Proceso,* no. 567 (14 September 1987): 6.

70. The founding parties included the Mexican Workers' Party (Partido Mexicano de los Trabajadores, or PMT), itself the product of the merger of five organizations in 1987; the PARM; the Frente Cárdenista de Reconstrucción Nacional (Cardenista Front of National Reconstruction, formerly the Partido Socialista de los Trabajadores}; and the Popular Socialist Party (Partido Popular Socialista, or PPS). *Latin American Weekly Report,* 16 June 1988, 10.

71. *Latin American Weekly Report,* 6 June 1988, 10.

72. *La Jornada,* 21 April 1988, 1.

73. *La Jornada,* 14 May 1988, 13. *Proceso,* no. 396 (4 April 1988): 17.

74. *Latin American Weekly Report,* 12 March 1987, 8.

75. *Proceso,* no. 451 (24 June 1985): 8.

76. *Latin American Weekly Report,* 10 December 1988, 3.

77. *Proceso,* no. 575 (9 December 1987): 9.

78. "Razón de estado y desobediencia civil," 49.

79. *Proceso,* no. 638 (23 January 1989): 17.

80. This organization had members from union locals 26, 14, 44, 11, and 10 of the union. *Proceso,* no. 594 (21 March 1988): 7; no. 550 (18 May 1987): 19.

81. *Proceso,* no. 612 (25 July 1988): 26–27.

82. Loyola Díaz, "La liquidación del feudo petrolero," 290.

83. *La Jornada,* 31 July 1988, 7; 19 August 1988, 17; 11 May 1988, 8.

84. See Gómez Tagle, "La demanda democrática."

85. Guillén López, "The Social Bases of the PRI," 255; "Corporativismo, no el (la) modelo," 47. This situation reflected a trend, begun in the late 1960s, characterized by a growing correlation between urbanization and votes for the PRI. Juan Molinar Horcasitas suggests that when this tendency

is extrapolated, the PRI would have 50 percent of the votes around the year 2000. Molinar Horcasitas, "Elecciones autoritarismo," 146, 150.

86. *La Jornada*, 19 August 1988, 7; Meyer, "El corporativismo Mexicano," 29.

87. Molinar Horcasitas, "Elecciones autoritarismo," 353; Grayson, *Mexican Labor Machine*, 62.

88. Whitehead, "Mexico's Economic Prospects,"?]] 57.

89. *La Jornada*, 17 October 1990, 17.

90. *La Jornada*, 3 December 1990, 1.

91. *La Jornada*, 30 July 1991, 7; *Latin American Weekly Report*, 20 September 1990, 4.

92. *El Día*, 15 May 1992, 22.

93. *La Jornada*, 26 July 1993, 7.

94. By 1990, some one billion U.S. dollars of PRONASOL's funding had come from the sale of state companies. Moguel, "¿Programa Nacional de Solidaridad para quién?" 24. Starting with an initial budget of US$640 million, its 1992 budget reached US$2.2 billion, 8 percent of the federal budget. *Latin America Weekly Report*, 16 August 1990, 6; *Unomásuno*, 20 July 1992, 9. Another source of PRONASOL funding has been the World Bank, a strong proponent of the elimination of what it views as inefficient redistributive mechanisms (public enterprises, generalized subsidies) and the establishment of more directly redistributive instruments. For World Bank funding, see note 101, below.

95. *El Financiero*, 23 April 1992, 6.

96. *Unomásuno*, 4 May 1992, 3; *El Día*, 8 April 1992, 7.

97. *El Día*, 8 April 1992, 7.

98. Moguel, "¿Programa Nacional de Solidaridad para quién?" 25; Angel Romero M., "Elecciones," 15; Dresser, *Neopopulist Solutions*, 24.

99. *Proceso*, no. 819 (13 July 1992): 14.

100. Ibid.

101. Between 1989 and 1993, the World Bank loaned $350 million to be used for this purpose in Mexico's poorest states. *Journal of Commerce*, 27 July 1993, 3. On the argument that the program has strengthened the presidency, see Bailey, "Centralism and Policy Change in Mexico," 101; Dresser, *Neopopulist Solutions*, 31; and Haber, "Political Change in Durango," 267.

102. *Miami Herald*, 3 January 1993, 9.

103. Ibid., 26.

104. *Unomásuno*, 4 May 1992, 6.

105. *La Jornada*, 28 April 1992, 19.

106. *Latin American Weekly Report*, 5 September 1991, 2; *El Financiero*, 28 May 1992, 34A.

107. *El Financiero*, 13 July 1992, 14.

108. Gómez Tagle, "Mexico 1991," 5.

109. *Proceso,* no. 819 (13 July 1991): 14. Heavy electoral spending has continued. The PRI is claimed to have spent a total of US$20 million for the 1992 campaign for the governorship of Chihuahua and the local elections in that state. Similar large amounts were spent in other 1992 campaigns. *Latin America Weekly Report,* 20 August 1992, 3.

110. Additional factors were the PRI's domination of the media and popular fears of political instability if the PRI did not retain power.

111. *La Jornada,* 24 August 1994, 45; 27 August, 11; *Unomasuno,* 8 August 1994, 11.

112. *El Financiero,* 19 August 1994, 30; 22 August 1994, 46.

113. *La Jornada,* 14 August 1994, 7.

114. *La Jornada,* 16 August 1994, 1.

115. *La Jornada,* 14 August 1994, 3; 25 August, p. 11.

116. Founded just after the 1988 federal election and also led by Cuauh-témoc Cárdenas, the PRD was unsuccessful in attracting support from many of the former FDN organizations.

117. *Mexico and NAFTA Report,* 10 June 1993, 2; *Mexico and Central America Report,* 9 May 1991, 6; *Latin American Weekly Report,* 28 June 1991, 6; 3 October 1991, 5; 26 March 1992, 26.

118. *Latin American Weekly Report,* 5 July 1990, 8. The threats were allegedly received from a police agent. The government has denied any involvement.

119. *Mexico and Central America Report,* 12 January 1989, 8. *La Jornada,* 29 December 1989, 20; *Proceso,* no. 670 (6 December 1989): 11; *Mexico and Central America Report,* 10 May 1990, 7; *Unomásuno,* 29 August 1989, 2; 29 September 1989, 25; *Unomásuno,* 22 August 1989; 29 September 1989, 25.

120. *Unomásuno,* 22 August 1989, 1; *Proceso,* no. 668 (21 August 1989): 12.

121. *Unomásuno,* 29 September 1989, 25; *Proceso,* no. 624 (17 October 1988): 77; no. 635 (2 January 1989): 22; *Latin American Weekly Report,* 26 January 1989, 26. It has been suggested that the left's defense of La Quina stemmed from the fact that La Quina had helped finance the presidential campaign of the FDN. *Latin American Weekly Report,* 2 February 1989, 8.

122. *El Día,* 25 September 1989, 3.

123. *Proceso,* no. 684 (11 December 1989): 8–9.

124. *Proceso,* no. 697 (12 March 1990): 18.

125. Barlón, "Semejanzas y diferencias en dos regiones indígenas," 19.

126. Human Rights Watch Americas, "Mexico: The New Year's Rebel-lion."

127. *Washinton Post,* 8 January 1995, 23.

128. *Latin American Weekly Report,* 17 March 1994, 110.

129. *La Jornada,* 4 December 1988, 1; *Unomásuno,* 5 February 1989, 5; *Proceso,* no. 706 (14 May 1990): 17.

130. *Proceso,* no. 713 (2 July 1990): 25.

131. *Latin American Weekly Report,* 4 December 1993, 514.

132. In the absence of an explict policy to ensure the dispersal of share-holding broadly throughout society, this result was perhaps inevitable. However, even when such policies are attempted, they face enormous obstacles for fiscally strapped governments. On the Chilean attempt at popular capitalism, see, Maloney, "Popular Capitalism in Chile."

133. While ALFA suspended repayment on the principal of its debt in 1983, other groups such as Cervecería Moctezuma were on the verge of bankruptcy. *Quarterly Economic Review of Mexico,* no. 3 (1983): 14; no. 3 (1984): 7. ALFA received a loan from the state bank BANOBRAS for 9 trillion pesos during the de la Madrid administration. *Proceso,* no. 812 (25 May 1992): 13.

134. According to a study carried out by the Instituto de Investigación Sociales of UNAM, the principal enterprises benefiting from this subsidy were ALFA, VISA, Tubos de Acero de México, CYDSA, Celanese Mexicana, Cervecería Moctezuma, and Central de Malta. *Proceso,* no. 580 (14 December 1985): 17.

135. The criteria for inclusion was direct exportation annually of a minimum of goods valued at $3 million or $1 million when exports account for the total sales of an enterprise. *El Mercado de Valores* 47, no. 20 (18 May 1987), 506. Manufacturers producing inputs included in exports could also be included.

136. *Mexico and NAFTA Report,* 15 April 1993, 4; *Wall Street Journal,* 19 January 1993, 15; 29 April 1993, 10.

137. *El Día,* 18 April 1992, 15.

138. In 1988, the most important exporting companies after PEMEX, with 55.9 percent of the value of total exports, were Chrysler of Mexico (6.4 percent), Ford Motor Company of Mexico (4.7 percent), GM of Mexico (4.6 percent), Companía Mexicana de Aviacíon (2.5 percent), TELMEX (2.3 percent), Peñoles (2.2 percent), Volkswagen of Mexico (1.4 percent), IBM of Mexico (1.4 percent), and Celanese Mexicana (.9 percent). *La Jornada,* 22 October 1988, 13.

139. *El Financiero,* 2 July 1992, 1.

140. *Unomásuno,* 6 June 1992, 7.

141. Camp, *Entrepreneurs and Politics,* 176–208.

142. This is a study carried out by Morera Camacho of the Instituto de Investigaciones Económicas of UNAM; quoted in *Unomásuno,* 22 June 1992, 6.

143. *La Jornada,* 7 July 1992, 2.

144. *La Jornada,* 5 May 1991, 29.

145. According to a report produced by the Mexican Banking Association. *Unomásuno,* 23 May 1991, 13.

146. *Proceso,* no. 623 (10 October 1988): 12; *La Jornada,* 1 April 1991, 10.

147. Mizrahi, "Rebels Without a Cause?" 12.

148. *Proceso,* no. 682 (27 December 1989): 15.

149. *Mexico and NAFTA Report,* 25 March 1993, 1. Top PRI officials affirmed that the pledges had been made. *Miami Herald,* 4 March 1993, 10. After considerable public outcry, their contributions were reduced to a third of a million each.

150. *Proceso,* no. 687 (1 January 1990): 23.

151. Camp notes that members of the CMHN claim the use of personal channels, especially to the president. Camp, *Entrepreneurs and Politics,* 171. The government's cultivation of the country's most powerful businessmen, initiated during the de la Madrid years, was not viewed in a positive light by all those in a position to benefit, however. There was an implicit political price attached to the government largesse involved in such actions as the bailout of ALFA: the company's directors were now expected to support the government. This was the assessment made by A. M. Sada Zambrano, former director of VITRO, about Bernardo Garza Sada and the implications of the government's rescue of ALFA. *Proceso,* no. 474 (2 December 1985): 7.

152. Luna, "Las associaciones empresariales Mexicanas," 5.

153. Ibid., 1, 3, 6.

154. *La Jornada,* 8 July 1988, 17; 3 October 1990, 22; 15 May 1992, 2. Luna, "Las associaciones empresariales Mexicanas," 9; *Unomásuno,* 26 May 1992, 10; *El Financiero,* 26 May 1992, 10; "Profiex," 17.

155. Luna, "Las associaciones empresariales Mexicanas," 9.

156. Ibid.

157. Mizrahi, "Rebels Without a Cause?" 10.

158. Mexico's largest financial group, BANAMEX/Accival, reported a loss of 555 million pesos for the forth quarter of 1994. *Wall Street Journal,* January 17 1995, 16.

159. *Wall Street Journal,* January 10 1995, 3.

160. *Wall Street Journal,* January 13, 1995, 30.

161. Mexico's largest financial group, BANAMEX/Accival, reported a loss of 555 million pesos for the forth quarter of 1994. *Wall Street Journal,* 17 January 1995, 16.

162. *Wall Street Journal,* 10 January 1995, 3.

163. *Wall Street Journal,* 13 January 1995, 30.

Chapter 8. From Statism to Neoliberalism

1. Echeverría's Caminos de Mano de Obra and de la Madrid's COPLA-MAR also emphasized the organized inclusion of popular communities. Dresser, *Neopopulist Solutions,* 13.

2. Suleiman and Waterbury, "Analysing Privatization."

3. Ibid, 12.

4. Ibid, 15.

5. Maloney, "Popular Capitalism in Chile," 18.

6. Kahler, "External Influence," 118.

7. Waterbury, *Exposed to Innumerable Delusions,* 155.

8. Kahler, "Orthodoxy and Its Alternatives," 59.

9. Haggard, "Politics of Adjustment," 176; Kaufman, "Stabilization and Adjustment," 75; Scott, "Cycles, Crises, and Classes," 129.

10. Waterbury, "Management of Long-Haul Economic Reform," 181; Suleiman and Waterbury, "Analysing Privatization," 19.

11. Rocha Geisa, "Redefining the Role of the Bourgeoisie," 90.

12. Smith, "Heterodox Shocks," 155.

13. *Latin America Weekly Report,* 24 May 1990, 11.

14. *Latin America Weekly Report,* 7 June 1990, 11; 9 August 1990, 11; 25 October 1990, 11.

15. *Latin American Weekly Report,* 18 February 1993, 57.

16. With the election of Fernando Cardoso as president of Brazil, there has been an invigorated commitment to privatization.

17. Kaufman, "Stabilization and Adjustment," 80–81.

18. Heterodox adjustment seeks to reduce political opposition by reducing inflation without provoking a recession. Stallings, "International Influence on Economic Policy," 74.

19. Haggard and Kaufman, "Political Economy of Inflation and Stabilization," 273.

20. *Latin American Weekly Report,* 3 May 1990, 9.

21. Waterbury, *Exposed to Innumerable Delusions,* 27.

22. Kaufman, *Politics of Debt,* 63.

23. *Latin American Weekly Report,* 23 September 1993, 435.

24. *Latin American Weekly Report,* 14 December 1989, 2.

25. This is despite the fact that they may well alienate that ally in the process of structural adjustment.

26. McCoy, "Venezuela," 220.

27. Bacha and Malan, "Brazil's Debt," 126; Fishlow, "Tale of Two Presidents," 101.

28. *Latin American Weekly Report,* 24 October 1991, 4.

29. None of Argentina's strategic state companies was privatized during the period of military rule, due to the bureaucratic resistance of the military men who were running them. Hence, despite the neoliberal rhetoric, no strategic state companies were privatized during this period. Flichman, "State and Capital Accumulation in Argentina."

References

Aguayo Quezado, Sergio. "The Inevitability of Democary in Mexico." In Riordan Roett, ed., *Political and Economic Liberalization in Mexico*. Boulder, Colo.: Lynne Rienner, 1993.

Aguilar Mora, Manuel. *El Bonapartismo Mexicano*. Vol. 1. Mexico City: Juan Pablo Editores, 1984.

Alonso, Angelina, and Roberto López. *El sindicato de trabajadores petroleros y sus relaciones en Pemex y el estado 1970–1985*. Mexico City: El Colegio de México, 1986.

Alonso, Antonio. *El movimiento ferrocarrilero en México, 1958–1959*. 7th ed. Mexico City: Ediciones Era, 1986.

Alvarez Bejár, Alejandro. "Economic Crisis and the Labor Movement in Mexico." In Kevin Middlebrook, ed., *Unions, Workers, and the State in Mexico*. San Diego: Center for U.S.-Mexican Studies, University of California, 1991.

Amparo Casar, María, and Wilson Peres. *El estado empresario en México: ¿Agotamiento o renovación?* Mexico City: Siglo XXI Editores, 1988.

Angel Abdala, Manuel. "The Regulation of Newly Privatized Firms: An Illustration from Argentina." Paper presented at the 18th International Congress of the Latin American Studies Association, 24–27 September 1992, Los Angeles.

Angel Centeno, Miguel. *Democracy Within Reason: Technocratic Revolution in Mexico*. University Park: Pennsylvania State University Press, 1994.

Angel Centeno, Miguel, and Sylvia Maxfield. "The Marriage of Finance and Order: Changes in the Mexican Elite." *Journal of Latin American Studies* 24 (February 1992): 17–85.

Angel Cruz B., Miguel. "La modernización de Pemex." *El Cotidiano* 3, no. 15 (January–February 1987): 11–14.

Angel Romero M., Miguel. "Elecciones: Nueva situación geopolítica." *El Cotidiano* 7, no. 39 (January–February 1991): 14–20.

Anglade, Christian, and Carlos Fortin. "The State and Capital Accumulation in Latin America: A Conceptual and Historical Introduction." In Anglade and Fortin, eds., *The State and Capital Accumulation in Latin America,* vol. 1. Pittsburgh: University of Pittsburgh Press, 1985.

Anglade, Christian, and Carlos Fortin. "Accumulation, Adjustment, and the Autonomy of the Latin American State." In Anglade and Fortin, eds., *The State and Capital Accumulation in Latin America,* vol. 2. Pittsburgh: University of Pittsburgh Press, 1990.

Armstrong, Philip, Andrew Glyn, and John Harrison. *Capitalism Since World War II.* London: Fontana Paperbacks, 1984.

Ashby, Joe C. *Organized Labor and the Mexican Revolution Under Lázaro Cárdenas.* Chapel Hill: University of North Carolina Press, 1967.

Aspe, Pedro, and José Cordoba. "Stabilization Policies in Mexico," unpublished manuscript, 1985.

Aspe Armella, Pedro. "Nuevos créditos y re-negotiación en apoyo el cambio estructural." *Comercio Exterior* 39, no. 5 (May 1989): 388–89.

Ayala, José L., Fidel Aroche R., and Luis Miguel Galindo P. "El papel del sector público en el dinámica de largo plazo de desarrollo económico, México. Un enfoque de interpretación y periodicación, 1925–1982." *Investigación Económica,* no. 182 (October–December 1986): 103–65.

Ayala Espino, José. *Estado y desarrollo: La formación de la economía mixta Mexicana (1920–1982).* Mexico City: Fondo de Cultura Económica, 1988.

Babai, Don. "The World Bank and the IMF: Rolling Back the State or Backing Its Role." In Raymond Vernon, ed., *The Promise of Privatization: A Challenge for U.S. Policy.* New York: Council on Foreign Relations, 1988.

Bacha, Edmar L., and Pedro S. Malan. "Brazil's Debt from the Miracle to the Fund." In Alfred Stepan, ed., *Democratizing Brazil.* New York: Oxford University Press, 1989.

Baer, M. Delal. "Mexico's Second Revolution: Pathways to Liberalization." In Riordan Roett, ed., *Political and Economic Liberalization in Mexico.* Boulder, Colo.: Lynne Rienner, 1993.

Bailey, John J. "Presidency, Bureaucracy, and Administrative Reform in Mexico: The Secretariat of Program and Budgeting." *Inter-American Economic Affairs* 34 (Summer 1980): 28–58.

―――. "Can the PRI Be Reformed? Decentralizaing Candidate Selection." In Judith Gentleman, ed., *Mexican Politics in Transition.* Boulder, Colo.: Westview, 1986.

―――. *Governing Mexico: The Statecraft of Crisis Management.* London: Macmillan, 1988.

―――. "Centralism and Policy Change in Mexico: The Case of National Solidarity." In Wayne A. Cornelius, Ann L. Craig, and Jonathan Fox, eds., *Transforming State-Society Relations in Mexico*. San Diego: Center for U.S.-Mexican Studies, University of California, 1994.

Ballance, Robert H. *International Industry and Business: Structural Change, Industrial Policy, and Industry Strategies*. London: Allen and Unwin, 1987.

BANAMEX. *Examen de la situación económica de México*. BANAMEX: Mexico City, various years.

Banco de México. *The Mexican Economy, 1992*.

———. *The Mexican Economy, 1993*.

———. *The Mexican Economy, 1994*.

Barbosa Cano, Fabio. "El Movimiento petrolero en 1938–1940." In Javier Aguilar García, coord., *Los Sindicatos nacionales en el México contemporaneo: Petroleros*, vol. 1. Mexico City: García Valades Editores, 1986.

———. "La restructuración de Pemex." *El Cotidiano* 7, no. 46 (March–April 1992): 20–33.

Barlón, Moisés J. "Semejanzas y diferencias en dos regiones indígenas del sur de México: Oaxaca y Chiapas a la luz de la revuelta del EZLN." Paper presented at the 17th International Congress of the Latin American Studies Association, March 10–12, 1994, Atlanta.

Basáñez, Miguel. *La lucha por la hegemonia en México, 1968–1990*. 8th ed. Mexico City: Siglo XXI Editores, 1990.

Basurto, Jorge. *Cárdenas y el poder sindical*. Mexico City: Ediciones Era, 1983.

———. *La clase obrera en la historia de México: Del avilocamachismo al alemanismo (1940–1952)*. Vol. 11. Mexico City: UNAM, 1984.

———. *La clase obrera en la historia de México en el régimen de Echeverría: Rebelión y independencia*. Vol. 14. Mexico City: Siglo XXI Editores, 1989.

———. "El nacionalismo revolucionario y la unificación de los electricistas." Cuadernos de investigación sociales, no. 19. Mexico City: UNAM, 1989.

———. *El proletariado industrial en México (1850–1930)*. Mexico City: UNAM, 1975.

Bennett, Douglas, and Kenneth Sharpe. "The State As Banker and Entrepreneur." In Sylvia Ann Hewlett and Richard Weinert, eds., *Brazil and Mexico: Patterns of Late Development*. Philadelphia: Institute for the Study of Human Issues, 1982.

Bensusan, Graciela. "Instituciones en crisis: El mundo del trabajo en transformación." In Graciela Bensusan and Carlos García, coords., *Estado y sindicatos: Crisis de un relación*. Mexico City: Universidad Aútonoma Metropolitana, 1989.

Bensusan, Graciela, and Carlos García. Introduction to Graciela Bensusan and Carlos García, coords., *Estado y sindicatos: Crisis de un relación*. Mexico City: Universidad Aútonoma Metropolitana, 1989.

Benveniste, Guy. *Bureaucracy and National Planning: A Sociological Case Study in Mexico*. New York: Praeger, 1977.

Bermúdez, Antonio J. *The Mexican National Petroleum Industry*. Stanford: Stanford University Press, 1963.

Besserer, Federico, Victoria Novelo, and Juan Luis Sariego. *El sindicalismo minero en México (1900–1952)*. Mexico City: Ediciones Era, 1983.

Biersteker, Thomas J. "Reducing the Role of the State in the Economy: A Conceptual Exploration of IMF and World Bank Prescriptions." *International Studies Quarterly*, no. 34 (1990): 477–92.

————. "The Logic and Unfulfilled Promise of Privatization in Developing Countries." In Louis Putterman and Dietrich Rueschemeyer, eds., *State and Markets in Developing Countries*. Boulder, Colo.: Lynne Rienner, 1992.

Bizberg, Ilán. "La crisis del corporativismo Mexicana." *Foro Internacional* 30, no. 4 (1990): 695–735.

————. *Estado y sindicalismo en México*. Mexico City: El Colegio de México, 1990.

Blair, Calvin P. "Nacional Financiera: Enterpreneurship in a Mixed Economy." In Raymond Vernon, ed., *Public Policy and Private Enterprise in Mexico*. Cambridge: Harvard University Press, 1964.

Bolsa Mexicana de Valores and Asociación Mexicana de Casas de Bolsas. *Mexico Company Handbook*. Austin: Reference Press, 1992.

Brailovsky, Vladimiro, Roland Clarke, and Natán Warman. *La política económica del desperdicio*. Mexico City: UNAM, 1989.

Brandenburg, Frank. *The Making of Modern Mexico*. Englewood Cliffs, N.J.: Prentice-Hall, 1964.

Bravo Mena, Luis Felipe. "Coparmex and Mexican Politics." In Sylvia Maxfield and Ricardo Anzaldúa Montoya, eds., *Government and Private Sector in Contemporary Mexico*. San Diego: Center for U.S.-Mexican Studies, University of California, 1987.

Butler, Stuart M. "Changing the Political Dynamics of Government." In Steve H. Hanke, ed., *Prospects for Privatization*. New York: Academy of Political Science, 1987.

Camacho, Manuel. *La clase obrera en la historia de México: el futuro inmediato*. 7th ed. Vol. 15. Mexico City: Siglo XXI Editores, 1989.

Camp, Roderic A. "Camarillas in Mexican Politics: The Case of the Salinas

Cabinet." *Mexican Studies/Estudios Mexicanos* 6, no. 1 (Winter 1990): 85–107.

———. *Entrepreneurs and Politics in Twentieth-Century Mexico.* New York: Oxford University Press, 1989.

———. *The Making of Government.* Tucson: University of Arizona Press, 1984.

———. "Political Liberalization: The Last Key to Economic Modernization in Mexico." In Riordan Roett, ed., *Political and Economic Liberalization in Mexico.* Boulder, Colo.: Lynne Rienner, 1993.

Carr, Barry. "Labor and the Political Left in Mexico." In Kevin J. Middlebrook, ed., *Unions, Workers, and the State in Mexico.* San Diego: Center for U.S.-Mexican Studies, University of California, 1991.

———. "The Mexican Left, the Popular Movements, and the Politics of Austerity." In Barry Carr and Ricardo Anzaldúa Montoya, eds., *The Mexican Left, the Popular Movements, and the Politics of Austerity.* San Diego: Center for U.S.-Mexican Studies, University of California, 1986.

———. "The PSUM: The Unification Process on the Mexican Left, 1984–1985." In Judith Gentleman, ed., *Mexican Politics in Transition.* Boulder, Colo.: Westview, 1986.

Carrillo Arronte, Ricardo. "The Role of the State and the Entrepreneurial Sector in Mexican Development." In Sylvia Maxfield and Ricardo Anzaldúa Montoya, eds., *Government and Private Sector in Contemporary Mexico.* San Diego: Center for U.S.-Mexican Studies, University of California, 1987.

Carrillo Castro, Alejandro, and Sergio García Ramírez. *Las empresas públicas en México.* Mexico City: Miguel Angel Porrúa, 1983.

Carsten Etenroth, Thomas, and Gabriela Gándara. "El plan Brady y la negotiación de la deuda Mexicana." *Comercio Exterior* 40, no. 4 (April 1990): 301–04.

"Carta de intención al Fondo Monetario Internacional." *El Trimestre Económico,* no. 198 (April–June 1983): 1127–32.

"Carta de intención del gobierno al FMI." *El Mercado de Valores* 44, no. 1 (2 January 1984): 29–30.

"Carta de intención del gobierno de México." *El Mercado de Valores* 45, no. 13 (April 1985): 293–94.

"Carta de intención del gobierno de México al FMI." *El Mercado de Valores* 46, no. 31 (4 August 1986): 751–55.

Carvaunis, Chris C. *The Foreign Debt/National Development Conflict.* New York: Quorum Books, 1986.

Castillo Flores, Angeles. "Cronología del cierre de Fundidora Monterrey." *El Cotidiano* 3, no. 12 (July–August 1986): 42–47.

Chalmers, Douglas A. "The Politicized State in Latin America." In James Malloy, ed., *Authoritarianism and Corporatism in Latin America*. Pittsburgh: University of Pittsburgh Press, 1977.

Clark, Marjorie Ruth. *Organized Labor in Mexico*. New York: Russell and Russell, 1973.

Cockcroft, James D. *Mexico: Class Formation, Capital Accumulation, and the State*. New York: Monthly Review, 1983.

Coleman, Kenneth M., and Charles E. Davis. "Preemptive Reform and the Mexican Working Class." *Latin American Research Review* 18, no. 1 (1983).

Colmenares, Francisco. "Pemex: Crisis y restructuración." Ph.D. diss., National Autonomous University of Mexico, Mexico City, 1989.

Commander, Simon, and Tony Killick. "Privatization in Developing Countries: A Survey of the Issues." In Paul Cook and Colin Kirkpatrick, eds., *Privatization in Less Developed Countries*. Brighton: Wheatsheaf, 1988.

"Comparencia del Alfredo del Mazo ante la Camara de Disputados." *El Mercado de Valores* 46, no. 47 (24 November 1986): 1099–1102.

Conaghan, Catherine, James A. Malloy, and Luis A. Abugattas. "Business and the Boys: The Politics of Neoliberalism in the Central Andes." *Latin American Research Review* 25, no. 2 (1990): 3–30.

"Conflictos obreros-patronales." *El Cotidiano* 7, no. 36 (July–August 1990): 52.

"Convenio del gobierno de México con el Fundo Monetario Internacional." *Comercio Exterior* 39, no. 4 (April 1989): 355–59.

Cook, Paul, and Colin Kirkpatrick. "Privatization in Less Developed Countries: An Overview." In Paul Cook and Colin Kirkpatrick, eds., *Privatization in Less Developed Countries*. Brighton: Wheatsheaf, 1988.

Coppedge, Michael. "Mexican Democracy: You Can't Get There from Here." In Riordan Roett, ed., *Political and Economic Liberalization in Mexico*. Boulder, Colo.: Lynne Rienner, 1993.

Cornelius, Wayne. "Political Liberalization in an Authoritarian Regime." In Judith Gentleman, ed., *Mexican Politics in Transition*. Boulder, Colo.: Westview, 1986.

Cornelius, Wayne, Judith Gentleman, and Peter H. Smith. "Overview of Political Change in Mexico." In Wayne A. Cornelius, Judith Gentleman, and Peter H. Smith, eds., *Mexico's Alternative Political Futures*. San Diego: Center for U.S.-Mexican Studies, University of California, 1989.

"Corporativismo, no el (la) modelo." *El Cotidiano* 7, no. 35 (May–June 1990):44–47.

Cortés A., Guadalupe. "Golpe al movimiento ferrocarrilero, 1948." In Víctor Durante Ponte, coord., *Las derrotas obreras, 1946–1952*. Mexico City: UNAM, 1984.

Cypher, James M. *State and Capital Accumulation in Mexico: Development Policy Since 1940*. Boulder, Colo.: Westview, 1990.

Dávila Mendoza, Miguel A. 1986. "La empresa pública como instrumento de desarrollo y sus necesidades financieras." *Empresa Pública* 1, no. 3 (1986): 11–22.

de la Madrid Hurtado, Miguel. *Primer informe de gobierno*. Anexo, 1983. Mexico City: Presidencia de la República.

"La deuda externa: Analysis de coyuntura." *El Cotidiano* 3, no. 12 (July–August 1986): 37–39.

El Día, 9 June 1986–6 July 1992.

Dresser, Denise. *Neopopulist Solutions to Neoliberal Problems: Mexico's National Solidarity Program*. San Diego: Center for U.S.-Mexican Studies, University of California, 1991.

———. "Bringing the Poor Back In: National Solidarity As a Strategy of Regime Legitimacy." In Wayne A. Cornelius, Ann L. Craig, and Jonathan Fox, eds., *Transforming State-Societal Relations in Mexico*. San Diego: Center for U.S.-Mexican Studies, University of California, 1994.

Economist, 14 June 1986–26 July 1986.

Ellison, Christopher, and Gary Gereffi. "Explaining Strategies and Patterns of Industrial Development." In Gary Gereffi and Donald L. Wyman, eds., *Manufacturing Miracles: Paths of Industrialization in Latin America and East Asia*. Princeton: Princeton University Press, 1990.

Escobar Toledo, Saúl. "Rifts in the Mexican Power Elite." In Sylvia Maxfield and Ricardo Anzaldúa Montoya, eds., *Government and Private Sector in Contemporary Mexico*. San Diego: Center for U.S.-Mexican Studies and the University of California, 1989.

Excelsior, 27 September 1989, 13 April 1992.

Fajnzylber, Fernando. 1989. "Sobre la impostergable transformación productiva de América Latina." *Pensamiento Iberoamericano*, no. 16 (July–December 1989): 85–106.

FERTIMEX. *Informes institutional de labores*. Mexico City: FERTIMEX, 1985–1986, 1986–1987.

Financial Times, 25 April–28 November 1986.

"El financiamiento y la promoción del Bancomext en 1987." *Comercio Exterior* 37, no. 3 (March 1987): 236–45.

El Financiero, 10 March 1987–24 August 1992.

Fishlow, Albert. "A Tale of Two Presidents: The Political Economy of Crisis Management." In Alfred Stepan, ed., *Democratizing Brazil.* New York: Oxford University Press, 1989.

Fitzgerald, E.V.K. *The State and Economic Development in Peru Since 1968.* Cambridge: Cambridge University Press, 1976.

Flichman, Guillermo. "The State and Capital Accumulation in Argentina." In Christian Anglade and Carlos Fortin, eds., *The State and Capital Accumulation in Latin America,* vol. 2. Pittsburgh: University of Pittsburgh Press, 1990.

Foweraker, Joe. "Popular Movements and the Transfomation of the Political System." In Wayne Cornelius, Judith Gentleman, and Peter H. Smith, eds., *Mexico's Alternative Political Futures.* San Diego: Center for U.S.-Mexican Studies, University of California, 1989.

——. Introduction to Joe Foweraker and Ann L. Craig, eds., *Popular Movements and Political Change in Mexico.* Boulder, Colo.: Lynne Rienner, 1990.

Fox, Jonathan. "Targeting the Poorest: The Role of the National Indigenous Institute in Mexico's Solidarity Program." In Wayne A. Cornelius, Ann L. Craig, and Jonathan Fox, eds., *Transforming State-Society Relations in Mexico.* San Diego: Center for U.S.-Mexican Studies, University of California, 1994.

Friedman, Milton. *Capitalism and Freedom.* Chicago: University of Chicago Press, 1962.

Gaítan Riveros, María Mercedes. 1984. "El movimiento minero 1950–1951." In Víctor Durante Ponte, coord., *Las derrotas obreras 1946–1952.* Mexico City: UNAM, 1984.

Gamer, Robert. *The Developing Nations: A Comparative Perspective.* 2d ed. Boston: Allen and Unwin, 1982.

Garavito, Rosa A., Guadalupe Montes de Oca, and Irma Rodríquez. 1984. "Pronafice, más que programa, un pacto." *El Cotidiano* 1, no. 6 (July–August 1984): 12–15.

Garza, Dionisio. "La democratización en la sección 147 (Monclova) del sindicato minero-metalúrgico." In Javier Aguilar García, coord., *Los sindicatos nacionales, minero-metalúrgicos,* vol. 2. Mexico City: García Valades Editores, 1987.

Gereffi, Gary. "Los nuevos desafíos de la industrialización: Observaciones sobre el sudeste Asiático y Latinoamérica." *Pensamiento Iberoamericano,* no. 16 (July–December 1989): 205–34.

Glade, William. "The Privatization and Denationalization of Public Enterprises." In G. Ram Reddy, ed., *Government and Public Enterprise: Essays in Honor of V. V. Ramanadham*. London: Frank Cass, 1983.

————. 1989. "Privatization in Rent-Seeking Societies." *World Development* 17, no. 5 (1989): 673–81.

Globe and Mail, 1 October 1983–9 June 1986.

Gómez, Leopoldo, and John Bailey. "La transición política y los dilemas del PRI." *Foro Internacional* 31, no. 1 (July–September 1990): 57–87.

Gómez Tagle, Silvia. *Insurgencia y democracia en los sindicatos electristas.* Mexico City: El Colegio de México, 1980.

————. "La demanda democrática del 6 de julio." Paper presented at the 15th International Congress of the Latin American Studies Association, 21–23 September 1989, Miami.

González Aguilar, Estinislao. *La crisis y los trabajadores.* Mexico City: Centro de Estudios de Trabajo, 1990.

González Fraga, Javier A. "Argentine Privatization in Retrospect." In William Glade, ed., *Privatization of Public Enterprises in Latin America.* San Francisco: ICS Press, 1991.

Grayson, George. *The Mexican Labor Machine: Power Politics and Patronage.* Washington, D.C.: Center for Strategic International Studies, 1989.

Green, María del Rosario. "Mexico's Economic Dependence." In Susan Kaufman Purcell, ed., *Mexican-U.S. Relations.* New York: Praeger, 1981.

Green, Rosario. *La deuda externa de México: 1973–1987. De la abundancia a la escasaz de créditos.* Mexico City: Editorial Nueva Imagen, 1988.

Greenberg, Martin Harry. *Bureaucracy and Development: A Mexican Case Study.* New York: Heath, 1970.

Gribomont, C., and M. Rimez. "La Política ecónomica del gobierno de Luis Echeverría (1971–1976): Un primer ensayo de interpretación." *El Trimestre Económico* 44, no. 176 (October–December 1977): 771–833.

Grindle, Merilee. *Bureaucrats, Politicians, and Peasants in Mexico.* Berkeley and Los Angeles: University of California Press, 1977.

————. "A New Political Economy: Positive Economics and Negative Politics." In Gerard M. Meier, ed., *Politics and Policymaking in Developing Countries.* San Francisco: ICS Press, 1991.

Grindle, Merilee, and John W. Thomas. *Public Choices and Policy Change.* Baltimore: Johns Hopkins University Press, 1991.

Grupo SIDERMEX. *Informes de labores.* Mexico City: Grupo SIDERMEX, 1985–1986, 1986–1987, 1988–1989.

Guillén López, Tonatiuh. "The Social Bases of the PRI." In Wayne A. Cornelius, Judith Gentleman, and Peter H. Smith, eds., *Mexico's Alternative*

Political Futures. San Diego: Center for U.S.-Mexican Studies, University of California, 1991.

Haber, Paul. "Political Change in Durango: The Role of National Solidarity." In Wayne A. Cornelius, Ann L. Craig, and Jonathan Fox, eds., *Transforming State Societal Relations in Mexico*. San Diego: Center for U.S.-Mexican Studies, University of California, 1991.

Haber, Stephen H. *Industry and Underdevelopment: The Industrialization of Mexico*. Stanford: Stanford University Press, 1989.

Haggard, Stephan. "The Politics of Adjustment: Lessons from the IMF's Extended Fund Facility." In Miles Kahler, ed., *The Politics of International Debt*. Ithaca: Cornell University Press, 1986.

Haggard, Stephan, and Robert Kaufman. "The Political Economy of Inflation and Stabilization in Middle-Income Countries." In Stephan Haggard and Robert R. Kaufman, eds., *The Politics of Economic Adjustment*. Princeton: Princeton University Press, 1992.

———. "The State in the Initiation of Market-Orientated Reform." In Louis Putterman and Dietrich Rueschemeyer, eds., *State and Market in Development*. Boulder, Colo.: Lynne Rienner, 1992.

Hamilton, Nora. *The Limits of State Autonomy*. Princeton: Princeton University Press, 1982.

Handelman, Howard. "Unionization, Ideology, and Political Participation Within the Mexican Working Class." In Mitchell A. Seligson and John A. Booth, eds., *Political Participation in Latin America: Politics and the Poor*, vol. 2. New York: Holmes and Meier, 1979.

Hansen, Roger D. *The Politics of Mexican Development*. Baltimore: Johns Hopkins University Press, 1980.

Hellman, Judith Adler. *Mexico in Crisis*. 3d ed. New York: Holmes and Meier, 1988.

Heraldo, 24 June 1989.

Hernández Guttierrez, Ignacio. "La burguesía comercial nativa y el capital extranjera." In Ramiro Reyes Esparza, Enrique Olivares Emilio Leyva, and Hernández G. Ignacio, *La burguesía Mexicana*. Mexico City: Editorial Nuestro Tiempo, 1978.

Human Rights Watch Americas. "Mexico: The New Year's Rebellion." 6, no. 3 (1 March 1994).

Ikenberry, G. John. "The International Spread of Privatization Policies: Inducements, Learning, and Policy Bandwagoning." In Ezra N. Suleiman and John Waterbury, eds., *The Political Economy of Public Sector Reform and Privatization*. Boulder, Colo.: Westview, 1990.

"Informe anual de labores de la Secofi." *El Mercado de Valores,* no. 42 (15 October 1984): 1033–35.

La Jornada, 11 May 1987–24 August 1993.

Journal of Commerce, 26 February 1993–28 July 1993.

Kahler, Miles. "External Influence, Conditionality, and the Politics of Adjustment." In Stephan Haggard and Robert R. Kaufman, eds., *The Politics of Economic Adjustment.* Princeton: Princeton University Press, 1992.

————. "Orthodoxy and Its Alternatives: Explaining Approaches to Structural Adjustment." In Joan M. Nelson, ed., *Economic Crisis and Policy Choice: The Politics of Adjustment in the Third World.* Princeton: Princeton University Press, 1990.

Kaufman, Robert R. "Stabilization and Adjustment in Argentina, Brazil, and Mexico." In Joan M. Nelson, ed., *Economic Crisis and Policy Choice: The Politics of Adjustment in the Third World.* Princeton: Princeton University Press, 1990.

————. *The Politics of Debt in Argentina, Brazil, and Mexico.* Berkeley, Calif.: Institute of International Studies, 1988.

————. "Mexican and Latin American Authoritarianism." In José Luis Reyna and Robert J. Weinert, eds., *Authoritarianism in Mexico.* Philadelphia: Institute for the Study of Human Issues, 1977.

Kelly de Escobar, Janet. "Venezuela: Letting in the Market." In Raymond Vernon, ed., *The Promise of Privatization: A Challenge for U.S. Policy.* New York: Council on Foreign Affairs, 1988.

Krueger, Anne. "Problems of Liberalization." In Armeane M. Choksi and Demetris Papageorgiou, eds., *Economic Liberalization in Developing Countries.* Washington, D.C.: World Bank, 1986.

La Botz, Dan. *The Crisis of Mexican Labor.* New York: Praeger, 1988. *Latin American Weekly Report,* 13 May 1983–30 March 1995.

"Ley Federal de las Entidades Parastatales." In *Marco Jurídico Básico.* Mexico City: PEMEX (Subdirección Técnica Administrativa), 1988.

Leyva, Marco Antonio, and Guillermo Campos. "Ferrocarriles, luz verde a la modernidad." *El Cotidiano* 21, no. 21 (January–February 1988): 46–61.

Looney, Robert E. *Mexico's Economy: A Policy Analysis and Forecast to 1990.* Boulder, Colo.: Westview, 1978.

López Aparicio, Alfonso. *El movimiento obrero en México.* Mexico City: Editorial Jus, 1952.

López, Carlos Roberto. "Crisis en la industria petrolera: El Conflicto

SRTPRM-Pemex." Primer coloquio sobre crisis, proceso de trabajo y clase obrera, Universidad Veracruzana, Xalapa, 1986.

―――. "Tres problemas obrero-patronales en la industria petrolera Mexicana, 1986–1987." Cuadernos Sobre Perspectiva Enérgetica, no. 110 (1987). El colegio de México.

"Lo que se dijo en Excelsior antes de la Asamblea Priista." *El Cotidiano* 1, no. 1 (July–August 1984).

Los Angeles Times, 22 June 1993.

Loyola Díaz, Rafael. "La liquidación del feudo petrolero en la politica moderna, México, 1988." *Mexican Studies/Estudios Mexicanos* 6, no. 3 (Summer 1990): 263–97.

Luna, Matilde, Ricardo Tirado, and Fransisco Valdés. "Businessmen and Politics in Mexico, 1982–1986." In Sylvia Maxfield and Ricardo Anzaldúa Montoya, eds., *Government and Private Sector in Contemporary Mexico.* San Diego: Center for U.S.-Mexican Studies, University of California, 1987.

Luna, Matilde. "Las associaciones empresariales Mexicanas y la apertura externa." Paper presented at the 17th International Congress of the Latin American Studies Association, 24–27 September 1992, Los Angeles.

―――. "La derecha empresarial." *El Cotidiano* 4, no. 24 (July–August 1988): 73–76.

Maloney, William F. "Popular Capitalism in Chile, 1985–1988." Paper presented at the 17th International Congress of the Latin American Studies Association, 24–27 September 1992, Los Angeles.

Manke, Richard B. *Mexican Oil and Natural Gas.* New York: Praeger, 1979.

Martínez Nava, Juan M. *Conflicto estado empresarios.* Mexico City: Editorial Nueva Imagen, 1984.

Maxfield, Sylvia. *Governing Capital: International Finance and Mexican Politics.* Ithaca: Cornell University Press, 1990.

―――. Introduction to Sylvia Maxfield and Ricardo Anzaldúa Montoya, eds., *Government and Private Sector in Contemporary Mexico.* San Diego: Center for U.S.-Mexican Studies, University of California, 1987.

McCoy, Jennifer L. "Venezuela: Austerity and the Working Class in a Democratic Regime." In Howard Handelman and Werner Baer, eds., *Paying the Costs of Austerity in Latin America.* Boulder, Colo.: Westview, 1989.

Méndez, Luis. "Espisodos de lucha obrera." *El Cotidiano* 5, no. 29 (May–June 1989): 63–69.

El Mercado de Valores (NAFINSA). May 1987–1 July 1989.

Mexico and Central America Report, 17 February 1984–20 August 1992.

Mexico and NAFTA Report, 18 February 1993–30 March 1995.

Mexico Update, 15 August 1984.

Meyer, Lorenzo. "Democratization of the PRI: Mission Impossible." In Wayne Cornelius, Judith Gentleman, and Peter H. Smith, eds., *Mexico's Alternative Political Futures.* San Diego: Center for U.S.-Mexican Studies, University of California, 1989.

―――. "El corporativismo Mexicano en los tiempos neoliberalismo." In Graciela Bensusan and Carlos García, coords., *Estado y sindicados: Crisis de un relación.* Mexico City: Universidad Autónoma Metropolitana, 1989.

Miami Herald, 3 January 1993–4 March 1993.

Micheli, Jordi. "Sindicatos y futuro: El neoliberalismo hoy." In Graciela Bensusan and Carlos García, coords., *Estado y sindicatos: Crisis de una relación.* Mexico City: Universidad Autónoma Metropolitana, 1988.

Middlebrook, Kevin J. "State-Labor Relations in Mexico: The Changing Economic and Political Context." In Kevin J. Middlebrook, ed., *Unions, Workers, and the State in Mexico* San Diego: Center for U.S.-Mexican Studies, University of California, 1991.

―――. "The CTM and the Future of State-Labor Relations." In Wayne Cornelius, Judith Gentleman, and Peter H. Smith, eds., *Mexico's Alternative Political Futures.* San Diego: Center for U.S.-Mexican Studies, University of California, 1989.

―――. "Political Liberalization in an Authoritarian Regime, Mexico, 1985–1986." In Guillermo O'Donnell, Philippe C. Schmitter, and Laurence Whitehead, eds., *Transitions from Authoritarian Rule: Prospects for Democracy,* vol. 2. Baltimore: Johns Hopkins University Press, 1986.

Minello, Nelson. *Siderlúrgica Lázaro Cárdenas: Las Truchas, historia de una empresa.* Mexico City: El Colegio de México, 1982.

Mizrahi, Yemile. "Rebels Without a Cause? The Politics of Entrepreneurs in Chihuahua." Paper presented at the 17th International Congress of the Latin American Studies Association, 24–27 September 1992, Los Angeles.

Moguel, Julio. "¿Programa Nacional de Solidaridad para quién?" *El Cotidiano* 7, no. 38 (November–December 1990): 23–27.

Molina, David A. "Pemex, la reprivaticación de facto." *El Cotidiano* 6, no. 32 (November–December 1989): 27–33.

Molinar Horcasitas, Juan Francisco. "Elecciones autoritarismo y democracia en México." M.A. thesis, El Colegio de México, 1989.

Molinar Horcasitas, Juan, and Jeffrey A. Weldon. "Electoral Determinants and Consequences of National Solidarity." In Wayne A. Cornelius, Ann

L. Craig, and Jonathan Fox, eds., *Transforming State-Societal Relations in Mexico*. San Diego: Center for U.S.-Mexican Studies, University of California, 1994.

Monsiváis, Carlos. "From '68 to Cardenismo: Towards a Chronicle of Social Movements." *Journal of International Affairs* 43, no. 2 (Winter 1990): 385–93.

Morris, Stephen D. "Political Reformism in Mexico: Past and Present." *Latin American Research Review* 28, no. 2 (1993): 191–205.

Mosely, Paul. "Privatization, Policy-Based Lending, and World Bank Behaviour." In Paul Cook and Colin Kirkpatrick, eds., *Privatisation in Less Developed Countries*. Brighton: Wheatsheaf, 1988.

Mosk, Sanford A. *Industrial Revolution in México*. Berkeley: University of California Press, 1954.

NAFINSA. *México en Cifras*. Mexico City: NAFINSA, 1991.

Nelson, Joan M. Introduction to Nelson, ed., *Economic Crisis and Policy Choice: Adjustment in the Third World*. Princeton: Princeton University Press, 1990.

Newell, Roberto G., and Luis Rubio F. *Mexico's Dilemma: The Political Origins of Economic Crisis*. Boulder, Colo.: Westview, 1984.

New York Times, 18 June 1986; 2, 24 January 1995.

News (Mexico City), 22 April–3 June 1992.

"Nuevas disposiciones para el funcionamiento de las entidades del sector parastatal." *El Mercado de Valores* 42, no. 21 (23 May 1983): 533–39.

O'Donnell, Guillermo A. *Modernization and Bureaucratic Authoritarianism: Studies in South American Politics*. Berkeley: Institute of International Studies, University of California, 1973.

O'Donnell, Guillermo A., and Philippe C. Schmitter. *Transitions from Authoritarian Rule: Tentative Conclusions About Uncertain Democracies*. Baltimore: Johns Hopkins University Press, 1986.

Ortiz Martínez, Guillermo. *La reforma financiera y la desincorporación bancaria*. Mexico City: Fondo de Cultura Económica, 1994.

Pacheco Méndez, Guadalupe. "Los sectores del PRI en las elecciones de 1988." *Mexican Studies/Estudios Mexicanos* 7, no. 2 (Summer 1991): 253–82.

Pastor, Manuel, Jr., and Carol Wise. "Peruvian Economic Policy in the 1980s: From Orthodoxy to Heterodoxy and Back." *Latin American Research Review* 27, no. 2 (1992): 83–117.

Peet, Richard. Introduction to Richard Peet, ed., *International Capitalism and Industrial Restructuring*. Boston: Allen and Unwin, 1987.

Pérez Linares, Rosalía. "El Charrismo sindical en la década de los sesenta:

el sindicato petrolero." In Ana María Prieto, coord., *Historia y cronicas de la clase obrera en México*. Mexico City: Escuela Nacional de Antropología e Historia and Instituto Nacional Antropología e Historia, n.d.

———. "Vigencia y formas del charrismo en el STPRM." In Javier Aguilar García, coord., *Los sindicatos nacionales en el México contemporaneo: Petroleros*, vol. 1. Mexico City: García Valades Editores, 1986.

"Perfil de la Jornada." *La Jornada*, 1–2 (April 1991).

Petras, James. "State Capitalism and the Third World." *Development and Change* 8, no. 1 (1977): 1–17.

Philip, George. "Public Enterprise in Mexico." In V. V. Ramandham, ed., *Public Enterprise and the Developing World*. London: Croom Helm, 1984.

Pineda Gómez, Francisco Javier. "Movimiento sindical y sistema de dominación en México (1936–1976)." Professional thesis, Escuela Nacional de Anthropología e Historia, 1981.

Pirages, Dennis C. "Tecnology, Ecology, and Transformations in the Global Political Economy." In Dennis C. Pirages and Christine Sylvester, eds., *Transformation in the Global Political Economy*. New York: St. Martin's Press, 1990.

Poder Ejecutivo Federal. *Plan Nacional de Desarrollo, 1983–1988*. Mexico City: SPP, 1983.

Poitras, Guy. "Welfare Bureaucracy and Clientele Politics in Mexico." *Administrative Studies Quarterly* 18, no. 1 (March 1973): 18–25.

"Política Actual en Materia de Inversión Extranjera." *Mercado de Valores* 68, no. 19 (October 1988): 22–24.

Poulantzas, Nicos. "The Problem of the Capitalist State." *New Left Review* (November–December 1969): 67–78.

Powell, J. Richard. *The Mexican Petroleum Industry, 1938–1950*. New York: Russell and Russell, 1972.

Powell, John Duncan. "Peasant Society and Clientelistic Politics." *American Political Science Review* 64 (June 1970): 411–25.

Prieto, Ana María. "Mexico's National *Coordinadoras* in a Context of Economic Crisis." In Barry Carr and Ricardo Anzaldúa Montoya, eds., *The Mexican Left, the Popular Movements, and the Politics of Austerity*. San Diego: Center for U.S.-Mexican Studies, University of California, 1986.

"Primer informe del Presidente Miguel de la Madrid, septiembre, 1983." *El Mercado de Valores* 53, no. 36 (5 September 1983): 909–22.

Proceso, 3 January 1983–17 August 1992.

"Profiex." *El Cotidiano* 1, no. 3 (December 1984–January 1985).

Puga E., Christina. "Los empresarios y la política en México." In Salvador

H. Cordero and Ricardo Tirado, coords., *Classes dominantes y estado de México*. Mexico City: UNAM, 1984.

Purcell, John F. H., and Susan Kaufman Purcell. "Mexican Business and Public Policy." In James M. Malloy, ed., *Authoritarianism and Corporatism in Latin America*. Pittsburgh: University of Pittsburgh Press, 1977.

Purcell, Susan Kaufman. "Business-Government Relations in Mexico: The Case of the Sugar Industry." *Comparative Politics* 13, no. 2 (1981): 211–33.

———. *The Mexican Profit-Sharing Decision*. Berkeley: University of California Press, 1975.

———. "Decision Making in a Authoritarian Regime: Theoretical Implications from a Mexican Case Study." *World Politics* 26, no. 1 (October 1973): 30–48.

Purcell, Susan Kaufman, and John F. Purcell. "State and Society in Mexico: Must a Stable Society be Institutionalized?" *World Politics* 30, no. 2 (January 1980): 194–227.

Quarterly Economic Review of Mexico, 1983–1986.

Quintano López, Enrique. "La bancarrota de Fundidora: Dimes y directos financieras." *El Cotidiano* 3, no. 12 (July–August 1986): 22–26.

Ramamurti, Ravi. *Privatization and the Latin American Debt Problem*. New Brunswick, N.J.: Transaction Publishers, 1992.

Ramírez Laiz, Juan Manuel. "Urban Struggles and Their Political Consequences." In Joe Foweraker and Ann L. Craig, eds., *Popular Movements and Political Change in Mexico*. Boulder, Colo.: Lynne Rienner, 1990.

"Razón de estado y desobediencia civil." *El Cotidiano* 4, no. 32 (23 January 1989): 47–51.

"Reformas constitucionales." *El Mercado de Valores* 43, no. 7 (14 February 1983): 164–68.

Remmer, Karen. "The Politics of Economic Stabilization: IMF Standby Programs in Latin America, 1954–1984." *Comparative Politics* 85 (October 1986): 777–800.

Reyes Esparza, Ramiro, Enrique Olivares, Emilio Leyva, and Hernández G. Leyva. *La burguesía Mexicana*. Mexico City: Editorial Nuestro Tiempo, 1978.

Reyna, José Luis, and Richard S. Weinert, eds. *Authoritarianism in Mexico*. Philadelphia: Institute for the Study of Human Issues, 1977.

Rivera Castro, José. "Periodizatión del sindicalismo petrolero." In Javier Aguilar García, coord., *Los sindicatos nacionales en el México contemporaneo: Petroleros*, vol. 1. Mexico City: García Valades Editores, 1986.

Rivera Flores, Antonio. "Union General de Obreros y Campesinos de Mexico." In Víctor Durante Ponte, ed., *Las derrotas obreros, 1946–1952.* Mexico City: UNAM, 1984.

Rocha Geisa, María. "Redefining the Role of the Bourgeoisie in Dependent Capitalist Development: Privatization and Liberalization in Brazil." *Latin American Perspectives* 21, no. 80 (Winter 1994): 72–98.

Rodríquez, Ma. Elena, and José Mauro Saldána. "El movimiento sindical en Fundidora Monterrey." In Javier Aguilar García, coord., *Los sindicatos nacionales en el México contemporaneo: Minero-metalúrgicos,* vol. 2. Mexico City: García Valades Editores, 1987.

Rodríquez F., Miguel A. "Consequences of Capital Flight for Latin American Debtor Countries." In Donald R. Lessard and John Williamson, eds., *Capital Flight and Third World Countries.* Washington, D.C.: Institute for International Economics, 1987.

Rodríquez Reyna, I. "La privatizatión de la petroquímica basica." *El Cotidiano* 6, no. 29 (May–June 1989): 16–22.

Roett, Riordan. "At the Crossroads: Liberalization in Mexico." In Riordan Roett, ed., *Political and Economic Liberalization in Mexico.* Boulder, Colo.: Lynne Rienner, 1993.

Ronfeldt, Donald. "Prospects for Elite Cohesion." In Wayne Cornelius, Judith Gentleman, and Peter H. Smith, eds., *Mexico's Alternative Political Futures.* San Diego: Center for U.S.-Mexican Studies, University of California, 1989.

Ross, Robert J. S. "The Relative Decline of Relative Autonomy: Global Capitalism and the Political Economy of State Change." In Edward S. Greenburg and Thomas F. Mayer, eds., *Changes in the State.* Newbury Park, Calif.: Sage, 1990.

Rubin, Jeffrey W. "Popular Mobilization and the Myth of State Corporatism." In Joe Foweraker and Ann L. Craig, eds., *Popular Movements and Political Change in Mexico.* Boulder, Colo.: Lynne Rienner, 1990.

Rubio, Luis. "Economic Reform and Political Change in Mexico." In Riordan Roett, ed., *Political and Economic Liberalization in Mexico.* Boulder, Colo.: Lynne Rienner, 1993.

Ruiz Dueñas, Jorge. "El redimensionamiento del sector parastatal, 1982–1989." *Foro Internacional* 30, no. 4 (1990): 789–811.

———. *Empresa pública: Elementos para el examen comparado.* Mexico City: Fondo de Cultura Ecónomica, 1988.

Saldívar, Américo. *Ideología y política de estado Mexicano (1970–1976).* Mexico City: Siglo XXI, 1980.

Salazar Segura, Antonio. "El movimiento sindical petrolera (1960–1980)." In Javier Aguilar García, coord., *Los sindicatos nacionales en el México contemporaneo: Petroleros,* vol. 1. Mexico City: García Valades Editores, 1986.

Salinas de Gortari, Carlos. "Discurso de toma de posesión." *Comercio Exterior* 38, no. 12 (December 1988): 1137–44.

————. *Quarto Informe de Gobierno.* Anexo, 1992. Mexico City: Presidencia de la República, 1993.

————. *Quinto Informe de Gobierno.* Anexo, 1993.

————. *Segundo Informe de Gobierno.* Anexo, 1990.

Saragoza, Alex M. *The Monterrey Elite and the Mexican State.* Austin: University of Texas Press, 1988.

Sariego, Juan Luis, Luis Reyadas, Miguel Angel Gómez, and Javier Farrera. *El estado y la minería Mexicana.* Mexico City: Fondo de Cultura Ecónomica, 1988.

Savas, E. S. *Privatization: The Key to Better Government.* Chatham, N.J.: Chatham House, 1987.

Saulniers, Alfred A. *Public Enterprise in Peru: Public Sector Growth and Reform.* Boulder, Colo.: Westview, 1988.

Schafer, Robert J. *Mexico: Mutual Adjustment Planning.* New York: Syracuse University Press, 1966.

Schmidt, Samuel. *The Deterioration of the Mexican Presidency: The Years of Luis Echeverría.* Tuscon: University of Arizona Press, 1991.

Schneider, Ben Ross. "Partly for Sale: Privatization and State Strength in Brazil and Mexico." *Journal of Interamerican Studies and World Affairs* 30, no. 4 (Winter 1988–1989): 89–110.

Scott, C. D. "Cycles, Crises, and Classes: The State and Accumulation in Peru." In Christian Anglade and Carlos Fortin, eds., *The State and Capital Accumulation in Latin America,* vol. 2. Pittsburgh: University of Pittsburgh Press, 1990.

SECOFI. *Legal Framework for Direct Foreign Investment.* Mexico City: SECOFI, 1990.

Secretaría de Hacienda y Credito Público. *Mexico: A New Economic Profile.* Mexico City, January 1991.

Secretaría de la Contraloría General de la Federación. *Restructuración del sector parastatal.* Mexico City, 1988.

SEMIP. *Informes de labores.* Mexico City: SEMIP, 1984–1985, 1985–1986, 1987–1988, 1988–1989.

Shabot, Esther. *Los orígines de sindicalismo ferrocarrilero.* Mexico City: Ediciones El Caballito, 1982.

Short, R. P. "The Role of Public Enterprises: An International Statistical Comparison." In Robert H. Floyd, Clive S. Gray, and R. P. Short, eds.,

Public Enterprise in Mixed Economies: Some Macroeconomic Aspects. Washington, D.C.: International Monetary Fund, 1984.

Smith, Peter H. "The 1988 Presidential Succession in Historical Perspective." In Wayne Cornelius, Judith Gentleman, and Peter H. Smith, eds., *Mexico's Alternative Political Futures.* San Diego: Center for U.S.-Mexican Studies, University of California, 1989.

Smith, William C. "Heterodox Shocks and the Political Economy of Democratic Transition in Argentina and Brazil." In William L. Canak, ed., *Lost Promises, Debt Austerity, and Development.* Boulder, Colo.: Westview, 1989.

El Sol de México (Mexico City), 23 February 1988–29 November 1989.

Spalding, Rose J. "Welfare Policymaking: Theoretical Implications of a Mexican Case Study." *Comparative Politics* 12, no. 4 (1980): 419–35.

Stallings, Barbara. "International Influence on Economic Policy: Debt Stabilization and Structural Reform." In Stephan Haggard and Robert R. Kaufman, eds., *The Politics of Economic Adjustment.* Princeton: Princeton University Press, 1992.

———. "Politics and Economic Crises: A Comparative Study of Chile, Peru, and Columbia." In Joan M. Nelson, ed., *Economic Crisis and Policy Choice: The Crisis of Adjustment in the Third World.* Princeton: Princeton University Press, 1990.

Stevens, Evelyn. *Protest and Response in Mexico.* Cambridge, Mass.: MIT Press, 1974.

Story, Dale. *Industry, the State, and Public Policy.* Austin: University of Texas Press, 1986.

———. *The Mexican Ruling Party: Stability and Authority.* New York: Praeger, 1986.

———. "The PAN, the Private Sector, and the Future of Mexican Opposition." In Judith Gentleman, ed., *Mexican Politics in Transition.* Boulder, Colo.: Westview, 1986.

———. "Industrial Elites in Mexico." *Journal of Interamerican Studies and World Affairs* 25, no. 3 (1983): 353–72.

Suárez, Antonio, and Eduardo Pérez, "Caída y recuperación: Los Salarios en México, 1987–1883." *El Cotidiano* 10, no. 59 (December 1993): 94–101.

Suleiman, Ezra N., and John Waterbury. "Analysing Privatization in Industrial and Developing Countries." Introduction to Suleiman and Waterbury, eds., *The Political Economy of Public Sector Reform and Privatization.* Boulder, Colo.: Westview, 1990.

Tamayo, Jorge. "Las entidades parastatales en México." *Investigación Económica,* no. 182 (October–December 1987): 255–78.

————. "Relación gobierno federal-entidadades parastatales en México." In Nuria Cunill and Juan Martin, eds., *Relación gobierno central—empresas públicas*. Caracas: Instituto Latinoamericano de Planificación Económico y Social y Centro de Administración para el Desarrollo, 1988.

Teichman, Judith A. *Policymaking in Mexico: From Boom to Crisis*. Boston: Allen and Unwin, 1988.

————. "The Mexican State and the Political Implications of Economic Restructuring." *Latin American Perspectives* 19, no. 2 (Spring 1992): 88–104.

Tello, Carlos. *La política económica en México, 1970–76*. Mexico City: Siglo XXI Editores, 1979.

Toye, John. "Is There a New Political Economy of Development?" In Christopher Colclough and James Manor, eds., *States or Markets? Neoliberalism and the Development Policy Debate*. Oxford: Clarendon Press, 1991.

Trebat, Thomas J. *Brazil's State-Owned Enterprises: A Case Study of the State as Enterpreneur*. Cambridge: Cambridge University Press, 1983.

Trejo Delarbre, Raúl. "Los trabajadores y el gobierno de Adolfo López Mateos (1958–1964)." In José Luis Reyna and Raúl Trejo Delarbre, eds., *La clase obrera en la historia de Adolfo Ruiz Cortines a Adolfo López Mateos (1952–1964)*. 4th ed., vol. 12. Mexico City: Siglo XXI Editores, 1988.

Unomásuno, 22 March 1985–20 July 1992.

U.S. Embassy. *Economic Trends Report, May 1989*. Mexico City: U.S. Embassy, May 1989.

Van de Walle, Nicolas. "Privatization in Developing Countries: A Review of the Issues." *World Development* 17, no. 5 (May 1989): 601–11.

Vargas, Sergio. "Recortes al gasto público." *El Cotidiano* 2, no. 7 (August–September 1985): 21–22.

Vargas Velázquez, Sergio, Victor Manuel Martínez Oregón, and Alejandro de la Torre Punzo. "La agonia Mexicana, cronología de una larga negociación." *El Cotidiano* 3, no. 12 (July–August 1986): 19–21.

Vásquez Rubio, Pilar. "Los telefonistas al filo de la Navaja." *El Cotidiano* 5, no. 25 (September–October 1988): 64–65.

————. "Telmex por los caminos de la productividad." *El Cotidiano* 7, no. 38 (November–December 1990): 10–14.

Vernon, Raymond. *The Dilemma of Mexico's Development*. Cambridge: Harvard University Press, 1963.

Villarreal, René. "Las empresas públicas en el desarrollo de México: Mitos y realidades." *Empresa Pública* 1, no. 1 (January–February 1986): 27–51.

Villarreal Arrambide, René. "La empresa pública y el desarrollo industrial en México." In Alejandro Cervantes Delgado, coord., *Ensayos sobre la modernidad nacional: La Empresa pública en la modernización económica de México.* Mexico City: Editorial Diana, 1989.

Wall Street Journal, 23 June 1986–29 April 1993.

Ward, Peter. *Welfare Politics in Mexico.* Cambridge: MIT Press, 1974.

Washington Post, 1 January 1995.

Waterbury, John. *Exposed to Innumerable Delusions: Public Enterprise and State Power in Egypt, India, Mexico, and Turkey.* Cambridge: Cambridge University Press, 1993.

————. "The Management of Long-Haul Economic Reform." In Joan Nelson, ed., *Fragile Coalitions: The Politics of Economic Adjustment.* Washington, D.C.: Overseas Development Council, 1989.

Weintraub, Sidney, and M. Delal Baer. "The Interplay Between Economic and Political Opening: The Sequence in Mexico." *Washington Quarterly* 15 (Spring 1992): 187–201.

Wernick, Rogério, L. F. "The Uneasy Steps Towards Privatization in Brazil." In William Glade, ed., *Privatization of Public Enterprise in Latin America.* San Francisco: CIS Press, 1991.

Whitehead, Laurence. "Mexico's Economic Prospects: Implications for Labor-State Relations." In Kevin Middlebrook, ed., *Unions, Workers, and the State in Mexico.* San Diego: Center for U.S.-Mexican Studies, and University of California, 1991.

Whiting, Van R., Jr. *The Political Economy of Foreign Investment in Mexico.* Baltimore: Johns Hopkins University Press, 1992.

Wilkinson, Bruce W. "Trade Liberalization, the Market Ideology, and Morality: Have We a Sustainable System?" In Ricardo Greenspun and Maxwell Cameron, eds., *The Political Economy of North American Free Trade.* New York: St. Martin's Press, 1993.

Witker, Jorge. "Relaciones y controles exterior de la empresa pública." In Marcos Kaplan, Francisco Osornio, Beatrice Bernal, Enrique Gurría, Jorge Witker, Ismael Eslava, Santiago Barajas, and Germán Rochas, *Regulación jurídica del intervencionismo estatal en México.* Mexico City: Fondo de Cultura Económica, 1988.

Witker, Jorge, and Ismael Eslava. "Aspectos generales del régimen legal aplicable a las entidades parastatales." In Marcos Kaplan et al., *Regulación jurídica del intervencionismo estatal en México.* Mexico City: Fondo de Cultura Economica, 1988.

Index